Directory of Dissertations in Accounting

Directory of Dissertations in Accounting

BY J. DAVID SPICELAND
Memphis State University

Markus Wiener Publishing
New York

ISBN 0-910129-39-8

Library of Congress Catalog
Card No. 86-40096

For information write to:
Markus Wiener Publishing, Inc.
2901 Broadway, New York, N.Y. 10025

Printed in the United States of America

Preface

The Directory of Accounting Dissertations identifies and classifies, by topic and methodology, dissertations in accounting since 1972. The purpose is to assist in the identification of relevant prior research by:

1. Doctoral students considering a potential dissertation topic as well as in developing the topic

2. Faculty supervisors of doctoral dissertations

3. Accounting reseachers approaching an area of research

Significant subjective judgement impacted the classification of the dissertations, typically on the basis of an abstract only. Frequently, the focus of a disseration overlapped two or more subject areas. Similarly, more than one research method was often employed in a study. In such cases, the classification is based on the dominant topic and/or methodology. In spite of the care taken in preparation of the data, some dissertations may be omitted or misclassified. Your comments are encouraged.

A description of the methodological categories follows:

Archival–Data obtained from existing data sources; e.g., library volumes, court cases, tax returns, etc. Does not include financial statement data (see Financial Statement Data-based).

Experimental–Manipulation of variables in either a laboratory or field environment. Includes computer simulations.

Field Study–Examines an issue through observation without interference. Includes cases studies and opinion surveys.

Financial Statement Data-based–Financial statement information from annual reports, 10K, or magnetic media (e.g., COMPUSTAT, NAARS, etc.)

Market-based–Examines security price or volume data.

Model-based–Centered around mathematical models and/or *a priori* analysis.

TABLE OF CONTENTS

DISSERTATIONS LISTED ALPHABETICALLY BY AUTHOR

Author	Title	School	Date	pp	Methodology	Topic
Abdallah, Wagdy Moustafa	AN INVESTIGATION OF THE MANAGEMENT ACCOUNTING FRAMEWORK FOR PERFORMANCE EVALUATION IN AMERICAN MULTINATIONAL ENTERPRISES	N Txs St	82	182	Field Study	Managerial
Abdeen, Adan Muhammed	THE ROLE OF ACCOUNTING IN THE ECONOMIC DEVELOPMENT OF SYRIA	Mss St	74	348	Field Study	International
Abdel-fattah, Zakaria F.	TRANSFER PRICING WITHIN A COMMERCIAL BANK	Arkansas	83	142	Field Study	Managerial
Abdoelkadir, Katjep K.	THE PERCEPTION OF ACCOUNTANTS AND ACCOUNTING STUDENTS ON THE ACCOUNTING PROFESSION IN INDONESIA	Txs A&M	82	328	Field Study	International
Abdolmohammadi, Mohammed J.	AN EVALUATION OF PRIOR PROBABILITY ASSESSMENT TECHNIQUES FOR THE APPLICATION OF BAYSIAN STATISTICS TO THE FIELD OF AUDITING	Indiana	82	148	Experimental	Auditing
Abdulkader, Abdullah	AN INVESTIGATION OF THE TIME SERIES PROPERTIES OF ACCOUNTING NUMBERS AT THE INDUSTRY LEVEL	Fla St	79	175	FinStData-based	Stochastic Properties
Abdullah, W. Moustafa	AN INVESTIGATION OF THE MANAGEMENT ACCOUNTING FRAMEWORK FOR PERFORMANCE EVALUATION IN AMERICAN MULTINATIONAL ENTERPRISES	N Txs St	82	182	Field Study	Managerial
Aboul-Ezz, Mohamed El-Said	THE RELATIONSHIP OF INCENTIVE STRUCTURE AND BUDGET STANDARD TO PERFORMANCE AND SOCIAL NORMATIVE INFLUENCE	Minnesota	84	253	Field Study	Managerial
Abraham, Stanley C.	THE PUBLIC ACCOUNTING PROFESSION: AN APPLICATION OF FUTURES RESEARCH METHODS TO IDENTIFYING AND CLARIFYING ITS PROBLEMS	S Calif	76	814	Field Study	Profession
Abu-Romman, Mohammed A.	PLANNING AND CONTROL IN COMPLEX MULTILEVEL ORGANIZATIONS: AN INTERDISCIPLINARY PERSPECTIVE	Wiscon	74	303	Model- based	Managerial

Author	Title	School	Date	pp	Methodology	Topic
Adam, Shiraz Tajdin Noormohame d	PREDICTIVE ABILITY OF ANNUAL CASH FLOW UNDER HISTORICAL COST AND CONSTANT DOLLAR ACCOUNTING	Simon Fraser	84		Model- based	Inflation
Adams, Barbara Louise	AN INVESTIGATION OF THE OBJECTIVES, METHODS, AND COST OF QUARTERLY REPORTING.	Tx A&M	81	97	Field Study	Interim Statements
Adams, Steven J.	IMPLICATIONS OF REPORTED ACCOUNTING INFORMATION ON CORPORATE EXPENDITURES FOR RESEARCH AND DEVELOPMENT	Cincinnati	81	191	FinStData-based	Research & Development
Adelberg, Arthur H.	NARRATIVE DISCLOSURES CONTAINED IN FINANCIAL REPORTS: AN EMPIRICAL EVALUATION OF THEIR UNDERSTANDABILITY	CUNY- Bar	77	495	Field Study	Financial
Adelsman, Rony Mark	ANALYSIS OF GROUP DECISION-MAKING MODELS UNDER VARYING INFORMATION CONDITIONS AND ASSUMPTIONS REGARDING INDIVIDUAL BEHAVIOR.	Purdue	77	199	Experimental	Managerial
Adibi-Adeyiga, Abidemi Janet	INDEPENDENT AUDITING OF BUDGETS OF MUNICIPALITIES: A POSSIBLE EXTENSION OF THE AUDIT FUNCTION.	Missouri	80	160	Field Study	Not-for-profit
Agudelo, Jaime	SOME EVIDENCE ON THE RELEVANCE OF CERTAIN EX POST ACCOUNTING SIGNALS	Okl St	79	69	FinStData-based	Financial
Aharony, Joseph	TIME EFFECTS IN EMPIRICAL STOCK VALUATION MODELS.	Northwest ern	74	169	Market- based	Financial
Ahern, John T.	A CONCEPTUAL FRAMEWORK FOR FORECAST DISCLOSURE	Kentucky	76	201	Model- based	Forecasts
Ahmed, Sania T.	AN EMPIRICAL INVESTIGATION OF INFORMATION CONTENT OF INFLATION ACCOUNTING DATA	Arkansas	83	243	Market- based	Inflation

Author	Title	School	Date	pp	Methodology	Topic
Aiyama, Toshikazu	INVENTORY POLICY WITH LOST SALES	N Car	84	119	Experimental	Managerial
Ajinkaya, Bipin B.	EFFECT OF COGNITIVE STRUCTURE AND MULTI SYSTEM CUES ON THE USE OF ACCOUNTING INFORMATION IN DECISION MAKING	Minnesota	76	262	Experimental	Financial
Akpa, Abimaje	COMMERCIAL LOAN DEFAULT RISK ASSESSMENT: PREDICTIVE ACCURACY OF ALTERNATIVE ACCOUNTING STRUCTURES IN AN INFLATIONARY ENVIRONMENT	S Calif	84		FinStData-based	Inflation
Al-Bassam, Sadik Mohammed	AN EVALUATION OF OPEC CONSERVATION REGULATION SYSTEMS OF THE HYDROCARBON RESOURCES: THE CASE OF KUWAIT.	Texas	80	648	Field Study	Not-for-profit
Al-Ghamdi, Saad Attieah	THE IMPACT OF INVENTORY VALUATION TECHNIQUES ON TIME SERIES BEHAVIOR OF FIRMS EARNINGS AND CASH FLOWS.	Oklahoma	80	72	FinStData-based	Stochastic Properties
Al-Rai, Ziad Khalil	THE IMPACT OF CORPORATE FORCAST'S ACCURACY OF EARNINGS PER SHARE ON THE STOCK MARKET EMPIRICAL ANALYSIS	NYU	83	156	Market- based	Forecasts
Al-Shuaib, Shaib A.	ACCOUNTING AND ECONOMIC DEVELOPMENT IN KUWAIT: DESCRIPTION AND ANALYSIS	Missouri	74	157	Field Study	International
Al-Tassan, Mohammad Saleh	CASH FLOW PREDICTION - A COMPARISON OF HISTORICAL COSTS AND CONSTANT DOLLAR ACCOUNTING INFORMATION	Missouri	83	157	FinStData-based	Inflation
Al-Yamani, Abdullah G.	ALTERNATIVE ACCOUNTING INCOME MEASURES AND DIVIDEND POLICY	Colorado	80	297	FinStData-based	Financial
Alberni, Carlos W.	IND. AND DEP. SHORTER THAN ANNUAL INC. VIEWS AS EXPRESSED IN APB OP. #28: INTERIM FIN. REPORT., MAY 1973. A THEOR. FRAMEWK. AND REVIEW OF EMP. WORK	Missouri	76	184	Model- based	Interim Statements

Author	Title	School	Date	pp	Methodology	Topic
Albrecht, William S.	**TOWARD A PROBABILISTIC ASSESSMENT OF INCOME**	Wiscon	75	182	Field Study	Financial
Alderman, Charles W.	**AN EMPIRICAL ANALYSIS OF THE IMPACT OF SELECTED AUDIT OPINION QUALIFICATION ON THE MARKET RISK COMPONENTS**	Tenn	77	168	Market- based	Auditing
Alexander, Robin A.	**A SIMULATION STUDY OF SOME TIME SERIES PROPERTIES OF EARNINGS**	Northwest ern	81	187	Experimental	Stochastic Properties
Alford, Robert M.	**SALES FORECASTING: AN ANALYSIS OF THE ACCURACY OF VARIOUS TIME SERIES FORECASTING TECHNIQUES IN SELECTED CONSUMER PRODUCT INDUSTRIES**	Txs A&M	78	201	Field Study	Forecasts
Alhumaid, Abdulrhman I.	**AN EMPIRICAL STUDY OF THE CHARACTERISTICS OF THE GOVERNMENTAL BUDGETARY PROCESS IN RICH AND UNCERTAIN ENVIRONMENTS: THE CASE OF SAUDI ARABIA.**	LSU	81	182	Field Study	Managerial
Alidina, Mohamed	**THE BUSINESS/HOBBY CLASSIFICATION - AN EMPIRICAL INVESTIGATION OF THE BUSINESS/HOBBY CLASSIFICATION BY THE TAX COURT FOR FEDERAL INCOME TAX PURPOSES**	Temple	84	154	Archival	Tax
Alkafaji, Yass A.	**AN EMPIRICAL INVESTIGATION INTO THE ASSOC. BETWEEN MAJOR POLITICO- SOCIO-ECONOMIC FACTORS AND ACCT. PRACTICE IN A SAMPLE OF WORLD COUNTRIES**	Miss St	83	226	Field Study	International
Allen, George Louis	**AN EMPIRICAL INVESTIGATION OF THE COMPLEMENTARY VALUE OF A STATEMENT OF CASH FLOWS IN A SET OF PUBLISHED FINANCIAL STATEMENTS (COMMUNICATION, SOLVENCY ANALYSIS, DECISION-MAKERS)**	Texas St	85	178	Field Study	Statement of Ch Fin Pos
Allen, Steven A.	**ACCOUNTING REGULATION AND INSIDER TRADING**	SUNY-Buf	82	437	Market- based	Financial
Alsultan, Sultan M.	**ACCOUNTING AND REPORTING PRACTICES OF MIXED (PUBLIC-PRIVATE) ENTERPRISES**	Missouri	80	199	Field Study	Financial

Author	Title	School	Date	pp	Methodology	Topic
Alsup, Rodney Glen	KENTUCKY COMMERCIAL BANK DIRECTORS -- THEIR LIABILITY AND INFORMATION REQUIREMENTS	Kentucky	84	188	Field Study	Bank Accounting
Alvara, Martenelli	THE ORGANIZATION AND EVOLUTION OF DOUBLE ENTRY BOOKKEEPING TO 1440	N Txs St	74	968	Archival	History
Alvis, John M.	AN EMP. INV. OF PERSONAL CHARACTERISTICS SIGNIFICANTLY AFFECTING EMPLOYMENT OFFERS FROM INTERNATIONAL ACCT. FIRMS TO ACCT. GRADUATES	Arkansas	83	220	Field Study	Profession
Alworth, Charles Houston	AN ANALYSIS OF THE USE AND USEFULNESS OF ZERO-BASE BUDGETING IN THE FORTUNE FIVE-HUNDRED INDUSTRIAL CORPORATIONS AND THE FIFTY STATE GOVERNMENTS IN THE U.S. THROUGH 1978.	Miss	79	217	Field Study	Managerial
Amenkhienam, Felix Ehichoya	TOWARD A THEORY OF INTERNATIONAL ACCOUNTING: AN EMPIRICAL EXAMINATION OF A MORPHOLOGICAL DECISION MODEL FOR FINANCIAL ACCOUNTING STANDARDS-SETTING IN DEVELOPING COUNTRIES	Miss	84	197	Field Study	International
Amry, Mohammed A.	PROGRAM BUDGETING MODEL FOR SAUDI ARABIAN ELEMENTARY EDUCATION: AN EMPHASIS ON PROGRAM COSTS FOR DECISIONS	Arizona	76	307	Field Study	Not-for-profit
Anderman, Steven G.	A MODEL OF ACCOUNTING AND REPORTING PRACTICES FOR PROFESSIONAL AND HONOR SOCIETIES	Nebraska	81	241	Field Study	Education
Anderson, Donald Terry	THE EFFECT OF PROBLEM-SOLVING STYLES ON ACCOUNTANTS' MATERIALITY DECISIONS.	Tx A&M	80	231	Experimental	Auditing
Anderson, Earl H.	THE NEW SMALL BUSINESSMAN AND ACCOUNTING INFORMATION	Nebraska	78	144	Field Study	Financial
Anderson, Kenneth E.	AN EQUITY ANALYSIS OF VARIOUS MINIMUM TAX STRUCTURES FOR INDIVIDUAL TAXPAYERS: AN EMPIRICAL STUDY	Indiana	83	309	Archival	Tax

Author	Title	School	Date	pp	Methodology	Topic
Anderson, Matthew J.	THE INVESTMENT DECISION - AN ANALYSIS USING VERBAL PROTOCOLS	Mich St	82	203	Experimental	Financial
Anderson, Philip Neil	AN EMPIRICAL STUDY OF RECENT CHANGES IN FEDERAL ESTATE TAXATION AND THEIR RELATED IMPACT ON THE FAMILY FARM	S Carol	85	93	Archival	Tax
Anderson, Thomas N., Jr.	AN EMPIRICAL INVESTIGATION INTO THE EXPECTANCY THEORY OF MOTIVATION IN AN ACCOUNTING ENVIRONMENT.	VPI	80	252	Experimental	Profession
Andrews, Wesley T.	THE DEVELOPMENT OF ACCOUNTING PRINCIPLES FOR BUSINESS COMBINATIONS 1932-1973	N Carol	76	342	Archival	History
Anthony, Joseph Harry	JOINT OPTION EQUITY ANALYSIS	Ohio St	84	123	Model- based	Financial
Anthony, Murray S.	AN EMP. INVEST. OF THE RELATIVE PREDICTIVE ASSISTANCE ABILITY OF SEVERAL ALT. NET INC. MEASURES W/ RESPECT TO STOCK PROP.-LIAB. INS. CO.	Missouri	75	232	Market- based	Financial
Antle, Ricky Lee	MORAL HAZARD AND AUDITOR CONTRACTS: AN APPROACH TO AUDITORS' LEGAL LIABILITY AND INDEPENDENCE.	Stanford	81	143	Model- based	Auditing
Anyane-Ntow, Kwabena	THE USE OF ACCOUNTING INFORMATION IN STRUCTURING DECISION MAKING AND THE MANAGEMENT OF STATE CONTROLLED BUSINESS ENTERPRISES IN GHANA: ACCOUNTING AND ECONOMIC DEVELOPMENT REVISITED.	Georgia	82	243	Field Study	Managerial
Anyanwa, Casimar I.	IDENTIFICATION AND EVALUATION OF FISCAL DISTRESS DISCLOSURE FACTORS IN MUNICIPAL FINANCIAL REPORTS	Missouri	77	204	Market- based	Financial Distress
Aono, June Yoshiko	DISCRIMINANT ANALYSIS WITH SEVERAL PATTERNS OF MISSING DATA.	Berkeley	82	262	FinStData-based	Financial

Author	Title	School	Date	pp	Methodology	Topic
Applewhite, George	INVESTIGATION OF THE NATURE OF ANNOUNCED AND UNAUDITED ANNUAL EARNINGS	NYU	77	144	Market- based	Auditing
Ariyo, Ademola	A SIGNAL DETECTION ANALYSIS OF AUDITORS' ANALYTICAL REVIEW JUDGEMENTS	Arizona	82	254	Model- based	Auditing
Arlinghaus, Barry Paul	AN EVALUATION OF THE IMPACT OF THE MINIMUM TAX PROVISIONS ON TAX EQUITY.	Cincinnati	79	208	Model- based	Tax
Armitage, Howard M.	TOWARD AN IMPROVED DISTRIBUTION ACCOUNTING INFORMATION SYSTEM THROUGH AN ENTITY RELATIONSHIP DATA MODELING APPROACH	Mich St	83	333	Field Study	Managerial
Armstrong, Mary Beth	INTERNALIZATION OF THE PROFESSIONAL ETHIC BY CERTIFIED PUBLIC ACCOUNTANTS: A MULTIDIMENSIONAL SCALING APPROACH	S Calif	84		Field Study	Ethics
Arnett, Stephen J.	COMPARISON OF COMPUTER ASSISTED INSTRUCTION VERSUS CONVENTIONAL INSTRUCTION IN A BEGINNING ACCOUNTING COURSE	S Calif	76	134	Experimental	Education
Arnold, Jerry L.	ACCOUNTING FOR THE INVESTMENT TAX CREDIT AS A POTENTIAL CAUSAL FACTOR IN THE CORPORATE INVESTMENT DECISION: AN EMPIRICAL ANALYSIS	Michigan	75	167	FinStData-based	Financial
Arrington, Cecil E.	A SOCIAL-COGNITIVE EXAMINATION OF GAPS BETWEEN PUBLIC EXPECTATIONS AND AUDIT PERFORMANCE	Fla St	80	242	Field Study	Auditing
Arvey, Richard E.	GROUPS VERSUS INDIVIDUALS: PERFORMANCE, RISK AND PROCESS	Wash	83	141	Experimental	Managerial
Asebrook, Richard J.	REPORTING OF EARNINGS FORECASTS BY CPA'S: AN ATTITUDINAL STUDY	Wiscon	74	218	Field Study	Forecasts

Author	Title	School	Date	pp	Methodology	Topic
Ashorn, Leroy W.	THE DEVELOPMENT OF A MODEL COST ACCOUNTING SYSTEM FOR DECISION-MAKERS IN THE COMMERCIAL TELEVISION INDUSTRY	Arkansas	74	194	Field Study	Managerial
Ashton, Alison Marie Hubbard	THE DESCRIPTIVE VALIDITY OF NORMATIVE DECISION THEORY IN AUDITING CONTEXTS.	Texas	79	190	Experimental	Auditing
Atamna, Said	AN EMPIRICAL INVESTIGATION OF THE USEFULNESS OF BUDGETED FINANCIAL STATEMENTS FOR INVESTORS	Missouri	74	137	FinStData-based	Financial
Atiase, Rowland Kwame	PREDISCLOSURE INFORMATIONAL ASYMMETRIES, FIRM CAPITALIZATION, FINANCIAL REPORTS, AND SECURITY PRICE BEHAVIOR.	Berkeley	80	143	Market- based	Financial
Atieh, Sulayman H.	A PROPOSED MODEL FOR THE AUDIT AND EVAL. OF THE OBJECTIVES AND ACCOMPLISHMENTS OF JORDANIAN GOV. EXPENDITURES PROGRAM	Arizona	75	360	Field Study	Not-for-profit
Atkinson, Anthony A.	ESSAYS ON CONTROL OF DECENTRALIZED DECISION MAKING	Carn Mel	77	186	Model- based	Managerial
Attaway, Alan N.	OPTIMIZING THE TAX RESULTS OF THE COMPLETE LIQUIDATION OF A CLOSELY HELD CORPORATION: A DECISION MODEL APPROACH	Cincinnati	83	264	Experimental	Tax
Atwood, K. Edward	CURRENT COST RELIABILITY: AN INVESTIGATION OF THE EFFECT OF CERTAIN MEASUREMENT CHOICES	Wiscon	83	285	Experimental	Inflation
Aukerman, Richard A.	THE EFFECT OF ACCOUNTING REGULATIONS EMANATING FROM SECURITIES AND EXCHANGE COMMISSION RULINGS ON ACCOUNTING EDUCATION	N Dak	75	152	Archival	Education
Austin, Kenneth R.	AN EMPIRICAL INVESTIGATION OF ASSET VALUATION METHODS AND THEIR IMPACT ON EQUITY INVESTORS' DECISIONS	Kentucky	79	236	Experimental	Financial

Author	Title	School	Date	pp	Methodology	Topic
Avard, Stephen L.	AN EMPIRICAL STUDY OF FINANCIAL ANALYSTS' VALUATIONS USING PROPOSED DISCLOSURES ABOUT OIL AND GAS PRODUCING ACTIVITIES	N Txs St	83	241	FinStData-based	Oil & Gas
Ayers, Frances Lynch	AN EMPIRICAL STUDY OF DIFFERENTIAL STOCK PRICE REACTIONS OF FIRMS TO THE ENACTMENTS OF THE INVESTMENT TAX CREDIT.	Iowa	82	193	Market- based	Tax
Azzeh, Jawad Jawdat	THE RELEVANCE OF FINANCIAL FORECASTS FOR FINANCIAL STATEMENTS USERS.	Nebraska	75	297	Archival	Forecasts
Baber, William Russell	MATHEMATICAL MODELS FOR INTERNAL CONTROL EVALUATION.	N Carol	80	181	Model- based	Auditing
Badawi, Ibrahim Mohamed	ORGANIZATION AND ADMINISTRATION OF PUBLIC ENTERPRISES FOR SOCIOECONOMIC DEVELOPMENT: THE EGYPTIAN EXPERIENCE, 1805-1975.	NYU	77	593	Field Study	Not-for-profit
Badi, Mahmoud Muhyadin	APPLICATION OF INPUT-OUTPUT ANALYSIS TO PLANNING REFINERY OPERATIONS: A THEORETICAL AND EMPIRICAL STUDY.	Oklahoma	79	167	Field Study	Managerial
Badran, Sanaa M.	AN INVESTIGATION OF THE EGYPTIAN AUDITORS' PERCEPTIONS OF THE INDEPENDENCE OF THE AUDITOR	Arkansas	83	163	Field Study	Auditing
Bahjatt, Mohammed F.	STOCK MARKET REACTION TO AUDIT OPINIONS CONTAINING REFERENCE TO OTHER AUDITORS: AN EMPIRICAL INVESTIGATION	Mich St	82	184	Market- based	Auditing
Bailey, Charles Daniels	EVALUATION OF INTERNAL ACCOUNTING CONTROLS: A LABORATORY STUDY OF THE EXPERT JUDGMENTS OF CERTIFIED INTERNAL AUDITORS AND INDEPENDENT CERTIFIED PUBLIC ACCOUNTANTS.	Ga St	81	157	Experimental	Auditing
Bailey, Kieffer Edwin, III	THE PERCEIVED CHARACTER OF EXTRAORDINARY ITEMS: A MULTIDIMENSIONAL SCALING APPROACH.	N Carol	76	282	Experimental	E.O.Items

Author	Title	School	Date	pp	Methodology	Topic
Bailey, Larry P.	AN EMPIRICAL EVALUATION OF THE QUALITY OF INTERIM FINANCIAL STATEMENTS	Penn	74	161	FinStData-based	Interim Statements
Bailey, William Tansley	AN EXAMINATION OF THE CREDIBILITY EFFECTS OF SELECTED AUDIT OPINIONS.	Texas	78	266	Experimental	Auditing
Baiman, Stanley	OPTIMAL FORECASTING IN SELECTED ORGANIZATIONAL MODELS.	Stanford	74	163	Model- based	Managerial
Baingridge, Dunham R.	PERCEPTIONS OF THE CPA'S ABILITY TO DETECT MISREPRESENTATIONS OF THE SMALLER BUSINESS'S FINANCIAL STATEMENTS	Lehigh	78	180	Field Study	Auditing
Bait-Elmel, Mohammed A.	THE ROLE OF ITC AND ACC. DEP. IN STIMULATING MORE INVESTMENT: THE USA CASE AND ITS IMPLICATIONS TO THE LIBYAN INCOME TAX SYSTEM	Kentucky	78	188	FinStData-based	Tax
Baker, Charles Richard	A RELATIONAL ANALYSIS OF STRUCTURE IN COMPLEX ORGANIZATIONS: THE CASE OF THE LARGE PUBLIC ACCOUNTING FIRM.	Berkeley	75	208	Model- based	Managerial
Baker, Jack D.	A STUDY OF MUNICIPALLY OWNED ELECTRIC UTILITIES' FINANCIAL REPORTING PRACTICES	Missouri	80	205	Field Study	Not-for-profit
Baker, Paul D.	THE RELATIONSHIP BETWEEN USE OF ACCOUNTING INFORMATION AND THE PERFORMANCE OF MUTUAL FUNDS	Ga St	74	175	Market- based	Mutual Funds
Baker, Richard Edward	AN EMPIRICAL INVESTIGATION OF THE EFFECT OF ACCOUNTING CHANGES ON INVESTOR BEHAVIOR.	Wiscon	74	318	Market- based	Accounting Changes
Baker, Robert Louis	BEHAVIOR OF CERTAIN STATISTICAL ESTIMATORS IN SAMPLING ACCOUNTING POPULATIONS.	S Carol	78	122	Model- based	Auditing

Author	Title	School	Date	pp	Methodology	Topic
Baldwin, Bruce A.	LINE OF BUSINESS DISCLOSURE REQUIREMENTS AND SECURITY ANALYSTS FORECAST ACCURACY	Ariz St	79	123	FinStData-based	Forecasts
Baldwin, Duane E.	AN INQUIRY INTO THE FEASIBILITY OF AUDITING PUBLISHED FINANCIAL PROJECTIONS	S Calif	75	195	Field Study	Auditing
Ballew, Van B.	ORGANIZATIONAL SIZE, TECHNOLOGY, AND FORMALIZATION IN PROFESSIONAL ACCOUNTING ORGANIZATIONS	Houston	77	164	Field Study	Profession
Balogun, Jacob Olakayode	THE REACTION OF THE SECURITY MARKET TO THE QUALITY OF SEGMENTAL DISCLOSURES: AN EMPIRICAL INVESTIGATION.	LSU	80	162	Market- based	Business Segments
Bamber, Edward Michael	EXPERT JUDGEMENT IN THE AUDIT TEAM: AN EXAMINATION OF SOURCE CREDIBILITY.	Ohio St	80	242	Experimental	Auditing
Banatte, Jean-Marie	AN ANALYSIS OF THE PRESIDENTS' LETTERS ACCOMPANYING ANNUAL FINANCIAL REPORTS IN THE TRANSPORTATION INDUSTRY	Missouri	77	171	Field Study	Financial
Banker, Rajiv Dushyant	STUDIES IN COST ALLOCATION AND EFFICIENCY EVALUATION.	Harvard	80	220	Field Study	Managerial
Banks, Doyle Wesley	AN EMPIRICAL ANALYSIS OF INFORMATION CONTENT IN ACCOUNTING LOSS CONTINGENCIES AND RELATED UNCERTAINTY QUALIFIED AUDIT OPINIONS.	Iowa	79	140	Market- based	Auditing
Bao, Ben Hsien	THE INFORMATION CONTENT OF CHANGING-PRICE ACCOUNTING DISCLOSURES MANDATED BY SFAS NO. 33 (IMPACTS, MARKET REACTIONS, RESPONSES)	Missouri	84	217	Market- based	Inflation
Bao, Da-Hsien	MULTIOBJECTIVE DECISION METHODS IN A CAPITAL BUDGETING CONTEST: A LABORATORY EXPERIMENT.	S Calif	81		Experimental	Managerial

Author	Title	School	Date	pp	Methodology	Topic
Baran, Arie	PRICE LEVEL EARNINGS: AN EMPIRICAL STUDY OF THEIR TIME-SERIES BEHAVIOR AND RELATIONSHIP TO SECURITY PRICE CHANGES	Berkeley	76	185	Market- based	Inflation
Barker, Robert L.	CERTIFICATION OF MGT. ACCOUNTANTS-A STUDY OF THE EVOLUTIION, THE UNDERLYING BODY OF KNOWLEDGE AND THE IMPORT. OF ACCT. PRAC. AND EDUCATION	Alabama	74	396	Field Study	Profession
Barkman, Arnold I.	A CRITICAL EVALUATION AND EXTENSION OF THE APPLICATION OF QUANTITATIVE TECHNIQUES TO THE FIELD OF AUDITING	Houston	74	176	Field Study	Auditing
Barnett, Andrew H.	COMMUNICATIONS IN AUDITING: AN EXAMINATION OF INVESTORS' UNDERSTANDING OF THE AUDITOR'S REPORT	Txs Tech	76	284	Experimental	Auditing
Barrack, John B.	AN EMPIRICAL STUDY OF COMMERCIAL BANK FINANCIAL REPORTING	Okl St	74	186	FinStData-based	Bank Accounting
Barron, Rhelda W.	AN EXPERIMENT TO DETERMINE THE EFFECT OF TEACHING METHODS ON ACHIEVEMENT AND ATTITUDE OF STUDENTS IN PRINCIPLES OF ACCOUNTING CLASSES.	Miss St	78	193	Experimental	Education
Bartczak, Norman Joseph	EFFECTS OF FINANCIAL DISCLOSURE ON CORPORATE BOND RISK PREMIUMS: A COMPARATIVE EMPIRICAL ANALYSIS.	Wash	78	365	Market- based	Bonds
Bartenstein, Edwin	PRODUCT COSTING UNDER CONDITIONS OF IDLE PLANT CAPACITY	S Calif	75	242	Archival	Managerial
Bartkowski, Richard J.	A STUDY OF ISSUES RELATED TO NONOPTIMUM EX POST BUDGETING	Pitt	82	278	Experimental	Managerial
Bartlett, Henry C.	AN ANALYSIS OF LINE OF BUSINESS FINANCIAL REPORTING	Indiana	75	290	Archival	Business Segments

Author	Title	School	Date	pp	Methodology	Topic
Bartlett, Roger Wallaco	POWER BASE ATTRIBUTION AND THE PERCEIVED LEGITIMACY OF MANAGERIAL ACCOUNTING.	Houston	80	245	Field Study	Managerial
Bartley, Jon W.	ACCOUNTING FOR THE COST OF CAPITAL: AN EMPIRICAL EXAMINATION	N Carol	78	277	FinStData-based	Financial
Barton, M. Frank, Jr.	THE EMPLOYMENT OF ACCOUNTING ASSOCIATE DEGREE GRADUATES OF THE TWO TECHNICAL INSTITUTES IN TENNESSEE.	Miss	75	177	Field Study	Profession
Barton, Thomas L.	RELEVANCE AND RELIABILITY IN AN EXPERIMENTAL LENDING ENVIRONMENT	Florida	84	160	Experimental	Financial
Basohlu, Basalet	AN EMPIRICAL STUDY ON SMOOTHING OF REPORTED ANNUAL CORPORATE INCOME THROUGH ACCOUNTING TREATMENT	Fla St	79	180	FinStData-based	Income Smoothing8:48 pm
Basu, Sanjoy	THE RELATIONSHIP BETWEEN INVESTMENT PERFORMANCE OF EQUITY SECURITIES AND THEIR PRICE-EARNINGS RATIOS: A TEST OF THE EFFICIENT MARKETS-EXPECTED RETURN MODEL.	Cornell	75	212	Market- based	Financial
Bates, Homer L	AN EMPIRICAL INVESTIGATION OF THE PREDICTIVE ABILITY OF SELECTED ACCOUNTING RISK MEASURES	Illinois	77	197	Market- based	Financial
Bathke, Allen William, Jr.	THE EFFECT OF CAPITAL STRUCTURE ON THE ASSOCIATION BETWEEN ACCOUNTING EARNINGS NUMBERS AND SECURITY RETURNS.	Fla St	82	350	Market- based	Financial
Baudin, Jerry J.	THE USEFULNESS AND PREDICTABILITY OF NET REALIZEABLE VALUES: AN EMPIRICAL STUDY	LSU	82	178	Field Study	Inflation
Bavish, Vinod Bapalal	CAPITAL BUDGETING FOR THE US-BASED MULTINATIONAL CORPORATIONS: AN ASSESSMENT OF THEORY AND PRACTICE.	Ohio St	79	167	Field Study	Managerial

Author	Title	School	Date	pp	Methodology	Topic
Baxter, Clifton A.	THE EFFECTS OF COMPUTER AUGMENTED INSTRUCTION ON ACHIEVEMENT IN THE COLLEGIATE PRINCIPLES OF ACCOUNTING COURSE	Georgia	74	129	Experimental	Education
Bayer, Frieda Anna Forcht	AN ANALYSIS OF THE RELATIONSHIP BETWEEN THE DISCRETIONARY ACTUARIAL FACTORS USED BY A FIRM AND CERTAIN FIRM-SPECIFIC VARIABLES (DEFINED BENEFIT, PENSION PLANS, EXPENSE ACCOUNTING)	Texas at Arlington	84	118	FinStData-based	Pensions
Bayes, Paul E.	EMPIRICAL INVESTIGATION OF THE EFFECTS OF HUMAN RESOURCE ACCOUNTING INFORMATION ON DECISION MAKING: RESULTS OF A MAIL SURVEY	Kentucky	83	205	Experimental	Hum.Resource Acct.
Bayless, Mark E.	THE DIFFERENTIAL ATTRACTIVENESS OF LOCATIONS AND THE SPATIAL PATTERN OF WAGES: THE CASE OF UNIVERSITY PROFESSORS	Wash	79	177	Field Study	Education
Bayou, Mohammed E.	AN INVESTIGATION OF ACCOUNTANTS' AND FINANCIAL ANALYSTS' ATTITUDES TOWARDS REPORTING SELECTED DEFERRABLE AND ACCRUABLE ITEMS	Cincinnati	82	328	Field Study	Financial
Bazaz, Mohammad Sadegh	THE ECONOMIC EFFECTS OF FASB STATEMENT NO. 2 ON SMALL FIRMS' R&D EXPENDITURES	Oklahoma	84	143	Field Study	Research & Development
Beam, Thomas J.	A COMPETITIVE BIDDING MODEL BASED ON ACCOUNTING INFORMATION	NYU	75	136	Experimental	Managerial
Bean, Russell D.	A STUDY OF THE USE OF FORMAL AND INFORMAL CASH BUDGETING IN THIRTY SMALL MFG FIRMS IN THE STATE OF COLORADO	Colorado	74	228	Field Study	Managerial
Beard, Larry H.	THE EFFECT OF PROJECTIONS OF ALTERNATIVE DISCLOSURES OF AN ACCOUNTING CHANGE: A BEHAVIORAL INVESTIGATION	Georgia	74	174	FinStData-based	Accounting Changes
Beatty, Randolph P.	A STUDY OF THE ACCOUNTING CLASSIFICATION OF CONVERTIBLE SECURITIES: A MARKET ANALYSIS	Illinois	82	153	Market- based	Financial

Author	Title	School	Date	pp	Methodology	Topic
Beck, Paul J.	A CRITICAL ANALYSIS OF THE REGRESSION ESTIMATOR IN AUDIT SAMPLING	Texas	77	259	Experimental	Auditing
Becker, Edward A.	A REEXAMINATION OF THE CONCEPT OF VARIABLE COSTS	Penn St	84	202	Field Study	Managerial
Beed, Teresa Kathryn	OCCUPATIONAL CHOICE OF COLLEGE ACCOUNTING SENIORS AS RELATED TO SELF-DESCRIPTIONS, ACCOUNTING STEREOTYPES, AND INTEREST LEVELS.	Colorado	81	120	Field Study	Profession
Beirne, Thomas Joseph, Jr.	AN INVESTIGATION INTO THE TAXATION OF UNDISTRIBUTED INCOME, SECTIONS 951 THROUGH 964 OF THE INTERNAL REVENUE CODE: THE CONTROLLED FOREIGN CORPORATION.	Oklahoma	81	149	Archival	Tax
Bell, Timothy Barnes	MARKET REACTION TO RESERVE RECOGNITION ACCOUNTING.	Okl St.	81	85	Market- based	Oil & Gas
Benbasat, Izak	AN EXPERIMENTAL EVALUATION OF THE EFFECTS OF INFORMATION SYSTEM AND DECISION-MAKER CHARACTERISTICS ON DECISION EFFECTIVENESS.	Minnesota	74	210	Experimental	Managerial
Bengharbia, Salem M.	AN EMPIRICAL INVESTIGATION OF THE DIFFERENTIAL MARKET RESPONSE TO QUARTERLY EARNINGS ANNOUNCEMENTS	LSU	82	133	Market- based	Quarterly Data
Benjamin, Wahjudi Prakarsa	ACCOUNTING POLICY INTERVENTIONS AND THE BEHAVIOR OF SECURITY RETURNS.	Missouri	80	146	Market- based	Financial
Benke, Ralph L.	A MULTIVARIATE ANALYSIS OF THE JOB SATISFACTION OF PROFESSIONAL EMPLOYEES IN BIG 8 PUBLIC ACCOUNTING FIRMS	Fla St	78	250	Field Study	Profession
Bennett, Jerome Vincent	AN INQUIRY INTO THE MEANINGS OF THE AUDITOR'S UNQUALIFIED OPINION TO STOCKHOLDERS, AUDITORS AND ACCOUNTANTS.	S Carol	76	179	Field Study	Auditing

Author	Title	School	Date	pp	Methodology	Topic
Bennett, Shelby Dill	JOINT FILING VERSUS SEPARATE FILING FOR SPOUSES: AN EMPIRICAL STUDY OF THE NORTH CAROLINA INDIVIDUAL INCOME TAX SYSTEM.	N Carol	80	274	Experimental	Tax
Benson, Vaughn Leon	A STUDY OF THE USEFULNESS OF SELECTED GAAP BASIS ACCOUNTING INFORMATION AND ITS ACTUAL USE IN THE SMALL PRIVATE COMPANY LOAN DECISION PROCESS	Nebraska	85	365	Experimental	Financial
Bentsen, Elesa J.W.	AN EXAMINATION OF THE FEDERAL INCOME TAX INCENTIVES FOR THE REHABILITATION OF HISTORIC PORPERTY	Texas	83	278	Experimental	Tax
Berk, Joel Lee	RELATIONSHIP BETWEEN MACROECONOMIC PROJECTIONS AND EARNINGS FORECASTS.	Columbia	78	177	FinStData-based	Forecasts
Berkshire, Stewart, Jr.	FACTORS WHICH INFLUENCE COST MANAGEMENT IN HOSPITALS	Santa Cl	75	128	Field Study	Not-for-profit
Bermudez, Andres	AN ANALYSIS OF INDUSTRIAL INCENTIVE TAXATION IN PUERTO RICO	Kent St	76	268	Field Study	Tax
Berry, Leonard E.	A SEARCH FOR A SET OF PERFORMANCE CRITERIA FOR USE IN A GOVERNMENTAL INTERNAL AUDIT MGMT. CONTROL SYSTEM: AN EMPIRICAL STUDY	Colorado	76	182	Field Study	Auditing
Berry, Maureen H.	ENTERPRISE VERSUS FUND ACCOUNTING: INCONGRUENCY AND DUALITY IN DEFENSE RELATED INDUSTRIES	UCLA	76	426	Model- based	Not-for-profit
Beshara, Robert Labib	NEWNESS AND IMPUTED ACCURACY OF MANAGEMENT FORECASTS: AN EMPIRICAL INVESTIGATION.	Florida	81	150	Market- based	Forecasts
Besser, Lance J.	BUDGETING RESPONSES TO INFLATION IN INSTITUTIONS OF HIGHER EDUCATION	Arkansas	83	293	Field Study	Not-for-profit

Author	Title	School	Date	pp	Methodology	Topic
Bettinger, Cynthia Ann Rabby	MANAGEMENT REPORTS: A STUDY OF COMPLIANCE WITH AICPA RECOMMENDATIONS AND OF THE USEFULNESS OF MANAGEMENT REPORTS TO FINANCIAL ANALYSTS.	La Tech	82	197	Field Study	Auditing
Bhamornsiri, Surasakdi	AN EMP. INV. INTO THE ASSOC. BETWEEN ACCT. RISK MEASURES ADJUSTED FOR CAPITALIZATION OF LEASE COMMITMENTS AND THE MARKET RISK MEASURES	Tenn	79	195	FinStData-based	Leases
Biddle, Gary Clark	ACCOUNTING METHODS AND MANAGEMENT DECISIONS: THE CASE OF INVENTORY COSTING AND INVENTORY POLICY.	Chicago	80		FinStData-based	Managerial
Biggs, Stanley F.	AN INVESTIGATION OF THE DECISION PROCESSES UNDERLYING THE ASSESSMENT OF CORPORATE EARNING POWER	Minnesota	78	355	Field Study	Managerial
Bindon, Kathleen Jo Ranney	INVENTORIES AND FOREIGN CURRENCY TRANSLATION REQUIREMENTS: AN EXPLORATORY STUDY.	Penn St	81	230	Field Study	Foreign Currency
Birkett, Brenda S.	PERCEPTIONS OF THE ROLE OF CORPORATE AUDIT COMMITTEES - NOW AND IN THE FUTURE	LSU	80	172	Field Study	Auditing
Birrer, George Eddy	IMPORTANCE OF SELECTED ACCOUNTING AND RELATED COURSES AS PREPARATION FOR A MANAGEMENT ACCOUNTING CAREER.	N Dak	81	106	Field Study	Education
Bishop, Ashton Coles, Jr.	ALLOWANCE FOR FUNDS USED DURING CONSTRUCTION, EARNINGS, AND THE BEHAVIOR OF STOCK PRICES OF ELECTRIC UTILITY COMPANIES.	Okl St.	79	80	Market- based	Financial
Bitner, Larry Newell	ACCOUNTING FOR CHANGING PRICES PER FASB 33 AND THE IMPACT ON INCOME SMOOTHING (INFLATION)	Geo Wash	85	116	FinStData-based	Inflation
Bizzell, Allen H.	A COMMUNICATION CONCEPTS ANALYSIS OF FINANCIAL REPORTING: IMPLICATIONS FOR ACCOUNTING THEORY AND PRACTICE	Miss St	76	384	Model- based	Financial

Author	Title	School	Date	pp	Methodology	Topic
Black, Robert L.	AN INVESTIGATION OF SOME FACTORS IN TAX PROBLEM-FINDING ABILITY	Minnesota	76	324	Experimental	Tax
Black, Thomas Gilbert	AN EMPIRICAL INVESTIGATION OF THE USEFULNESS OF GENERAL PRICE-LEVEL INFORMATION FOR STOCK INVESTMENT DECISIONS.	Missouri	79	181	Market- based	Inflation
Blank, Mark M.	SOCIALIZATION IN PUBLIC ACCOUNTING FIRMS	Penn St	84	241	Field Study	Social
Blann, Jack Ralph	AN INVESTIGATION OF THE INFORMATION CONTENT AND PREDICTIVE ABILITY OF SELECTED ACCOUNTING INCOME NUMBERS.	Wash	78	112	FinStData-based	Financial Ratios
Blocher, Edward J.	A GOAL PROGRAM MODEL FOR AUDIT SAMPLING DECISIONS	Texas	74	256	Model- based	Auditing
Block, Linda Joyce	SEC INCOME TAX DISCLOSURE AND MARKET RISK ADJUSTMENTS.	Purdue	78	165	Market- based	Deferred Taxes
Bloom, Robert	PERSPECTIVES ON THE OBJECTIVES OF FINANCIAL STATEMENTS	NYU	76	336	Model- based	Financial
Bodnar, George H.	A BEHAVIORAL ANALYSIS OF COST ALLOCATION IN RESPONSIBILITY ACCOUNTING SYSTEMS	Penn	75	130	Field Study	Managerial
Boes, Richard Fred	INVESTOR REACTION TO PREFERENTIAL TAXATION-THE OIL INDUSTRY AND THE TAX REFORM ACT OF 1969.	Mich St.	78	126	Market- based	Tax
Bokemeier, L. Charles	AN INVESTIGATION OF THE CRITERIA FOR THE RECOGNITION OF SELECTED REVENUES AND EXPENDITURES/EXPENSES IN STATE GOV'T ACCOUNTING	Kentucky	83	311	Field Study	Not-for-profit

Author	Title	School	Date	pp	Methodology	Topic
Boland, Richard James, Jr.	PROTOCOLS OF INTERACTION IN THE DESIGN OF INFORMATION SYSTEMS: AN EVALUATION OF THE ROLE OF THE SYSTEMS ANALYST IN DETERMINING INFORMATION REQUIREMENTS.	Case Wes	76	217	Experimental	Systems/ Computers
Boley, Richard Dale	THE USE OF FLOWCHARTS AS AN ANALYTICAL AND EDUCATIONAL APPROACH TO THE DETERMINATION OF CONSOLIDATED CORPORATE TAXABLE INCOME.	Texas	76	307	Experimental	Tax
Bomber, Linda S.	THE INFORMATION CONTENT OF ANNUAL EARNINGS RELEASES: A TRADING VOLUME APPROACH	Ohio St	83	237	Market- based	Financial
Bond, James G.	AN EMPIRICAL INVESTIGATION OF COURT-DETERMINED DEBT-EQUITY ATTRIBUTES FOR FEDERAL INCOME TAX PURPOSES	S Carol	77	175	Archival	Tax
Boockholdt, James Lee	A MANAGEMENT ORIENTED DESIGN METHODOLOGY FOR DISTRIBUTED BUSINESS SYSTEMS UTILIZING A RING NETWORK OF MINICOMPUTERS.	Alabama	77	258	Field Study	Systems/ Computers
Boodai, Khalid M.	AN INCOME DETERMINATION MODEL FOR INCOME SHARING INVESTMENT COMPANIES	Missouri	80	392	Field Study	Financial
Booker, Quinton	AN EMPIRICAL INVESTIGATION OF THE ATTITUDES OF MISSISSIPPI CPAs AND BANKERS CONCERNING SELECTED ASPECTS OF SSARS	Miss St	84	193	Experimental	Auditing
Boren, Adrian W.	AN INVESTIGATION INTO THE ASSOCIATION BETWEEN ACCOUNTING VARIABLES AND STOCK MARKET RETURNS: THE MEXICAN CASE	VPI	82	180	Market- based	Financial
Boritz, Jefim E.	EXPERTISE IN REVIEW AND PLANNING BY EXTERNAL AUDITORS	Minnesota	83	404	Experimental	Auditing
Borthick, Alice F.	SELECTION OF COMPUTERS FOR SMALL ACCOUNTING SYSTEMS: AN INTERACTIVE MULTI-CRITERIA APPROACH	Tenn	82	166	Model- based	Systems/ Computers

Author	Title	School	Date	pp	Methodology	Topic
Bostrom, Donald E.	SEGMENT DEFINITION FOR FINANCIAL REPORTING BY DIVERSIFIED FIRMS	N Txs St	74	231	Model- based	Business Segments
Bostwick, William Jackson	PREDICTION OF EARNINGS, SIX YEARS AFTER GRADUATION, OF A GROUP OF GEORGIA STATE UNIVERSITY MBA'S.	Ga St	80	194	Field Study	Education
Bottin, Ronald R.	AN ANALYSIS OF THE DESIREABILITY OF INCORPORATING CPA FIRMS	Missouri	74	189	Field Study	Profession
Bourne, Frances Yvonne	A BUDGET MODEL FOR SMALL MANUFACTURING COMPANIES.	Okl St.	78	389	Model- based	Managerial
Bourne, Lowell D.	ORDER EFFECTS IN ACCOUNTING VARIANCE REPORTS: A LABORATORY EXPERIMENT	Wash U	76	155	Experimental	Managerial
Bowen, Robert Michael	VALUATION OF CAPITALIZED INTEREST ON CONSTRUCTION EXPENDITURES IN THE ELECTRIC UTILITY INDUSTRY.	Stanford	78	214	Model- based	Interest Capitalization
Bowlin, William Frank	A DATA ENVELOPMENT ANALYSIS APPROACH TO PERFORMANCE EVALUATION IN NOT-FOR-PROFIT ENTITIES WITH AN ILLUSTRATIVE APPLICATION TO THE U.S. AIR FORCE (UNITED STATES) (EFFICIENCY)	Texas	84	298	Field Study	Not-for-Profit
Bowman, Betty R.	A VIDEO TUTORIAL APPROACH TO THE TEACHING OF ACCOUNTING	VPI	77	136	Experimental	Education
Bowman, Robert G.	AN EMPIRICAL INVESTIGATION OF THE DEBT EQUIVALENCE OF LEASES	Stanford	78	151	FinStData-based	Leases
Boyd, James H.	TAX PLANNING FOR COMPENSATION FOR THE OWNER-OPERATOR OF A SMALL BUSINESS CORPORATION: A DECISION MODEL APPROACH	Texas	76	462	Experimental	Tax

Author	Title	School	Date	pp	Methodology	Topic
Boyd, Joseph L.	AN EMPIRICAL INVESTIGATION OF REASONABLE COMPENSATION DETERMINATION IN CLOSELY-HELD CORPORATIONS	S Carol	77		Archival	Tax
Boyett, Arthur S., III	THE EFFECTS OF AUDITORS' REPORTS ON INTERNAL ACCOUNTING CONTROLS UPON INVESTMENT ANALYSES MADE BY FINANCIAL ANALYSTS AND BANK LOAN OFFICERS: AN EMPIRICAL STUDY.	Tx Tech	80	145	Experimental	Auditing
Boyles, Jesse V.	ACCOUNTING FOR LONG-LIVED PRODUCTIVE RESOURCES - THE DEVELOPMENT AND EVALUATION OF GENERAL ENERGY SYSTEMS MEASUREMENT PROCEDURES	Florida	75	232	Model- based	Financial
Boynton, William C.	AN ANALYSIS OF THE RELIABILITY OF MGMT. EARNINGS FORECAST PUBLISHED IN ALTERNATIVE FORMATS AND INVESTIG. OF SELECTED MGMT. FORECAST DISCL. PRACTICES	Mich St	76	170	FinStData-based	Forecasts
Bozanich, Peter Kenneth	AN INQUIRY INTO COST VARIABILITY AT THE COST CENTER LEVEL OF SELECTED SOUTH CAROLINA HOSPITALS.	S Carol	76	169	Field Study	Not-for-profit
Bracken, Robert M.	THE ACCOUNTING PROFESSION'S SPECIFICATION OF PROCEDURES AND ACTIONS FOLLOWING INITIATIONS OF SELECTED LEGAL ACTIONS INVOLVING ALLEGATIONS OF ILLEGAL OR IMPROPER MANAGEMENT ACTS: 1939-1978	Miss St	83	270	Field Study	Profession
Brackner, James Walter	A STUDY OF THE FRAMEWORK FOR THE TREATMENT OF CONTINGENT LOSSES	Alabama	84	300	Field Study	Financial
Bradley, Bryce T.	DETERMINATION OF RELEVANT FINANCIAL INFORMATION AND MINIMUM PACKET DESIGN FOR SELECTED NEBRASKA HOSPITALS	Nebraska	79	245	Field Study	Not-for-profit
Brady, Thomas J.	INFLATION ACCOUNTING AND STATEMENT OF FAS NO. 33: AN EMPIRICAL STUDY OF ACCOUNTING DISCLOSURE AND REPORTING SIGNIFICANCE	Saint Louis	81	176	Model- based	Inflation
Braide, January Miller	PERFORMANCE EVALUATION AND DECISION MAKING: AN ANALYTICAL APPROACH	Missouri	81	224	Model- based	Managerial

Author	Title	School	Date	pp	Methodology	Topic
Braun, Robert M.	CONCERNING ACCOUNTING FOR UNCERTAINTIES	NYU	80	146	Field Study	Financial
Bravo Herrera, Fernando	AN EMPIRICAL ANALYSIS OF THE PREDICTIVE ABILITY OF ALTERNATIVE INCOME MEASURES.	Berkeley	77	148	FinStData-based	Financial
Brecha, Sonia A.	COMPARITIVE FORECASTING FROM TWO ACCOUNTING INCOME MEASURES	Kent St	83	190	FinStData-based	Forecasts
Brecht, Howard David	REGRESSION ANALYSIS USING LINEAR PROGRAMMING: A STUDY OF ESTIMATION CHARACTERISTICS AND STATISTICAL PROPERTIES.	Texas	74	151	Model- based	Financial
Bremser, Wayne G.	AN EMPIRICAL STUDY OF THE CONSISTENCY STANDARD IN FINANCIAL ACCOUNTING AND DISCRETIONARY ACCOUNTING CHANGES	Penn	74	165	Market- based	Accounting Changes
Brewer, Carl Wm.	THE NATURE OF AUDIT RISK INDICATORS AND THEIR EFFECT ON THE INTENSITY OF AUDIT WORK PERFORMED.	Houston	81	163	Field Study	Auditing
Briner, Russell F.	AN EMPIRICAL STUDY OF THE ASSOCIATION BETWEEN ALTERNATIVE MEASURES OF EPS AND BEHAVIOR OF SECURITY PRICES 1969-1972	Okl St	76	142	Market- based	Financial
Bristol, James Tadsen	PREDICTING MUNICIPAL REVENUE BOND RATINGS WITH FINANCIAL RATIOS AND OTHER ECONOMIC DATA.	Texas	78	206	FinStData-based	Financial Ratios
Brock, Barbara H.	AN EXAMINATION OF THE UNIFORM SYSTEMS OF ACCOUNTS FOR ELECTRIC CORPORATIONS AS PRESCRIBED BY THE NEW YORK PUBLIC SERVICE COMMISSION WITH CONSIDERATION OF MAJOR POLITICAL, ECONOMIC, STATUTORY AND LEGAL INFLUENCES, 1906-1977.	NYU	79	631	Archival	Not-for-profit
Broden, Berry C.	ETHICS IN TAX PRACTICE	Maryland	77	438	Experimental	Ethics

Author	Title	School	Date	pp	Methodology	Topic
Brook, Edna Mae	THE EFFECTIVENESS OF THREE TECHNIQUES USED IN TEACHING FIRST SEMESTER ACCOUNTING PRINCIPLES TO TECHNICAL JR. COLLEGE STUDENTS	Arizona	74	167	Experimental	Education
Brooks, Eugene H.	INTEGRATED MUNICIPAL ACCOUNTING INFORMATION SYSTEMS	N Carol	83	221	Field Study	Not-for-profit
Brooks, John E.	AN EMPIRICAL INVESTIGATION OF THE USEFULNESS OF EARNINGS IN PREDICTING FUTURE ENTERPRISE CASH FLOWS	Mich St	81	151	FinStData-based	Cash Flows
Broom, Lowell S.	AN INQUIRY INTO THE ABILITY OF ASR 190 RULE 3-17 TO ACCOMPLISH ITS OBJECTIVES WITHIN THE STEEL INDUSTRY AND PAPER INDUSTRY	La Tech	80	146	FinStData-based	Inflation
Brown, Barbara	AN EXAM. OF THE UNIF. SYS. OF ACCTS. FOR ELEC. CORP. AS PRES. BY THE N.Y. PUB. SERV. COM. W/CONSID.. OF MAJOR POL., ECON. STAT. AND LEGAL INFL. 1905-1977	SUNY-Buf	79	631	Field Study	Managerial
Brown, Clifton E.	HUMAN INFORMATION PROCESSING FOR DECISIONS TO INVESTIGATE COST VARIANCES	Florida	78	205	Experimental	Managerial
Brown, Howard J.	PROFESSIONAL ETHICS IN REQUIRED AUDITING COURSES IN THE EDUCATION OF PUBLIC ACCOUNTANTS	NYU	75	212	Field Study	Ethics
Brown, James France, Jr.	PLANNING POLICIES AND EFFECTIVENESS OF FIRMS ENGAGED IN SYSTEMATIC PLANNING PROCESSES: A CROSS-VALIDATION STUDY.	Tenn	81	228	FinStData-based	Managerial
Brown, Paul R.	A DESCRIPTIVE ANALYSIS OF SELECT INPUT BASES OF THE FINANCIAL ACCOUNTING STANDARDS BOARD	Texas	79	286	Field Study	Financial
Brown, Robert M.	CHANGES TO LIFO ACCOUNTING AND SECURITY PRICES: AN EMPIRICAL INVESTIGATION	Geo St	77	176	Market- based	Inventories

Author	Title	School	Date	pp	Methodology	Topic
Brown, Ronald D.	THE USEFULNESS OF FINANCIAL RATIOS FOR PREDICTING COMMON STOCK PERFORMANCE ON CANADIAN MANUFACTURING FIRMS	Syracuse	78	190	Market- based	Financial Ratios
Brown, Surdo	A GENERAL APPROACH FOR THE DETERMINATION OF MATERIALITY	Wiscon	79	190	Experimental	Financial
Brownell, Peter	PARTICIPATION IN BUDGETING, LOWS OF CONTROL AND ORGANIZATIONAL EFFECTIVENESS	Berkeley	79	158	Experimental	Managerial
Brownlee, Earl R.	AN INVESTIGATION AND ANALYSIS OF THE USEFULNESS OF THE SCFP TO SELECTED EXTERNAL USERS OF CORPORATE FINANCIAL INFORMATION	Ga St	75	246	Field Study	Statement of Ch Fin Pos
Brugger, Karl A.	IMPACT OF FASB 2 ON INDUSTRIAL RESEARCH AND DEVELOPMENT EXPENDITURES	Ariz St	78	108	FinStData-based	Research & Development
Bryan, Edward L.	THE DEVELOPMENT OF A FINANCIAL REPORTING MODEL FOR NOT FOR PROFIT AND TRADE PROFESSIONAL ASSOCIATIONS	Geo Wash	80	226	Model- based	Not-for-profit
Bryant, Murray J.	AUDITOR JUDGEMENT: SIMULATION AND INFORMATION SEARCH PROCESSES	Cincinnati	83	389	Experimental	Auditing
Bryson, Roscoe E.	ROBERT M. TRUEBLOOD-CPA: THE CONSUMMATE PROFESSIONAL	Ga St	76	315	Archival	History
Bublitz, Bruce Orval	OPERATIONISM AS THE BASIS OF ACCOUNTING INCOME CONSTRUCTS: A PHILOSOPHICAL AND EMPIRICAL INVESTIGATION INCLUDING A MARKET ASSOCIATION TEST OF REPLACEMENT COST AND IMPLICIT INTEREST ACCOUNTING	Illinois	82	372	Market- based	Inflation
Buchanan, Phillip G.	INCOME SMOOTHING UNDER THE SUCCESSFUL EFFORTS AND FULL COST METHODS IN THE OIL AND GAS INDUSTRY	Temple	83	156	FinStData-based	Oil & Gas

Author	Title	School	Date	pp	Methodology	Topic
Buchman, Thomas A.	REPORTING OF EXTRAORDINARY ITEMS AND THE BEHAVIOR OF SECURITY PRICES	Illinois	76	158	Market- based	E.O.Items
Buckley, Charles E.	A STUDY OF INTERNSHIPS IN PUBLIC ACCOUNTING: STATUS, TRENDS, AND AN EVALUATION FROM THE VIEWPOINT OF PRACTITIONERS	Oklahoma	74	250	Field Study	Profession
Buehlmann, David M.	THE IMPORTANCE OF LEADERSHIP STYLE ON THE JOB SATISFACTION, TURNOVER PERCEPTION, AND PERFORMANCE OF STAFF ACCOUNTANTS IN LARGE PUBLIC ACCOUNTING FIRMS	Illinois	75	190	Field Study	Profession
Bullen, Maria L.	AN EMPIRICAL STUDY OF SOURCES OF JOB SATISFACTION IN THE BIG EIGHT CPA FIRM	UCLA	82	538	Field Study	Profession
Bullock, James H.	A MODEL-SYSTEMS APPROACH TO THE PLANNING AND CONTROL OF MAINTENANCE COSTS	Okl St	74	221	Model- based	Managerial
Bulmash, Gary F.	AN INQUIRY INTO THE BACKGROUND OF AND CIRCUMSTANCES LEADING TO THE ESTABLISHMENT OF THE CASB	Maryland	74	350	Archival	History
Burgstahler, David Curtis	CROSS-SECTIONAL AND CROSS-TEMPORAL DIFFERENCES IN THE RELATIONSHIP BETWEEN ANNUAL EARNINGS AND SECURITY RETURNS.	Iowa	81	197	Market- based	Financial
Burke, Mimi	ATTITUDES TOWARD PARTICIAPTION IN THE STANDARD-SETTING PROCEDURES OF THE FASB	Txs A&M	78	115	Field Study	Financial
Burke, Richard Collingwood	SOME PARAMETERS OF FINANCIAL ANALYSIS BEHAVIOR: AN INTERCULTURAL EVALUATION UNDER EXPERIMENTAL CONDITIONS.	Wash	76	147	Experimental	Financial
Burnaby, Priscilla A.	THE INFORMATION CONTENT OF RESERVE RECOGNITION ACCOUNTING	Txs A&M	82	118	Market- based	Oil & Gas

Author	Title	School	Date	pp	Methodology	Topic
Burns, Jane Offutt	THE DOMESTIC INTERNATIONAL SALES CORPORATION: AN EMPIRICAL INVESTIGATION.	Penn St	76	281	Field Study	Tax
Burrows, Ronnie J.	ACCOUNTING AND REPORTING PRACTICE OF NATIONAL LABOR UNIONS	Penn St	80	405	FinStData-based	Financial
Burton, Eric J.	AN INQUIRY INTO THE SOCIO-ECONOMIC ACCOUNTING INFORMATION NEEDS OF FEDERAL LEGISLATORS	Illinois	76	129	Field Study	Social
Bush, James L.	A STUDY OF THE CASH MANAGEMENT PRACTICES OF SELECTED FOOD PROCESSING FIRMS IN ARKANSAS	Arkansas	77	162	Field Study	Managerial
Butler, Daniel L.	A HISTORY OF THE CPA PROFESSION IN LOUISIANA	LSU	76	143	Archival	History
Butler, David H.	SELECTING THE FORM OF SMALL BUSINESS ORGANIZATION: A DETERMINISTIC INCOME TAX PLANNING MODEL	Cincinnati	78	254	Experimental	Tax
Byars, Richard B.	DECISION CRITERIA FOR GIFTS UNDER THE 1976 TAX REFORM ACT	N Txs St	77	96	Experimental	Tax
Bylinski, Joseph Henry	COST EFFECTIVE AUDITING FOR MANAGEMENT FRAUD: A DECISION THEORETIC APPROACH.	Ohio St	80	200	Model- based	Auditing
Byrd, David Blackwell	GUIDELINES FOR DETERMINING THE NATURE OF PROCEDURES FOR UNAUDITED FINANCIAL STATEMENT ENGAGEMENTS.	Arkansas	79	165	Field Study	Auditing
Byrd, Sandra Darlene	THE ARKANSAS CERTIFIED PUBLIC ACCOUNTANT AND THE AMERICAN INSTITUTE OF CERTIFIED PUBLIC ACCOUNTANTS' CODE OF PROFESSIONAL ETHICS.	Arkansas	79	141	Field Study	Ethics

Author	Title	School	Date	pp	Methodology	Topic
Cain, James E.	A FINANCIAL ANALYSIS INTO THE NATURE OF CORPORATE GIVING	Oklahoma	82	132	Archival	Tax
Cairns, Scott N.	AN EMPIRICAL INVESTIGATION INTO THE EFFECTS ON TAX EQUITY OF SELECTED ALTERNATIVE METHODS OF TAXING CAPITAL GAINS AND LOSSES	Illinois	83	198	Archival	Tax
Caldwell, Charles William	THE DEVELOPMENT OF A DISCRIMINANT MODEL FOR USE IN PREDICTING CORPORATE DIVIDEND INCREASES.	Fla St	79	195	FinStData-based	Financial
Callaghan, David Richard	THE SECURITY OF COMPUTER ACCOUNTING SOFTWARE: THE USE OF FIRMWARE.	Massach	78	195	Model- based	Systems/ Computers
Campbell, David R.	FORECAST UPDATING: AN EMPIRICAL STUDY	Georgia	75	135	Market- based	Forecasts
Campbell, Jane E.	AN EMP. INV. OF THE IMPACT ON THE DECISION PROCESSES OF LOAN OFFICERS OF SEPARATE ACCT. STDS. FOR SMALLER OR CLOSELY HELD COMPANIES	Tenn	81	311	Field Study	Financial
Campbell, Penelope S.	COST VARIANCE ANALYSIS: A RELIABILITY THEORY APPLICATION	Ohio St	82	96	Experimental	Managerial
Campbell, Terry Lee	THE CERTIFIED PUBLIC ACCOUNTING PROFESSION - AN EXPLORATORY INDUSTRY STUDY.	Indiana	80	370	Field Study	Profession
Campbell, Walter M.	AN EMPIRICAL EXAMINATION OF THE RELATIONSHIP BETWEEN AUDIT COMMITTEES AND THE DISPLACEMENT OF ACCOUNTING FIRMS	N Txs St	82	225	Field Study	Auditing
Campbell, William Dennis	A MEAN-VARIANCE-SKEWNESS APPROACH TO ALLOCATING FACULTY RESOURCES.	Pitt	80	215	Model- based	Education

Author	Title	School	Date	pp	Methodology	Topic
Cantz, Keith W.	AN EMPIRICAL TEST OF A CANNING-BASED THEORETICAL APPROACH FOR THE DEVELOPMENT OF ACCOUNTING RISK SURROGATES	Iowa	75	142	Market- based	Financial
Capettini, Robert Joseph	SOME SOCIAL INFLUENCE VARIABLES AFFECTING THE INTERNAL ALLOCATION OF CAPITAL RESOURCES.	Illinois	75	121	Experimental	Managerial
Capps, Robert S.	A STUDY OF THE EXTENT TO WHICH GENERALLY ACCEPTED AUDITING STANDARDS CAN BE APPLIED TO AUDITS OF CORPORATE EARNINGS FORECASTS	Geo Wash	78	153	Archival	Auditing
Cargile, Barney Ray	THE USE OF SOCIAL RESPONSIBILITY INFORMATION IN THE IVESTMENT DECISION MAKING PROCESS: AN EMPIRICAL EXAMINATION.	Missouri	79	324	Experimental	Social
Carlson, Frederic J.	AN EMPIRICAL INVESTIGATION OF THE CITIZENS' USE OF MUNICIPAL ACCOUNTING INFORMATION	Saint Louis	83	257	Field Study	Not-for-profit
Carney, Keith T.	THE IMPORTANCE OF SELECTED COST ACCOUNTING TOPICS TO CAREERS IN PUBLIC ACCOUNTING	N Col	76	152	Field Study	Education
Carpenter, Jon Robert	THE USE OF DEFENSIVE INTERVALS IN CORPORATE FAILURE PREDICTION AND AUDITORS' GOING CONCERN EVALUATIONS.	VPI	81	212	FinStData-based	Auditing
Carpenter, Vivian Laverne	THE INCENTIVES FOR THE EVOLUTION OF PERFORMANCE-ORIENTED ACCOUNTING INFORMATION SYSTEMS IN THE GOVERNMENTAL SETTING (THEORY, PRODUCTION, PRINCIPAL-AGENT MODEL, ECONOMIC, SPECIAL INTEREST GROUPS)	Michigan	85	297	Field Study	Systems/Computers
Carr, Janice Lynn	THE ACCELERATED COST RECOVERY SYSTEM: AN EXAMINATION OF ITS EFFECTS ON INCOME-PRODUCING PROPERTY (FISCAL POLICY, INVESTMENTS DEPRECIATION)	Ariz St	85	187	Archival	Tax
Carruth, Paul Joseph	BEHAVIORAL AND ATTITUDINAL IMPLICATIONS OF DIFFERENT STYLES OF PERFORMANCE EVALUATION: AN EMPIRICAL STUDY.	LSU	79	114	Experimental	Managerial

Author	Title	School	Date	pp	Methodology	Topic
Carter, Charles Edward	IMPACT ON THE LENDING DECISION OF THE AUDITORS' REVIEW REPORT ON FINANCIAL FORECASTS - AN EMPIRICAL INVESTIGATION	Missouri	84	196	Experimental	Forecasts
Carter, Donald G.	ROLE CONFLICTS IN THE DIVISION CONTROLLER'S OFFICE	Berkeley	77	458	Field Study	Managerial
Carter, Jack L.	AUDITOR USE OF GENERAL INFORMATION IN JUDGEMENTS OF THE APPLICATION OF ACCOUNTING PRINCIPLES	Cincinnati	80	225	Field Study	Auditing
Carter, William K.	AN ALTERNATIVE TO CONVENTIONAL INDUSTRY DEFINITIONS IN MODELING EARNINGS GENERATION PROCESSES	Okl St	77	128	FinStData-based	Financial
Casey, Cornelius John, Jr.	THE COGNITIVE EFFECT OF VARIATION IN ACCOUNTING INFORMATION LOAD: A STUDY OF BANK LOAN OFFICERS.	Ohio St	78	158	Experimental	Financial
Cashell, James Douglass	AN EMPIRICAL INVESTIGATION OF THE EFFECTS ON INTERNAL AUDITORS' AUDIT PLANNING DECISIONS ATTRIBUTABLE TO THE AVAILABILITY OF REGRESSION ANALYSIS DATA AS ANALYTICAL REVIEW EVIDENCE	Cincinnati	84	221	Field Study	Auditing
Caspari, John A.	AN EMPIRICAL INVESTIGATION INTO THE BEHAVIOR OF INDIRECT COSTS IN RELATION TO TYPE OF PROCUREMENT INSTRUMENT	Missouri	76	184	Field Study	Managerial
Cassell, Michael N.	A CONTRIBUTION MODEL OF BENEFIT-COST RELATIONSHIPS FOR CREDIT CARD OPERATIONS IN COMMERCIAL BANKS	Georgia	76	204	Field Study	Managerial
Cavanagh, Walter Forbes	THE ECONOMIC EFFECTS OF DEFINED BENEFIT PENSION FUNDING POLICY ON THE VALUE OF THE FIRM	NYU	85	144	Model- based	Pensions
Cerva,John A	EVALUATION OF CAPITAL INVESTMENT DECISION MODELS IN LIGHT OF POSITED SECURITY VALUATION MODELS	Northwestern	76	251	Model- based	Financial

Author	Title	School	Date	pp	Methodology	Topic
Chalos, Jean-Pierre	A DECISION THEORY EXPERIMENT IN THE ASSESSMENT OF FINANCIAL DISTRESS	Illinois	82	114	Experimental	Managerial
Chaloupecky, KentE.	ACCOUNTING FOR MARKETABLE EQUITY SECURITIES	Missouri	77	293	FinStData-based	Investments
Chan, James L.	ORGANIZATIONAL CONSENSUS REGARDING THE RELATIVE IMPORTANCE OF RESEARCH OUTPUT INDICATORS	Illinois	76	136	Model- based	Education
Chan, Yee Ching Lilian	MULTIFACTOR RETURN MODEL BASED ON INTERIM FINANCIAL STATEMENTS	Virginia	84	315	Model- based	Interim Statements
Chaney, Paul K.	MORAL HAZARD IN FINANCIAL MARKETS: ESSAYS ON RESOURCE ALLOCATION, GOVERNMENT LOAN GUARANTEES, AND CONDITIONAL VARIANCE INVESTIGATION	Indiana	83	140	Model- based	Managerial
Chang, Davis L.	AN EMPIRICAL ANALYSIS OF THE EFFECTS OF INACCURACY OF A COST STANDARD ON INVESTIGATION AND EVALUATION DECISIONS	Pitt	74	191	Experimental	Managerial
Chant, Peter D.	THE PREDICTABILITY OF NET INCOME AND ITS COMPONENTS	Northwestern	78	200	FinStData-based	Financial
Chapman, William C.	AN EVAL. OF THE STAFF FUNC. OF INTERNAL AUDITING AND INST. RES. IN INSTITUTIONS OF HIGHER ED.: AND A COMP. OF THE COMBINED ACTIONS OF THESE STAFF FUNCTIONS WITH THE INTERNAL AUDIT STAFF FUNCTION IN PRIV. BUSINESS ENTERPRISE	Oklahoma	82	173	Field Study	Auditing
Charlton, Richard E., Jr.	COST/BENEFIT ANALYSIS OF MUNICIPAL FINANCIAL REPORTING AND AUDITS: A CASE STUDY (MICHIGAN PUBLIC ACT #2 OF 1968)	Mich St	76	335	Field Study	Not-for-profit
Chatham, Thomas West	DEVELOPMENT OF A STANDARD COST ACCOUNTING SYSTEM FOR THE COMPUTER CENTER OF A COMMERCIAL BANK.	La Tech	80	201	Field Study	Managerial

Author	Title	School	Date	pp	Methodology	Topic
Chee, Yong Hee	A NEGOTIATION FRAMEWORK FOR TECHNOLOGY IMPORTERS IN LESS-INDUSTRIALIZED COUNTRIES.	Wash	79	104	Model- based	Managerial
Cheever, John K.	INVESTOR ACTIONS AND FORECASTED EARNINGS IN AN EFFICIENT MARKET	S Calif	75		Market- based	Forecasts
Chen, Kung-Hong	REMOVING THE APPEARANCE OF CERTAINTY FROM ACCOUNTING INFORMATION: A BEHAVIORAL EXPERIMENT	Texas	74	303	Experimental	Financial
Cheng, Cheng-shing	JOINT COST ALLOCATION AND DECISION MAKING: THE MARGINAL REVENUE APPROACH	Illinois	83	297	Model- based	Managerial
Cheng, Peter	EXISTENCE OF OPTIMAL NASH CONTRACTS OF A PRINCIPLE AGENT MODEL SINGLE AND MULTIPERIOD CONSIDERATIONS	Mich St	82	311	Model- based	Financial
Cheng, Thomas Tong	IMPACT OF THE FAS 8 STANDARD-SETTING PROCESS ON SECURITY RETURNS OF MULTINATIONALS.	Missouri	81	210	Market- based	Foreign Currency
Cheng, Ting-Wong	AN INVESTIGATION OF THE JUSTIFICATION AND SELECTION OF ALTERNATIVE DEPRECIATION METHODS	Missouri	74	195	Field Study	Depreciation
Cherny, Julius	FUND FLOW, LIQUIDITY AND FINANCIAL FLEXIBILITY MEASURES THROUGH A PHASE SPACE APPROACH TO ACCOUNTING	NYU	83	281	Field Study	Statement of Ch Fin Pos
Cherry, Alan Abraham	TESTING THE EFFECTS OF SOCIAL ACCOUNTING INFORMATION ON DECISION MAKING AND ATTITUDES: A LABORATORY EXPERIMENT.	UCLA	78	233	Experimental	Social
Cheung, Joseph K.	THE PREDICTIVE RELEVANCE OF ACCOUNTING NUMBERS	Michigan	77	152	Market- based	Financial

Author	Title	School	Date	pp	Methodology	Topic
Chevalier, Gilles	UNIVERSALITY OF ACOUNTING PRINCIPLES AND PRACTICES AND THE NEEDS OF USERS OF ACCOUNTING INFORMATION	Illinois	75	294	Experimental	Financial
Chewning, Eugene G. Jr.	ACCOUNTING INFORMATION LOAD AND DECISION MAKERS' DECISION CUE UTILIZATION LEVELS	S Carol	84	139	Experimental	Standard-setting
Chiang, Hung-Fu	MANPOWER SMOOTHING-A STUDY OF A GROUP DECISION PROCESS.	UCLA	75	202	Field Study	Managerial
Cho, Paek Je	THE RELATIVE ASSO. BETW. FIRM'S SYST. RISK AND ACCT. SIGNALS DERIVED FROM ALT. METHODS: CAPITAL. VS. FTNOTE DISCL. OF L-TERM LEASES TO THE FIN. ST.	Illinois	77	169	Market- based	Leases
Choi, Sung Kyu	DIFFERENTIAL INFORMATION CONTENT OF PUBLICLY ANNOUNCED EARNINGS THEORETICAL AND EMPIRICAL ANALYSIS	Iowa	85	142	Market- based	Financial
Chope, Roger Allen	MARKET AND INDUSTRY FACTORS, ACCOUNTING POLICY, AND THE TIME SERIES PROPERTIES OF ACCOUNTING EARNINGS.	Oregon	81	132	Market- based	Oil & Gas
Chow, Chee Woo	AN INVESTIGATION OF THE WEALTH IMPACTS OF THE 1933 AND 1934 SECURITIES ACTS' FINANCIAL DISCLOSURE REQUIREMENTS.	Oregon	81	217	Market- based	Financial
Christensen, John Asmus	COMMUNICATION AND COORDINATION IN AGENCIES: AN APPROACH TO PARTICIPATIVE BUDGETING.	Stanford	79	137	Model- based	Managerial
Christie, Andrew Allan	THE TIME SERIES BEHAVIOR OF THE VARIANCE OF COMMON STOCK PRICES.	Stanford	81	190	Market- based	Stochastic Properties
Christmore, Patricia C.	A COMPUTER SIMULATION MODEL UTILIZING SELECTED FINANCIAL PLANNING VARIABLES	Oklahoma	75	205	Experimental	Tax

Author	Title	School	Date	pp	Methodology	Topic
Chumley, Delbert W.	AN INQUIRY INTO THE EQUITY METHOD OF ACCOUNTING FOR INVESTMENTS IN COMMON STOCK WITH EMPHASIS ON THE IMPACT OF APB OPINION NO. 18	Arkansas	75	88	FinStData-based	Investments
Chung, Yu to	A MODEL OF GOVERNMENT BUDGETING IN A DEVELOPING COUNTRY, HONG KONG	Indiana	75	232	FinStData-based	Not-for-profit
Cianciolo, Salvatore T.A.	PRIVATE INVESTORS' BEHAVIORAL RESPONSE TO FINANCIAL FORECASTS AND RELATED AUDITORS' REPORTS	Mich St	75	179	Experimental	Forecasts
Cirtin, Arnold Lee	NETWORK ANALYSIS--A TOOL FOR AUDIT PLANNING AND CONTROL.	Cincinnati	74	185	Model- based	Auditing
Clancy, Donald Keith	AN ANALYSIS OF ALTERNATIVE REPORTING CONCEPTS OF CONVERTIBLE DEBENTURES.	Penn St	76	214	Market- based	Bonds
Clark, Corolyn Elizabeth	AN EXPERIMENT TO DETERMINE THE EFFECTS OF A BEHAVIOR MODIFICATION INTERVENTION PROGRAM ON ANXIETY LEVELS AND ACHIEVEMENT OF STUDENTS IN PRINCIPLES OF ACCOUNTING CLASSES (STRESS)	Temple	85	147	Experimental	Education
Clark, Myrtle W.	ACCOUNTING INCONSISTENCIES AND INFORMATIONAL VALUE	S Carol	78	195	FinStData-based	Financial
Clark, Ronald L.	COLLECTION AND EVALUATION OF EVIDENCE CONCERNING THE CONTINUED EXISTENCE STATUS OF AUDIT CLIENTS	Alabama	82	139	FinStData-based	Auditing
Clark, Wilbur R	EVALUATIONS OF UNAUDITED FINANCIAL STATEMENTS' STANDARDS	Missouri	80	156	Field Study	Auditing
Clay, Raymond J.	AN ANALYSIS OF SELECTED ANNUAL REPORTS AS AN INPUT INTO THE INVESTMENT DECISION PROCESS OF BANK TRUST INVESTMENT OFFICERS	Kentucky	74	161	Field Study	Financial

Author	Title	School	Date	pp	Methodology	Topic
Clowery, Grant M.	THE SUPPLY OF AND DEMAND FOR ACCOUNTANTS: AN EMPIRICAL ANALYSIS	Chicago	83		Field Study	Profession
Coakley, James R.	ANALYTICAL REVIEW: A COMPARISON OF PROCEDURES AND TECHNIQUES USED IN AUDITING	Utah	82	443	Field Study	Auditing
Coats, Jay Hartwell	.0	Pitt	75	124	Experimental	Managerial
Coffee, Carl D.	AN EXPLORATORY AND HEURISTIC INVESTIG. INTO THE IMPACT OF INCONSISTENT ACCT. PRACTICES IN THE COAL EXTRACTION INDUSTRY: A SURVEY APPROACH	Kentucky	83	162	Field Study	Financial
Coffey, William J.	GOVERNMENT REGULATIONS AND PROFESSIONAL PRONOUNCEMENTS: A STUDY OF THE SEC AND AICPA FROM 1934-1974	NYU	76	282	Archival	History
Colgan, Joseph C.	AN EMPIRICAL ANALYSIS OF TECHNICAL KNOWLEDGE NEEDED BY TAXPAYER SERVICE SPECIALISTS IN THE AREAS OF PARTNERSHIPS, CORPORATIONS, AND SUBCHAPTER S CORPORATIONS.	N Tex St	81	276	Field Study	Tax
Collins, Dennis John	ANALYTICAL REVIEW IN AUDITING: THE PROBLEM OF MODEL VALIDITY.	Iowa	79	156	Experimental	Auditing
Collins, Everett F.	AN EMPIRICAL STUDY OF THE EFFECTS OF BUDGET CHARACTERISTICS AND PERSONALITY VARIABLES ON BUDGETING RESPONSE	Houston	74	226	Field Study	Managerial
Collins, James F.	FINANCIAL REPORTING METHODS AND MANAGEMENT DECISIONS: AN EMPIRICAL EXAMINATION OF INFORMATION INDUCTANCE.	Northwestern	78	159	FinStData-based	Financial
Collins, James R.	AN EMPIRICAL INVESTIGATION INTO THE ASSOCIATION BETWEEN THE FINANCIAL BATH AND INCOME SMOOTHING	Tenn	79	200	FinStData-based	Income Smoothing8:48 pm

Author	Title	School	Date	pp	Methodology	Topic
Collins, Julie Haney	AN ANALYSIS OF THE EFFECT OF INTEGRATION ON THE PRIVATE PENSION TAX SUBSIDY	Florida	83	218	Archival	Tax
Collins, Lane G.	AN INVEST. INTO THE NATURE OF FIN. ACCT. BASED ON A PRIORI INTERPRETATION AND ADAPT. OF MEAS. CONSTRUCTS: A COMPENDIUM OF MEAS. THEORY FOR FIN. ACCT.	S Calif	78		Model- based	Financial
Collins, William A.	AN EMPIRICAL EXAMINATION OF THE ASSOCIATION BETWEEN EPS AND STOCK PRICE MOVEMENTS	Wash	75	90	Market- based	Earnings Per Share
Colson, Robert Henry	MANAGEMENT ACCOUNTING IN PROFIT CENTERS: THE EFFECTS OF OPERATING CONTEXT AND MANAGEMENT STYLE	Ohio St	80	209	Field Study	Managerial
Colvard, Robert Gene	A FRAMEWORK FOR FARMLAND VALUATION UNDER THE 1976 TAX REFORM ACT.	Georgia	81	136	Archival	Tax
Committe, Bruce E.	STRUCTURING A PUBLIC ACCOUNTING AUDIT INDEPENDENCE THEORY FROM A DOCUMENT STUDY OF U.S. CONGRESSIONAL TESTIMONY	Alabama	83	437	Archival	Auditing
Compton, Ted R.	AN INVESTIGATION OF THE USE OF ACCOUNTING PARAPROFESSIONALS IN AUDITING: AN EXPLORATORY RESEARCH.	Cincinnati	80	125	Experimental	Auditing
Conn, Carolyn Terrell	AN ANALYSIS OF THE EFFECTS OF THE REDUCTION AND ELIMINATION OF THE PERCENTAGE DEPLETION ALLOWANCE FOR U.S. OIL AND GAS PRODUCERS.	Arkansas	78	112	Field Study	Oil & Gas
Conway, Lucian G.	CHURCH INFORMATION SYSTEMS: AN EMPIRICAL INVESTIGATION OF THE EFFECTIVENESS OF CHURCH INFORMATION SYSTEMS IN PROVIDING DATA FOR DECISIONS	LSU	75	324	Field Study	Not-for-profit
Cooper, William David	CARMAN G. BLOUGH: A STUDY OF SELECTED CONTRIBUTIONS TO THE ACCOUNTING PROFESSION.	Arkansas	80	271	Archival	History

Author	Title	School	Date	pp	Methodology	Topic
Corbett, Barker D.	REPORTING EXPENDITURES FOR POLLUTION ABATEMENT FACILITIES-A CASE STUDY IN SOCIAL RESPONSIBILITY ACCOUNTING	Florida	75	173	Field Study	Social
Cornick, Michael F.	A STUDY TO SEE IF BANKERS PERCEIVE DIFFERENCES IN THE INFORMATIONAL CONTENT OF THE DIFFERING ACCOUNTING TREATMENTS FOR INFLATION	N Carol	80	173	Field Study	Inflation
Correia, Ernest V.	ASR 190 REPLACEMENT COST DISCLOSURE AND THE PULP AND PAPER INDUSTRY- AN ATTITUDINAL STUDY	Miss	77	271	Field Study	Inflation
Corriher, Jacob D.	A STUDY OF THE IMPACT OF POLLUTION CONTROL UPON ACCOUNTING	Alabama	76	335	Field Study	Social
Cottell, Philip G.	LIFO LAYER LIQUIDATION: POSSIBLE REASONS FOR THE DECISION	Kentucky	82	227	FinStData-based	Managerial
Courtenay, Stephen M.	AN EMPIRICAL STUDY OF ACCOUNTING INFORMATION, FORCED CONVERSIONS AND SECURITY PRICES	Arkansas	82	181	Market- based	Financial
Courtis, John K.	FORECASTING FINANCIAL RATIOS: A PROSPECTUS- BASED INVESTIGATION	Minnesota	74	395	Market- based	Financial Ratios
Covaleski, Mark Anthony	THE RELATIONSHIP OF NURSES' PERCEIVED BUDGET BEHAVIOR TO HOSPITAL AND NURSING DEPARTMENT SYSTEMIC CHARACTERISTICS.	Penn St	78	219	Field Study	Not-for-profit
Cowen, Scott S.	THE DEVELOPMENT OF A FINANCIAL ACCOUNTING MODEL FOR THE COST OF CAPITAL	Geo Wash	75	205	Model- based	Financial
Cox, Billie Don	AN ANALYSIS OF THE BALANCE SHEET CLASSIFICATION OF PREFERRED STOCK.	Missouri	80	152	FinStData-based	Financial

Author	Title	School	Date	pp	Methodology	Topic
Cox, Clifford Theodore	SYSTEMATIC DIFFERENCES BETWEEN VOLUNTARY FORECAST DISCLOSURE AND NONDISCLOSURE FIRMS AND THE INFORMATION CONTENT IN INVOLUNTARY MANAGEMENT FORECAST DISCLOSURES.	Iowa	81	149	Market- based	Forecasts
Cox, Ellen F.	SECURITY RETURN BEHAVIOR CONCURRENT WITH DISTORTED FINANCIAL STATEMENT DATA	Berkeley	82	168	Market- based	Financial
Cox, James S.	THE EFFECTS OF INFLATION UPON DEPRECIABLE ASSETS-A FIELD STUDY	Pitt	74	93	Field Study	Inflation
Cox, Michael A.	AN EMPIRICAL STUDY OF DIFFERENCES IN PRIMARY EPS UNDER ALTERNATIVE CRITERIA FOR DECIDING COMMON STOCK EQUIVALENCY OF CONVERTIBLE BONDS	Okl St	82	177	Market- based	Earnings Per Share
Craft, Clifford Justin, III	AN EXAMINATION OF THE DECISIVE DECISION STYLE IN TASKS USING ACCOUNTING INFORMATION	S Calif	84		Model- based	Financial
Craig, Darryl L.	THE RELATIONSHIP BETWEEN ACCOUNTING METHODS, EARNINGS-PRICE RATIOS AND MARKET RETURNS	Kansas	83	190	Market- based	Financial
Crain, Gilbert W.	AN INVESTIGATION OF THE USAGE AND COMPREHENSION OF MUNICIPAL ACCOUNTING REPORTS IN TWO MONTANA CITIES	Illinois	78	172	Field Study	Not-for-profit
Cready, William Montgomery	AN EMPIRICAL INVESTIGATION INTO THE RELATIONSHIP BETWEEN THE VALUE OF ACCOUNTING EARNINGS ANNOUNCEMENTS AND EQUITY INVESTOR ENDOWMENT SIZES (TRANSACTION VOLUME, SPEED OF ADJUSTMENT, INFORMATION CONTENT)	Ohio St	85	185	Market- based	Financial
Creech, Janie L.	AN EVALUATION OF CURRENT GOVERNMENTAL ESTIMATING METHODS FOR DETERMINING CONSTRUCTION EQUIPMENT USAGE RATES	American	74	274	Field Study	Not-for-profit
Cress, James L.	A STUDY OF THE EFFECTS OF PRICE-LEVEL ADJUSTMENTS ON THE INCOME STATEMENTS OF BANKRUPT COMPANIES	Kent St	79	228	FinStData-based	Inflation

Author	Title	School	Date	pp	Methodology	Topic
Cress, William Peter	A STUDY OF THE RELATIONSHIP BETWEEN BUDGET-RELATED PLANNING AND CONTROL POLICIES AND PROCEDURES AND FIRM PERFORMANCE AND SELECTED FIRM CHARACTERISTICS.	N Tex St	80	486	Field Study	Managerial
Crichfield, Timothy Ryan	COST VARIANCE INVESTIGATION DECISION MODELS.	Cornell	79	168	Model- based	Managerial
Crockett, James R.	THE IMPACT OF THE EVOLUTION TO MGMT. AUDITING OF PERSONNEL REQUIREMENTS OF DEPT. OF DEFENSE INTERNAL AUDIT AGENCIES	Miss St	74	218	Field Study	Auditing
Croll, David Bruce	A BEHAVIORAL INVESTIGATION INTO THE INITIAL REACTIONS OF SELECTED FINANCIAL STATEMENT USERS TO PUBLISHED CORPORATE PROFIT FORECASTS.	Penn St	74	254	Experimental	Forecasts
Crosby, Michael Alan	BAYESIAN STATISTICS IN AUDITING: A COMPARISON OF PROBABILITY ELICITATION TECHNIQUES AND SAMPLE SIZE DECISIONS.	Ohio St	78	178	Experimental	Auditing
Crowley, Robert M.	A STUDY OF ACCOUNTING AND REVIEW SERVICES BY CERTIFIED PUBLIC ACCOUNTANTS.	Nebraska	79	203	Archival	Profession
Crum, Robert P.	THE SHORT RUN NEUTRALITY OF SELECTED VALUE-ADDED TAX FORMS WITH RESPECT TO FINANCING	Kentucky	83	315	Experimental	Tax
Cummings, Robert R.	AN EVALUATION OF THE EFFECTS OF VARIATIONS IN COST ACCT. TECHNIQUES ON PUBLISHED FINANCIAL STATEMENTS OF SELECTED FIRMS IN THE STEEL INDUSTRY	Miss	76	226	FinStData-based	Managerial
Cunningham, Billie Marie	AN ANALYSIS OF THE VARIABLES INFLUENCING THE OUTCOMES OF FEDERAL COURT CASES INVOLVING ANTITRUST ACTION AGAINST ACCOUNTANCY AND OTHER PROFESSIONS BROUGHT UNDER THE SHERMAN ACT	N Tex St	80	214	Archival	Profession
Cunningham, Gary M.	AN ACCOUNTING RESEARCH FRAMEWORK FOR MULTINATIONAL ENTERPRISES	Texas	76	292	Model- based	Financial

Author	Title	School	Date	pp	Methodology	Topic
Curatola, Anthony P.	AN ALTERNATIVE AUTOMATIC INDEXING MODEL AND AN EMP. INV. INTO THE RELATIONSHIP BETWEEN NOMINAL INTEREST RATES AND EXPECTED INFLATION	Txs A&M	81	179	Market- based	Tax
Czarsty, Steven L.	AN IN DEPTH ANALYSIS OF HUMAN RESOURCE ACCOUNTING WITH EMPHASIS ON THE BASIS FOR MEASURING THE VALUE OF HUMAN RESOURCES	Geo Wash	75	194	Model- based	Hum.Resourc e Acct.
D'Souza, Rudolph E.	MARKET MODEL WITH FIRST ORDER AUTOREGRESSIVE COEFFICIENTS FOR BETA ESTIMATION AND PREDICTION	S Carol	83	216	Market- based	Stochastic Properties
Daley, Lane A.	AN EMPIRICAL STUDY OF DIFFERENCES IN PRIMARY EPS UNDER ALTERNATIVE CRITERIA FOR DECIDING COMMON STOCK EQUIVALENCY OF CONVERTIBLE BONDS	Wash	82	297	Market- based	Earnings Per Share
Dalton, Michael A.	AN INVESTIGATION OF THE USES OF EXTERNAL ACCOUNTING INFORMATION IN STOCK PURCHASE RCOMMENDATIONS	Ga St	79	205	Field Study	Financial
Damtew, Desta	COMPARATIVE STUDY OF THE APPLICATION OF SELECTED MANAGEMENT ACCOUNTING TECHNIQUES IN SOME COMMERCIAL BANKS IN ETHIOPIA AND THE COMMONWEALTH OF KENTUCKY.	Kentucky	80	256	Field Study	Managerial
Danese, Stephen	AN EMP. INV. OF THE EFFECTS OF THE REVENUE/EXPENSE & ASSET/LIAB. CONCEPTS OF EARNINGS & ALT. MEAS. BASES ON COMPAR. FIN. ANALYSIS	Georgia	80	157	FinStData-based	Financial
Danos, Paul P.	CONFIRMABILITY LEVEL FINANCIAL STATEMENTS: A THEORETICAL AND EMPIRICAL ASSESSMENT	Texas	74	127	Field Study	Financial
Daroca, Frank Peter, Jr.	LEADERSHIP AND INFORMATIONAL INFLUENCES ON GROUP DECISION MAKING IN A PARTICIPATIVE BUDGETING CONTEXT: A LABORATORY EXPERIMENT.	Illinois	81	85	Experimental	Managerial
Dau, Khalifa A.	PROBABILISTIC INCOME DETERMINATION THEORY: A MODIFICATION OF THE TRADITIONAL MODEL	LSU	75	263	Experimental	Financial

Author	Title	School	Date	pp	Methodology	Topic
Davidson, David	COMPUTER SIMULATION MODELS FOR EVAL. POTENTIAL TAX SAVINGS OF FED. REV. CODE SEC. 6166,6166A, AND 2032A WHEN ELECTIONS ARE MUTUALLY EXCLUSIVE	N Col	82	167	Experimental	Tax
Davidson, Lewis Franklin	BEHAVIORAL DETERMINANTS IN ROLE RELATIONSHIPS: AN EXTENSION OF THE INTERNAL CONTROL REVIEW IN AUDIT SITUATIONS.	Penn St	74	301	Experimental	Auditing
Davies, Jonathan J.	ACCOUNTANTS' CIVIL LIABILITY TO THIRD PARTY FINANCIAL STATEMENT USERS-A CASE FOR UNIFORMITY	LSU	75	159	Archival	Profession
Davis, Dale Allen	ANALYTICAL TECHNIQUES FOR IMPROVEMENT OF INTERNAL DECISION-MAKING IN INSTITUTIONS OF HIGHER EDUCATION.	Michigan	78	271	Field Study	Education
Davis, Darrel Wilber	AN EMPIRICAL INVESTIGATION OF THE ASSOCIATION BETWEEN REPORTED EARNINGS AND CORPORATE BOND PRICES	Okl St	75	127	Market- based	Bonds
Davis, Harry	THE GROSS MARGIN RATIO OF FIFO AND LIFO FIRMS: IMPLICATIONS FOR OPERATIONALIZING THE TRUEBLOOD CRITERION AND INSIGHT INTO PRICE ADJ. LAGS	Columbia	78	209	FinStData-based	Inventories
Davis, Henry Holbrook	EFFECT OF ENVIRONMENTAL UNCERTAINTY ON THE INFORMATION CONTENT OF FINANCIAL STATEMENTS	N Car	84	186	Field Study	Financial
Davis, James R	AN INQUIRY INTO THE NATURE OF MANAGEMENT AUDITING AND THE FEASIBILITY OF ITS PERFORMANCE BY CPA'S	Ga St	74	232	Field Study	Auditing
Davis, Lee Edward	THE DEFINITION, MEASUREMENT, AND ANALYSIS OF THE INTERNAL REVENUE CODE'S ARRANGEMENTS.	Georgia	81	515	Archival	Tax
Davis, Robert R	AN EMPIRICAL EVALUATION OF THE INFORMATION CONTENT OF "SUBJECT TO" OPINIONS	SUNY-Buf	82	143	Market- based	Auditing

Author	Title	School	Date	pp	Methodology	Topic
Davis, Stanley Ward	A METASCIENTIFIC INQUIRY INTO THE ONTOLOGICAL AND EPISTEMOLOGICAL ASSUMPTIONS OF CURRENT ACCOUNTING RESEARCH	Penn St	84	196	Field Study	Profession
Dawkins, Louis E.	A STUDY OF ACCOUNTING GRADUATES AND ACCOUNTING PROGRAMS AT SELECTED ARKANSAS COLLEGES AND UNIVERSITIES	Arkansas	82	213	Field Study	Education
Dawkins, Sarah E.	AN INQUIRY CONCERNING ITHE SELECTION, ROTATION AND RETENTION OF INDEPENDENT AUDITORS	LSU	78	155	Field Study	Auditing
Dawley, Donald L.	A STUDY OF AUDITOR DATA PROCESSING KNOWLEDGE REQUIREMENTS FOR COMPUTER BASED MANAGEMENT INFORMATION SYSTEMS	Geo Wash	82	305	Field Study	Auditing
Dawson, Ted	AN EMPIRICAL INVESTIGATION OF RELATIONSHIPS OF SELECTED FIRM ATTRIBUTES AND PERFORMANCE VARIABLES TO VOLUNTARY ACCOUNTING CHANGES	Oregon	77	143	FinStData-based	Accounting Changes
De Jong, Douglas V.	THE VALUE OF THE FIRM AND ITS OBLIGATIONS: IMPLICATIONS FOR ACCOUNTING.	Michigan	80	138	Model- based	Financial
De Moville, Wiggens B.	AN INVESTIGATION OF THE TIME SERIES PROPERTIES OF SALES AND OPERATING EXPENSES OF SELECTED FIRMS	Txs Tech	78	174	FinStData-based	Stochastic Properties
DeAngelo, Linda Elizabeth	AN ECONOMIC ANALYSIS OF THE AUDITOR-CLIENT CONTRACTUAL RELATIONSHIP.	Wash	80	212	Model- based	Auditing
Debessay, Araya	AN EMPIRICAL INVESTIGATION OF THE IMPACT OF REPLACEMENT COST DISCLOSURES ON CAPITAL MARKET EQUILIBRIUM	Syracuse	79	197	FinStData-based	Inflation
DeCelles, Michael D.	AN EXAMINATION OF THE FACTORS AFFECTING THE JUDICIAL ASSESSMENT OF CONTINUITY OF INTEREST IN CORPORATE REORGANIZATIONS	Oklahoma	83	205	Archival	Financial

Author	Title	School	Date	pp	Methodology	Topic
Deck, Alan Bruce	AN EXPLANATORY INVESTIGATION OF THE FACTORS AFFECTING A FIRM'S SELECTION OF ACCOUNTING POLICIES	Alabama	84	154	Field Study	Financial
Defeo, John V.	A STUDY OF THE DURATION OF THE SECURITY MARKET REACTION TO THE RELEASE OF ACCOUNTING EARNINGS REPORTS	Illinois	83	163	Market- based	Financial
Degnan, Theodore	A COMPUTER CODED CONTENT ANALYSIS STUDY OF TAX CASES INVOLVING VALUATIONS OF LARGE HOLDINGS OF PUBLICLY TRADED STOCK	S Carol	83	187	Archival	Tax
Deines, Dan Stuart	A TEST FOR THE SIMILARITY OF ANALYSTS' AND INVESTORS' EXPECTATIONS SUBJECT TO THE RELEASE OF MANDATED ACCOUNTING DISCLOSURES	Nebraska	85	94	Market- based	Financial
Deitrick, James W.	AN EXAMINATION OF CHANGES IN THE UTILITY OF INTERIM FINANCIAL INFORMATION	Tenn	77	173	Field Study	Interim Statements
Demotses, Andrew J.	THE LOCATION MODEL: DISCRIMINATION AND CLASSIFICATION WHEN THE DATA CONTAINS BOTH BINARY AND CONTINUOUS VARIABLES	Massach	79	222	FinStData-based	Financial
Dennis, David K.	DECISION MAKING BY CPA'S IN CONFLICT SITUATIONS: A STUDY OF ROLE CONFLICT RESOLUTION	Cincinnati	75	242	Field Study	Profession
Dennis, Hubert L.	THE EFFECTS OF GENERAL PRICE-LEVEL ADJUSTMENTS UPON SELECTED FINANCIAL RATIOS AND MEASURES	Kentucky	76	155	FinStData-based	Inflation
Dennis-Escoffier, Shirley	THE IMPACT OF FEDERAL INCOME TAX ON CAPITAL BUDGETING EQUIPMENT DECISIONS: A COMPARATIVE STUDY OF HOTELS IN SELECTED RESORT CITIES OF THE UNITED STATES, CANADA, AND THE BAHAMAS.	Miami	81	138	Field Study	Tax
Dereshiwsky, Mary Irene	ALIGNMENT OF SPECIAL-INTEREST SUBJECTS IN THE ACCOUNTING STANDARD-SETTING PROCESS: AN INVESTIGATION (FASB, DISCUSSION MEMOS)	Massach	85	364	Field Study	Standard-setting

Author	Title	School	Date	pp	Methodology	Topic
DeRidder, Jerome J.	COMPARISON OF SEVEN FUNDAMENTAL FEATURES OF THE STATEM. OF CHANGES IN FINANCIAL POSITION IN THE U.S., CANADA, U.., NEW ZEALAND, AND AUSTRALIA	Nebraska	80	220	FinStData-based	International
Devine, Wilfred Francis	THE INFLUENCE OF CONSTITUENCY INPUT IN SETTING ACCOUNTING STANDARDS	Temple	85	232	Field Study	Standard-setting
DeVries, Joann S.	AN ANALYSIS OF ESTATE ADMINISTRATION AND PLANNED REDUCTION IN FEDERAL ESTATE TAXES AND COSTS FOR ESTATES VALUED AT LESS THAN $120,000	Okl St	75	196	Archival	Tax
Dhaliwal, Dan Singh	THE IMPACT OF IMPROVED FINANCIAL DISCLOSURE ON THE COST OF EQUITY CAPITAL.	Arizona	77	130	FinStData-based	Financial
Dharan, Bala Ganga	TIME SERIES ANALYSIS OF INVENTORY DECISIONS AND ACCOUNTING EARNINGS.	Carn Mel	81	186	FinStData-based	Inventories
Diamond, Michael A.	THE EFFECT OF SUPPLEMENTAL REPLACEMENT COST DISCLOSURES ON BANK LOAN DECISIONS: AN EMPIRICAL ANALYSIS	UCLA	78	185	Field Study	Inflation
Dickens, Thomas L.	EFFECTS OF 1981 AND 1982 TAX LEGISLATION ON CONVENTIONAL APARTMENT INVESTMENT THROUGH THE CORPORATE AND PARTNERSHIP FORMS	Txs A&M	83	238	Experimental	Tax
Dickinson, Harry Dawideit	LEADER BEHAVIOR AND TURNOVER IN BIG-EIGHT CPA FIRMS.	Georgia	81	190	Field Study	Profession
Dietrich, James Richard	RECOGNITION AND MEASUREMENT OF GAINS AND LOSSES ON LONG TERM CORPORATE DEBT IN PERIODS OF INFLATION: AN EMPIRICAL STUDY OF SECURITY RETURNS.	Carn Mel	81	350	Market- based	Inflation
Dillard, Jesse F.	THE APPLICATION OF A VIC MODEL TO CORRECT DECISIONS WITHIN LARGE CPA FIRMS	S Carol	76	248	Experimental	Profession

Author	Title	School	Date	pp	Methodology	Topic
Dillaway, Manson Peter	A STUDY OF CONTEMPORARY LEADERSHIP MODELS IN CPA FIRM AUDIT TEAMS.	Florida	80	140	Experimental	Auditing
Dilley, Steven Charles	ACCOUNTING FOR EXTERNALITIES: CONDUCTING A SOCIAL AUDIT AND PREPARING A SOCIAL RESPONSIBILITY ANNUAL REPORT FOR A PUBLIC UTILITY.	Wiscon	72	180	Field Study	Social
Dillon, Gadis J.	THE ROLE OF ACCOUNTING IN THE STOCK MARKET CRASH OF 1929	Michigan	77	367	FinStData-based	History
Dillon, Ray D.	AN EMPIRICAL EVALUATION AND EXTENSION OF THE POSTAUDIT OF CAPITAL EXPENDITURES	Txs Tech	74	226	Field Study	Managerial
Dinius, Sara Holton	THE ROLE OF PERSONALITY CHARACTERISTICS IN THE CHOICE OF ACCOUNTING AS A MAJOR AND IN SUCCESS IN ACCOUNTING COURSES.	Auburn	74	322	Field Study	Education
Dirsmith, Mark W.	ATTITUDES OF SELECTED DECISION-MAKERS TOWARDS INFORMATION PROVIDED BY THE FINANCIAL ACCOUNTING SYSTEM	Northwest ern	75	335	Field Study	Financial
Dittenhofer, Mortimer A.	ACCOUNTING PRINCIPLES IN STATE GOVERNMENT	American	74	333	Field Study	Not-for-profit
Dittman, David Arthur	A LIMITED COST-BENEFIT ANALYSIS OF THE DIPLOMA NURSING SCHOOL DILEMMA: A CASE STUDY OF THE CONTINUE/DISCONTINUE DECISION.	Ohio St	73	224	Field Study	Managerial
Dodd, Peter Raymond	THE MARKET FOR CORPORATE CONTROL AND STOCKHOLDER WEALTH.	Rochester	80	126	Market- based	Financial
Dodson, Nita Jean Jones	IMPLEMENTATION OF A STANDARD FINANCIAL MANAGEMENT SYSTEM IN SMALLER TEXAS COUNTIES.	Texas	80	175	Field Study	Not-for-profit

Author	Title	School	Date	pp	Methodology	Topic
Dombrowski, Robert F.	FACTORS AFFECTING THE POSSIBLE CONVERSION OF THE LOUISIANA INHERITANCE TAX TO AN ESTATE TAX.	La Tech	75	175	Experimental	Tax
Donahue, Marlene S.	AN EMPIRICAL INVESTIGATION OF THE OPINIONS OF SELECTED FINANCIAL STATEMENT USERS, ACCOUNTING ACADEMICIANS, AND CPA'S TOWARD THE INDEP. AUDITOR'S RESP. FOR THE DETECTION, PREVENTION AND DISCLOSURE OF FRAUD	Nebraska	79	283	Field Study	Auditing
Donelly, David P.	AN ANALYSIS OF THE IMPORTANCE OF THE TREASURY REGULATIONS AND OTHER FACTORS ON SECTION 482 COURT CASE OUTCOMES	Illinois	83	144	Archival	Tax
Dontoh, Alex Kwesi	PUBLIC INFORMATION STRUCTURES: AN ANALYSIS OF THE STEWARDSHIP FUNCTION	NYU	84	258	Model- based	Financial
Doran, Benjamin Michael	A MARKET BASED ASSESSMENT OF THE INFORMATION CONTENT OF SUPPLEMENTAL RESERVE ACCOUNTING DATA IN THE EXTRACTIVE PETROLEUM INDUSTRY	Iowa	84	111	Market- based	Oil & Gas
Dorr, Patrick B.	THE IMPACT OF THE TAX REFORM ACT OF 1976 AND OTHER PROPOSED LEGISLATION ON INVESTMENT IN REAL ESTATE TAX SHELTERS.	N Tex St	79	273	Experimental	Tax
Doty, Edwin A.	ALTERNATIVE INFORMATION REPRESENTATION: A GRAPHIC APPROACH	Massach	81	216	Experimental	Statement Presentation
Dougherty, Frank P.	ALTERNATIVE METHODS OF EVALUATING INVESTMENT DECISIONS: WILL DIFFERENT DECISIONS EMERGE?	Penn St	76	202	Experimental	Managerial
Douglas, Sharon M.	AN EXAMINATION OF UNDERREPORTING OF HOURS BY ACCOUNTANTS WITHIN AN EXPANDED EXPECTANCY THEORY FRAMEWORK	Oregon	77	205	Field Study	Profession
Douma, Irene K.	IS THE CERTIFIED PUBLIC ACCOUNTANT A PROFESSIONAL? THE PERCEPTION OF CPA'S, FIN. EXEC., BANKERS, FIN. ANALYSIS, AND ATTORNEYS	CUNY-Bar	82	269	Field Study	Profession

Author	Title	School	Date	pp	Methodology	Topic
Doupnik, Timothy S.	ACCOUNTING IN AN INFLATIONARY ECONOMY: A STUDY OF THE BRAZILIAN SYSTEM OF MONETARY CORRECTION	Illinois	83	345	Experimental	Inflation
Dowell, Claud D.	AN EMPIRICAL EVALUATION OF THE COST AND EQUITY METHODS OF ACCOUNTING FOR LONG-TERM INVESTMENTS IN COMMON STOCK	Mich St	74	125	Market- based	Investments
Downes, David Howard	THE INVESTMENT PERFORMANCE OF UNSEASONED NEW ISSUES.	Cornell	75	185	Market- based	Financial
Dozier, Donald D.	AN ANALYSIS AND EVALUATION OF REPORTS BY MANAGEMENT	Missouri	81	170	Field Study	Managerial
Driscoll, Donna Ann	A GENERAL THEORY OF AUDITOR INDEPENDENCE AND EMPIRICAL TEST OF INDEPENDENCE IN FACT	S Calif	84		Field Study	Auditing
Drummings, Sandra T.	AN EXAMINATION OF THE MATERIALITY JUDGEMENT POLICIES OF PUBLIC ACCOUNTANTS	Wiscon	82	176	Experimental	Auditing
Drury, Donald H.	AN EXAMINATION OF DIFFERENCES IN FINANCIAL REPORTING BETWEEN CANADA AND THE U.S.: AN EMPIRICAL ANALYSIS	Northwestern	76	383	FinStData-based	International
Duangploy, Orapin	THE SENSITIVITY OF EARNINGS PER SHARE TO DIFFERENT FOREIGN CURRENCY TRANSLATION METHODS.	Missouri	77	324	Experimental	Foreign Currency
DuBois, Donoly A.	FULL-COST ACCOUNTING FOR EXPLORATION AND DEVELOPMENT COSTS OF PETROLEUM COS.: ITS EFFECT ON STOCK MARKET PRICES	Missouri	74	106	Market- based	Oil & Gas
Dudley Lola W.	AN ADAPTATION OF CAPITAL INVESTMENT THEORY TO MISSISSIPPI RIVER DELTA FARMS	Arkansas	82	172	Field Study	Managerial

Author	Title	School	Date	pp	Methodology	Topic
Duke, Donald E.	A PROPOSAL FOR ADDITIONAL DISCLOSURE REQUIREMENTS IN FINANCIAL REPORTS FOR COMMERCIAL BANKS	Georgia	74	166	Model- based	Financial
Duke, Gordon Leon	AN EMPIRICAL INVESTIGATION OF THE POWER OF STATISTICAL SAMPLING PROCEDURES USED IN AUDITING UNDER DIFFERENT MODELS OF CHANGE OF ERROR PATTERNS.	Georgia	80	414	Experimental	Auditing
Dukes, Roland Edward	MARKET EVALUATION OF ACCOUNTING INFORMATION: A CROSS-SECTIONAL TEST OF INVESTOR RESPONSE TO EXPENSING RESEARCH AND DEVELOPMENT EXPENDITURES.	Stanford	74	147	Market- based	Research & Development
Duncan, William A.	AN ANALYTICAL INVESTIGATION OF SHORT-TERM TRUSTS: PLANNING AND POLICY IMPLICATIONS	Texas	83	355	Experimental	Tax
Dungan, Christopher W.	A MODEL OF AN AUDIT JUDGMENT IN THE FORM OF AN EPXERT SYSTEM	Illinois	83	208	Experimental	Auditing
Dunn, William M.	THE DEVELOPMENT, DESIGN, AND TESTING OF A PERFORMANCE MEASUREMENT MODEL FOR A NOT-FOR-PROFIT ORGANIZATION	Florida	76	246	Field Study	Not-for-profit
Dworin, Lowell	INFLATION AND CORPORATE TAXATION: AN ECONOMIC ANALYSIS.	Michigan	77	169	Experimental	Tax
Dykes, Linda Muckenfuss	AN EXAMINATION OF THE IMPORTANCE OF CERTAIN ATTRIBUTES TO CLIENTS' SELECTIONS OF ACCOUNTING FIRMS.	Ga St	81	220	Field Study	Auditing
Dykxhoorn, Hans J.	AN EMPIRICAL INVESTIGATION OF WIRTSCHAFTSPRUFER INDEPENDENCE	Mich St	78	298	Experimental	Auditing
Earnest, Kenneth Roger	TRANSFER PRICING: AN EXPECTANCY THEORY INVESTIGATION.	Texas	78	268	Experimental	Managerial

Author	Title	School	Date	pp	Methodology	Topic
Ebey, Carl Finley	LONG-RANGE FINANCIAL PLANNING: ITS EXISTENCE AND IMPORTANCE AT CATHOLIC COLLEGES AND UNIVERSITIES.	Indiana	80	244	Field Study	Not-for-profit
Edmonds, Thomas Paul	AN EMPIRICAL INQUIRY INTO THE EFFECT OF AUDITOR INVOLVEMENT ON THE PREDICTIVE CAPACITY OF INTERIM FINANCIAL INFORMATION.	Ga St	79	207	Field Study	Auditing
Egenold, Robert V.	INTER-FIRM COMPARISON--A STUDY WITH SPECIAL EMPHASIS ON THE COMMERCIAL CATTLE FEEDING INDUSTRY	Txs A&M	74	165	Field Study	Agricultural
Eggleton, Ian Richard Carfrae	PATTERNS, PROTOTYPES, AND PREDICTIONS.	Chicago	79		Experimental	Managerial
Ehrenreich, Keith B.	HUMAN RESOURCES ACCOUNTING: AN EXPLORATORY FIELD STUDY	S Calif	75		Field Study	Hum.Resourc e Acct.
Eichenseher, John Walter	CONCENTRATION IN THE MARKET FOR AUDIT SERVICES: AN ANALYSIS ACROSS CLIENT INDUSTRY SUBMARKETS.	Michigan	80	136	FinStData-based	Auditing
Eisenman, Seymour L.	ATTEST INDEPENDENCE AND MANAGEMENT ADVISORY SERVICES.	NYU	75	385	Field Study	Auditing
El-Arabi, Abdussalan	THE EFFECTS OF ACCOUNTING ALTERNATIVVES ON LENDING DECISIONS OF COMMERCIAL BANKS	LSU	77	310	Experimental	Financial
El-Badadawi, Mohammed H.	THE DISCLOSURE OF UNCERTAINTY IN ACCOUNTING NUMBERS: INFORMATIONAL AND BEHAVIORAL ISSUES	S Calif	80		Experimental	Financial
El-Gawhary, Ali Mohamed	THE ASSOCIATION BETWEEN CORPORATE SOCIAL PERFORMANCE AND FINANCIAL PERFORMANCE IN GHE MARKET: AN EMPIRICAL STUDY.	Mich St.	80	138	Market- based	Social

Author	Title	School	Date	pp	Methodology	Topic
El-Gehawe, Abdelsalam Ali	AN ANALYSIS OF EFFECTIVENESS AUDITING FOR GOVERNMENTAL PROGRAMS IN THE UNITED STATES AND SWEDEN WITH APPLICATION TO LIBYA.	Missouri	80	98	Field Study	Not-for-profit
El-Leithy, Fouad M.	ON THE ASSOCIATION BETWEEN FINANCIAL RATIOS AND SYSTEMATIC RISK UNDER ALTERNATIVE REPLACEMENT-COST MODELS	Okl St	82	11	Market- based	Inflation
El-Maksy, Mostafa M.	A THEORETICAL AND EMPIRICAL INVESTIGATION OF THE EFFECTS OF FASB STATEMENT 33 ON LENDING DECISIONS	NYU	83	292	Experimental	Inflation
Elgers, Pieter Thomas	ACCOUNTING-BASED RISK MEASURES AND THE SYSTEMATIC RISK OF EQUITY SECURITIES: TESTS OF ASSOCIATION AND PREDICTIVE ABILITY.	Maryland	78	179	Market- based	Financial
Elhassy, Juma'a	SCHEMATIC FACES AND FINANCIAL PREDICTIONS: SENSITIVITY TO SELECTED CONSTRUCTION ASSUMPTIONS	Oklahoma	80	116	Experimental	Financial
Eliraqi, Iraqi A.	THE IMPACT OF EGYPTIAN INVESTMENT INCENTIVES ON THE INVESTMENT DECISIONS OF MULTINATIONAL ENTERPRISES	Arkansas	82	146	Model- based	Managerial
Elkhorouf, Farouk W.	A COMPARISON OF THE ABILITY OF FINANCIAL RATIOS BASED ON DIFFERENT ACCOUNTING STANDARDS TO PREDICT BANKRUPTCY	Illinois	82	179	FinStData-based	Financial Ratios
Elliott, John A.	THE ASSOCIATION OF QUALIFIED AUDIT OPINIONS AND SECURITY RETURNS	Cornell	82	220	Market- based	Auditing
Ellison, David J.	A STUDY OF ACCOUNTING INFORMATION SYSTEMS OF FARM SUPPLY COOPERATIVES	Arkansas	74	179	Field Study	Systems/ Computers
Elmadfai, Abdulfattah O.	AN INTEGRATED THEORY OF ACCOUNTING USING CAPITAL/EXPENSE DECISIONS IN THE PETROLEUM INDUSTRY AS A SPECIAL APPLICATION	LSU	76	263	Model- based	Oil & Gas

Author	Title	School	Date	pp	Methodology	Topic
Elmallah, Amin A.	THE EVALUATION AND SELECTION OF INDUSTRIAL RESEARCH AND DEVELOPMENT PROJECTS	Illinois	74	275	Model- based	Managerial
Elsea, John Edward	A COMPARISON OF ACHIEVEMENT IN ELEMENTARY ACCOUNTING BETWEEN STUDENTS TAUGHT BY THE SELF-PACED METHOD AND STUDENTS TAUGHT BY THE TRADITIONAL METHOD.	N Colo	73	225	Field Study	Education
Emore, James Robert	THE INFORMATION CONTENT OF LEASE DISCLOSURES-A CLOSER EXAMINATION	Kent St	84	184	Experimental	Leases
Engle, Terry J.	THE CONGRUENCY OF AUDIT TRAINING BETWEEN LARGE PUBLIC ACCOUNTING FIRMS AND COLLEGES AND UNIVERSITIES	Missouri	83	251	Field Study	Education
Englebrecht, Ted Dewin	AN EMPIRICAL INVESTIGATION INTO THE VALUATION OF CLOSELY HELD CORPORATIONS BY THE TAX COURT FOR ESTATE AND GIFT TAX PURPOSES.	S Carol	76	176	Archival	Tax
Engler, Calvin	AN INDEPTH INQUIRY INTO CURRENT PRATICES IN ACCOUNTING FOR BUSINESS COMBINATIONS	CUNY-Bar	77	186	FinStData-based	Business Combinations
Engstrom, John G.	AN INVESTIGATION INTO THE ACCOUNTING INFORMATION NEEDS OF PARTICIPANTS IN THE MUNICIPAL BUDGET PROCESS	Indiana	77	234	Field Study	Not-for-profit
Enis, Charles Richard	THE IMPACT OF REPLACEMENT COST INFORMATION UPON THE INVESTMENT DECISIONS OF INDIVIDUAL INVESTORS.	Maryland	81	291	Experimental	Inflation
Ensly, Chula G.	TOWARD THE DEVEL. OF A MODEL TO EVAL. THE EFFECT OF THE ACRS AS ENACTED BY THE ECON. RECOVERY ACT OF 1981 ON STATE OF FLA. CORP. TAX RETURNS	LSU	83	303	Archival	Tax
Ernst, John D.	ACCT. CHANGES: AN EVAL. OF THE INC. SMOOTHING AND RELATED HYP. UNDERLYING AN IDENTIFICATION OF CHAR. THAT MOTIVATE ACCT. CHANGES	Ga St	75	199	Market- based	Accounting Changes

Author	Title	School	Date	pp	Methodology	Topic
Espahbodi, Hassanali	AN EMPIRICAL INVESTIGATION INTO THE INFORMATION NEEDS OF FINANCIAL STATEMENT USERS: EVALUATION OF ALTERNATIVE ACCOUNTING MEASURES IN THE PREDICTION OF CASH FLOWS.	Alabama	81	143	FinStData-based	Financial Ratios
Espahbodi, Reza	A COST BENEFIT ANALYSIS OF ACCOUNTING FOR INFLATION	Alabama	80	130	FinStData-based	Inflation
Etebari-Khorasgani, Ahmad	AN ASSESSMENT OF THE STOCK MARKET EFFECTS OF PROPOSED ACCOUNTING CHANGES IN THE OIL AND GAS INDUSTRY.	N Tex St	79	155	Market- based	Oil & Gas
Etherington, Lois Deane	AN EXPERIMENTAL STUDY OF HUMAN INFORMATION PROCESSING OF NUMERICAL DATA INVOLVING BASIC STATISTICAL CONCEPTS.	Wash	77	204	Experimental	Financial
Euske, Kenneth J.	AGREEMENT WITH AND CONTROL OVER BUDGETARY MEASURES AS RELATED TO MANAGERIAL PERFORMANCE AND SATISFACTION	Ariz St	78	211	Field Study	Managerial
Evens, John Henry	ECONOMETRIC MODELS OF AUDITING IN THE ACCOUNTABILITY ENVIRONMENT	Carn Mel	79	155	Model- based	Auditing
Everett, John O.	EVALUATING SELECTED ESTATE PLANNING TOOLS: A PROBABILISTIC SIMULATION APPROACH.	Okl St.	78	544	Model- based	Tax
Ewing-Chow, Frank D.	AN INVESTIGATION INTO COGNITIVE STYLES AND PATTERNS OF BEHAVIOR WITHIN AN INVESTMENT FRAMEWORK	S Calif	77		Experimental	Financial
Fairchild, Joseph V.	COMP. FOR USE OF CAPTIAL ASSETS DURING PERIODS OF RAPID INFLATION: AN EVAL. OF DEPT. OF DEFENSE PROCEDURES VS. CURRENT COMMERCIAL PRACTICES	LSU	75	261	Field Study	Inflation
Faircloth, Archie W.	RATINGS OF THE RELEVANCE OF CURRENT REPLACMENT COST AND THEIR EFFECT ON RATINGS OF PROFITABILITY AND LIQUIDITY	Kentucky	77	220	FinStData-based	Inflation

Author	Title	School	Date	pp	Methodology	Topic
Faisal, Abdullah M.	THE EFFECT OF ACCOUNTING FOR THE COST OF INTEREST ON THE PREDICTIVE ABILITY OF FINANCIAL RATIOS	Oklahoma	79	173	FinStData-based	Financial Ratios
Fane, Gary R.	THE DEVELOPMENT AND EVALUATION OF A UNIFORM HOSPITAL COST ACCOUNTING INFORMATION SYSTEM	Florida	74	241	Field Study	Not-for-profit
Fantl, Irving L.	A STUDY OF THE INFLUENCE OF DIFFERENT METHODS OF CORPORATE TAXATION ON THE DIVIDEND POLICIES OF PUBLICLY HELD CORPORATIONS IN FRANCE, THE FEDERAL REPUBLIC OF GERMANY AND THE UNITED KINGDOM.	NYU	74	287	Archival	Tax
Farmer, Larry E.	A SIMULATION MODEL FOR PREDICTING AND MANAGING INDIVIDUAL INCOME TAX REVENUES IN THE STATE OF ARKANSAS	La Tech	75	164	Experimental	Tax
Farmer, Martha K.	AN EMPIRICAL INVESTIGATION INTO THE CAPITAL MARKETS' RESPONSE TO ALTERNATIVE ACCOUNTING METHODS	S Carol	77	218	Market- based	Financial
Farmer, Timothy Alan	AN ANALYSIS OF MULTI-ATTRIBUTE UTILITY THEORY AS A MODEL OF INTERNAL CONTROL EVALUATIONS BY EXTERNAL AUDITORS	Ohio State	84	173	Model- based	Auditing
Farrar, Robert H.	THE INTEGRATED MGMT. CONTROL AUDIT: A STUDY OF SELECTED ASPECTS OF THE NEED, MEANS, AND FEASIBILITY OF MODERNIZING STATE POST-AUDITING	Massach	78	191	Field Study	Auditing
Farrelly, Gail E.	TOWARD THE EXPLICIT DISCLOSURE OF RISK IN FINANCIAL REPORTING	Geo Wash	81	210	FinStData-based	Financial
Fasci, Martha Alicia	THE EFFECT OF THE NATURE OF INFORMATION ON THE CHOICE OF DECISION PARADIGMS IN A COLLEGE OR UNIVERSITY.	Texas	77	214	Field Study	Education
Fay, Jack R.	DEVELOPMENT OF GENERAL CRITERIA APPLICABLE FOR THE ESTABLISHMENT OF A NEW ACCOUNTING PRACTICE	Arkansas	76	128	Field Study	Profession

Author	Title	School	Date	pp	Methodology	Topic
Fazzi, Charles	MEASURING THE EFFECT OF ALTERNATIVE INFLATION ACCOUNTING SYSTEMS ON FINANCIAL RATIOS	Penn St	83	410	Experimental	Inflation
Fedorowicz, Jane	MODELING AN AUTOMATIC BIBLIOGRAPHIC SYSTEM: A ZIPFFIAN APPROACH.	Carn Mel	81	128	Model- based	Education
Feibelkorn, George A.	THE ROLE OF THE CPA IN THE ACCT. COMMUN. PROCESS AS PERCEIVED BY SOPHIS- TICATED USERS, WITH AN EMP. ANALYSIS OF FACTORS AFFECTING MGMT'S CREDI- BILITY WITH CPA CREDIBILITY	Ga St	77	178	Field Study	Profession
Feller, Robert E.	AN EMP. STUDY OF SELECTED CAUSES AND EFFECTS OF SEMIRIGID PRICES IN THE PETROLEUM REFINING IND. WITH EMPHASIS ON THE PERIOD 1963-1973	Arkansas	75	263	FinStData- based	Oil & Gas
Fellingham, John C.	THE VALUE OF IMPROVED ESTIMATES OF SYSTEMATIC SECURITY RISKINESS FOR INVESTOR DECISIONS	UCLA	75	116	Market- based	Financial
Ferris, Kenneth R.	FORECAST DISCLOSURE OF EARNINGS: AN EMPIRICAL STUDY OF THE EFFECTS OF MANAGERIAL BEHAVIOR	Ohio St	74	199	Field Study	Managerial
Fertuck, Leonard J.	A TEST OF THE EFFICIENT MARKET HYPOTHESIS USING AUDITOR CHANGES	Cornell	77	89	Market- based	Auditing
Fesmire, Walker E.	A COMPARISON OF THE ADVOCATIONS OF HENRY SWEENY IN " STABILIZED ACCOUNTING" TO RECENT PRICE LEVEL REPLACEMENT COST ACTIVITY	Miss	82	296	Archival	Inflation
Fields, Kent T.	A DESCRIPTIVE STUDY OF STATEMENT OF FAS #12	Txs A&M	77	216	Field Study	Investments
File, Richard Garrison	AUDITOR PREDICTION OF CLIENT FIRM FAILURE.	Texas	81	211	Experimental	Auditing

Author	Title	School	Date	pp	Methodology	Topic
Fisher, Ted Lance	AN ANALYSIS OF THE FACTORS THAT HAVE CONTRIBUTED TO THE USE OF LEVERAGED FINANCING WITH NON-RECOURSE LOANS IN TAX SHELTERS.	Okl St.	77	222	Experimental	Tax
Fitzgerald, Michael N.	A METHODOLOGY FOR THE ANALYSIS AND SELECTION OF TAX SHELTERED INVESTMENTS	Saint Louis	83	346	Archival	Tax
Flaherty, Daniel J.	THE RELATIVE EFFECTIVENESS OF CLOSED CIRCUIT TELEVISION AS A COMMUNICATION MEDIUM FOR INSTRUCTION IN ACCOUNTING	Txs A&M	74	154	Experimental	Education
Fleenor, William C.	INVESTORS' REACTION TO THE REPLACEMENT COST INFORMATION PROVIDED AS A RESULT OF ASR #190: SOME EMPIRICAL RESULTS	LSU	78	164	Market- based	Inflation
Fleming, Mary Madonna Katzer	IMPLICATIONS OF BUDGETARY PRESSURE IN CPA FIRMS.	S Calif	79		Field Study	Auditing
Fleming, Robert J.	AN EMPIRIACL STUDY OF THE INFORMATIONAL RELATIONSHIP BETWEEN CONVENTIONAL DISCLOSURE AND THE REQUIREMENTS OF ASR 190	Miss	82	264	FinStData-based	Inflation
Flesher, Dale L.	A GENERALIZED OPERATIONS AUDIT MODEL AND AUDIT PROGRAM FOR A SMALL NON-PROFIT HOSPITAL	Cincinnati	75	242	Field Study	Auditing
Flesher, Tonya Kay	AN ANALYSIS OF THE TAX OPINIONS OF JUDGE LEARNED HAND AND HIS CONTRIBUTIONS TO THE DEVELOPMENT OF THE FEDERAL TAX SYSTEM.	Miss	79	383	Archival	Tax
Fletcher, John Cameron	A DELPHI EVALUATION OF A RAILROAD'S SOCIAL COSTS AND BENEFITS.	Colorado	81	242	Experimental	Social
Flory, Steven M.	AN INQUIRY INTO SELECTED PROBLEMS OF AUDITING COMPUTER-BASED ACCOUNTING SYSTEMS	LSU	76	240	Field Study	Auditing

Author	Title	School	Date	pp	Methodology	Topic
Flowers, Vincent S.	CONCEPTUAL FOUNDATION FOR HUMAN RESOURCE ACCOUNTING.	N Tex St	74	246	Archival	Hum.Resource Acct.
Fonfeder, Robert	AN EMPIRICAL INQUIRY INTO THE VALUE OF LIMITED REVIEW OF QUARTERLY STATEMENTS.	NYU	80		FinStData-based	Auditing
Foote, Paul S.	CORPORATE PROFITABILITY: DETERMINANTS AND FORECASTS	Mich St	83	469	FinStData-based	Forecasts
Ford, Donald H.	AN EXPERIMENT ON NONRESPONSE AND IMPROPER RESPONSE TO RECEIVABLE CONFIRMATIONS	N Colo	74	94	Experimental	Auditing
Foroughi, Tahirih T.	PRIVATE INDUSTRIAL DEVELOPMENT AND EVOLUTION AND CHANGE OF ACCOUNTING EDUCATION AND PROFESSION IN IRAN	Oregon	75	452	Field Study	History
Fortin, Karen A.	A COMPARISON OF ACCOUNTING ENTROPY MEASURES AND FINANCIAL RISK MEASURES	S Carol	79	185	FinStData-based	Financial
Foster, George J.	THE ASSOCIATION BETWEEN ACCOUNTING EARNINGS AND STOCK PRICES OF INSURANCE COMPANIES	Stanford	75	151	Market- based	Financial
Foster, Taylor William, III	AN EMPIRICAL INVESTIGATION OF THE ACCOUNTING FOR STOCK OPTIONS.	Penn St	74	250	FinStData-based	Financial
Fowler, Anna Cook	CHARITABLE REMAINDER TRUSTS UNDER THE POST-1969 TAX LAW: EFFECTS OF CHANGES IN THE LAW ON THEIR USE, A MODEL FOR TAX PLANNING, AND SUGGESTIONS FOR REVISIONS.	Texas	77	417	Field Study	Tax
Fox, James G.	A COMPARATIVE STUDY OF SELECTED AREAS OF THE ACCOUNTING THOUGHT OF WILLIAM ANDREW PATTON AND PREVAILING ACCT. THOUGHT 1915 TO 1970	Geo Wash	74	435	Model- based	History

Author	Title	School	Date	pp	Methodology	Topic
Frakes, Albert H.	ACHIEVEMENT OF SELECTED EDUC. OBJECTIVES IN INTRO. ACCT. AND OTHER VARIABLES AS PREDICTORS OF PERFORMANCE IN THE FIRST INTERMED. ACCT. COURSES	Wash	74	232	Experimental	Education
Frantz, Irving L.	A STUDY OF THE INFLUENCE OF DIFFERENT METH. OF CORP. TAX. ON THE DIVIDEND POLICIES OF PUB. HELD CORP. IN FRANCE, THE FED. REP. OF GERMANY, AND THE U. KINGDOM	NYU	74	287	Archival	Tax
Frazier, Katherine Beal	WORD-FREQUENCY CONTIGUITIES IN NARRATIVE ACCOUNTING DISCLOSURES.	S Carol	81	142	FinStData-based	Communication
Frecka, Thomas Jean	THE EFFECTS OF COMPLEX CAPITAL STRUCTURES ON THE MARKET VALUE OF FIRMS.	Syracuse	78	205	Market- based	Financial
Freedman, Martin	AN ANALYSIS OF INDUSTRIAL SOCIAL COSTS: A TAXONOMIC APPROACH	Illinois	75	259	Field Study	Social
Freeman, Jack Louis	REPLACEMENT COST DATA AND CAPITAL MARKET EQUILIBRIUM.	Michigan	81	134	Market- based	Inflation
Freeman, Robert N.	ACCOUNTING AND MARKET ESTIMATES OF RISK DUE TO UNANTICIPATED INFLATION	Texas	77	215	Market- based	Inflation
Fried, Haim D.	AN EXAMINATION OF THE AGGREGATION PROBLEM IN ACCOUNTING UNDER THE PREDICTIVE ABILITY CRITERION	NYU	78	160	FinStData-based	Financial
Friedberg, Alan H.	INTERNAL AUDITOR'S RESPONSES TO EXTERNAL AUDITORS' CRITICISMS OF THE SYSTEM OF INTERNAL CONTROLS	Florida	83	213	Field Study	Auditing
Friedlob, George Thomas	VARIABLE COSTING AS AN INCOME MEASUREMENT MODEL AT THE BUSINESS CYCLE UPPER TURNING POINT.	Miss	81	216	FinStData-based	Managerial

Author	Title	School	Date	pp	Methodology	Topic
Friedman, Laurence A.	THE THEORY AND THE FORMAT OF AN INCOME STATEMENT TO ACCOMPANY EXIT-PRICE FINANCIAL STATEMENTS	Kansas	75	188	Model- based	Inflation
Friedman, Mark Edward	THE EFFECT ON ACHIEVEMENT OF USING THE COMPUTER AS A PROBLEM SOLVING TOOL IN THE INTERMEDIATE ACCOUNTING CURRICULUM.	NYU	78	257	Experimental	Education
Fries, Clarence E.	A COMPARITIVE ANALYSIS OF EARNINGS FORECAST MODELS AUGMENTED FOR INTERINDUSTRY DEPENDENCIES AND PHASED FOR ECONOMIC CYCLES	Tenn	83	330	FinStData-based	Forecasts
Frigo, Mark Louis	INFLATION AND THE TAXATION OF INCOME AND CAPITAL WITHIN THE NONFINANCIAL CORPORATE SECTOR: AN EMPIRICAL STUDY.	N Ill	81	189	FinStData-based	Tax
Fry, Nichola E.	AN EMPIRICAL EVALUATION OF FIVE PRICE LEVEL ADJUSTED INCOME CONCEPTS AS ALTERNATIVES TO HISTORICAL COSTS	Miss St	78	280	FinStData-based	Inflation
Fulks, Daniel Lee	THE APPLICATION OF HUMAN RESOURCE QUANTIFICATION MODELS TO THE PROFESSIONAL SPORTS INDUSTRY AND THE IMPACT UPON RELATED INCOME TAX ISSUES.	Ga St	80	231	Experimental	Tax
Gaber, Brian G.	AN EMPIRICAL STUDY OF AUDIT JUDGEMENT IN PROGRAM PLANNING	Wiscon	83	299	Experimental	Auditing
Gabhart, David L.	AN INQUIRY INTO CONSTRUCTION OF ACCOUNTING PREDICTORS OF FUTURE MUNICIPAL FINANCIAL INSOLVENCY	Mich St	77	180	FinStData-based	Not-for-profit
Gaertner, James F.	A STUDY OF PROPOSED ALTERNATIVES FOR ACCOUNTING FOR BUSINESS COMBINATIONS	Txs A&M	77	180	Experimental	Business Combinations
Gaffney, Mary Anne	CONSOLIDATED VERSUS FUND-BY-FUND COUNTY ACCOUNTING REPORTS: THE PERSPECTIVES OF CONSTITUENTS	Maryland	84	237	Field Study	Not-for-Profit

Author	Title	School	Date	pp	Methodology	Topic
Gallun, Rebecca A.	REVENUE FORECASTING MODELS FOR SMALL MUNICIPALITIES IN TEXAS	Txs A&M	79	178	Model- based	Not-for-profit
Gamble, George O.	CONCEPTS OF CAPITAL MAINTENANCE IN A CONCEPTUAL FRAMEWORK FOR FINANCIAL REPORTING	Penn St	80	171	FinStData-based	Financial
Gangolly, Jagdish Shivshanker	TOWARDS A BEHAVIORAL THEORY OF TRANSFER PRICING.	Pitt	77	187	Experimental	Managerial
Gangouli, Gourganga	A COMPARATIVE ANALYSIS OF THE CONTENTS OF SOME OPERATIONAL AUDITING COURSES AND THE OPINIONS OF TWO GROUPS OF PROF. ON THE CONTENT ELEMENTS	Miss	83	448	Field Study	Auditing
Gardner, Robert L.	CUMULATIVE INCOME AVERAGING: AN ALTERNATIVE TO THE CURRENT INCOME AVERAGING PROVISIONS	Texas	79	319	Archival	Tax
Garsombke, Henry P.	THE RELATIONSHIP BETWEEN CORPORATE DISCLOSURE AND RISK: A THEORETICAL AND EMPIRICAL ANALYSIS	S Calif	76	207	Market- based	Financial
Gatley, Mary Sue	AN ANALYSIS OF THE ESTATE TAX CONSEQUENCES TO NONRESIDENT ALIENS INVESTING IN THE UNITED STATES.	Houston	81	304	Archival	Tax
Gaumnitz, Bruce	INCOME DETERMINATIONS AND CLOSED-END INVESTMENT COMPANIES	Wiscon	82	253	Market- based	Financial
Gavin, Thomas A.	THE CONSIDERATION OF FINANCIAL ACCT. AND INTERNAL CONTROL ISSUES BY BOARDS OF TRUSTEES OF VOL. SHORT-TERM GEN. HOSP.: AN EMPIR. INVEST.	Tenn	82	353	Field Study	Not-for-profit
Gean, Gilbert Farrell	A STUDY OF THE DESIRABILITY OF DEFERRED TAX ACCOUNTING FOR DEPRECIATION TIMING DIFFERENCES.	Ga St	81	212	Field Study	Deferred Taxes

Author	Title	School	Date	pp	Methodology	Topic
Geary, Kent M.	AN EMPIRICAL INV. OF THE RELATIONSHIP BETWEEN CERTAIN AUDITOR JUDGEMENTS AND STRUCTURE IN THE AUDIT PROCESS	Cincinnati	82	208	Experimental	Auditing
Geary, William Thomas	AN EXAMINATION OF EXPERT-CLIENT INTERACTION IN MANAGEMENT INFORMATION SYSTEMS DESIGN ACTIVITIES USING A ROLE THEORETIC APPROACH.	Northwest ern	76	375	Experimental	Systems/ Computers
Geiser, Eugene G.	COST-BENEFIT ANALYSIS OF DENTAL CARE PROGRAMS FOR SCHOOL CHILDREN	NYU	75	270	Model- based	Managerial
Gelinas, Ulric Joseph, Jr.	PRIVACY AUDITS AND THE CERTIFIED PUBLIC ACCOUNTANT.	Massach	78	303	Model- based	Auditing
Geller, Arthur Neal	FINANCIAL LEASES AND MARKET-DETERMINED IMPACT: SOME EMPIRICAL EVIDENCE.	Syracuse	77	135	Market- based	Leases
Gheyara, Kelly Framroze	THE REPLACEMENT COST DISCLOSURE REQUIREMENTS OF ASR-190: A TEST FOR INFORMATION	Okl St	79	45	Market- based	Inflation
Giacoletti, Robert R.	A COMPARISON BETWEEN STATE GOVERNMENT AUDITORS AND PRIVATE SECTOR CPA AUDITORS ON THE ATTRIBUTE OF INDEPENDENCE IN FACT.	Kentucky	81	192	Field Study	Auditing
Giacomino, Don Edward	AN ANALYSIS AND EMPIRICAL TEST OF THE USE OF SELECTED MANAGEMENT ACCOUNTING TECHNIQUES IN HIGHER EDUCATION CONTROLLERSHIP.	Kentucky	78	182	Field Study	Managerial
Gibbins, Michael	PERSUASIVE COMMUNICATION AND ACCOUNTING.	Cornell	76	269	Experimental	Communicati on
Gibson, Robert W.	THE UNIFORMITY PROBLEM AND THE STATE OF AUSTRALIAN CO. FINANCIAL REPORTING	Cincinnati	76	404	FinStData- based	International

Author	Title	School	Date	pp	Methodology	Topic
Gift, Michael J.	INFORMATION CONTENT OF MGMT. FORECASTS: RISK SHIFT AND MEAN EARNINGS SHIFT EFFECTS ON EQUILIBRIUM SECURITY PRICES	Florida	83	134	Market- based	Forecasts
Gillespie, Jackson Floyd	A MARKOVIAN MANPOWER PLANNING, HUMAN RESOURCE VALUATION MODEL.	VPI	78	289	Model- based	Hum.Resource Acct.
Gillett, John W.	AN EMPIRICAL INVESTIGATION INTO THE INFORMATION CONTENT OF FINANCIAL ACCOUNTING STANDARDS BOARD STATEMENT NO. 33 CURRENT COST REPORTING REQUIREMENTS	N Txs St	82	151	Field Study	Inflation
Gingras, Russell T.	AM EMPIRICAL EVALUATION OF THE STOCK PRICE REACTION TO ERRORS IN MANAGEMENT FORECASTS OF EPS	Mich St	74	184	Market- based	Forecasts
Giroux, Gary Alan	FINANCIAL FORECASTING IN COMMERCIAL BANKS: AN INDUSTRY SURVEY.	Texas Tech.	79	146	Field Study	Forecasts
Givoly, Dan	THE INFORMATIONAL CONTENT OF QUARTERLY REPORTS	NYU	75	177	Market- based	Quarterly Data
Glazer, Alan S.	AN INVESTIGATION OF THE EFFECTS OF ALTERNATIVE AUDITORS' REPORTS ON INVESTMENT BEHAVIOR IN THE PRESENCE OF LITIGATIOUS UNCERTAINTIES	Penn	78	254	Experimental	Auditing
Glezen, G. William, Jr.	A STUDY OF COMPETITIVE CHARACTERISTICS AND ACTIONS OF PUBLIC ACCOUNTING FIRMS AND IMPLICATIONS FOR SOCIETY AND THE ACCOUNTING	Arkansas	79	145	Experimental	Auditing
Glick, John R.	THE USEFULNESS OF FINANCIAL ACCOUNTING INFORMATION IN PLANNING AND CONTROL ASPECTS OF ACCOUNTING MANAGEMENT	Colorado	75	278	Field Study	Managerial
Glover, Robert I.	SELECTED PROBLEMS OF FOREIGN CURRENCY TRANSLATION	Arkansas	75	153	FinStData-based	Foreign Currency

Author	Title	School	Date	pp	Methodology	Topic
Godfrey, L. Howard	AN INQUIRY INTO THE SIGNIFICANCE AND DISCLOSURE OF YEAR-TO-YEAR VARIATIONS IN PENSION EXPENSE REPORTED BY SELECTED CORPORATIONS	Alabama	75	258	FinStData-based	Pensions
Godfrey, Robert F.	THE EFFECT OF MODE OF PROBLEM SOLVING ON STUDENT ACHIEVEMENT IN PRINCIPLES OF ACCOUNTING 1	Ohio St	77	128	Experimental	Education
Godwin, Larry B.	AN EMPIRICAL STUDY OF THE DISCLOSURE NEEDS OF FINANCIAL STATEMENT USERS	Colorado	74	419	Field Study	Financial
Goetz, Joseph F.	AN INQUIRY INTO THE NATURE OF THE INCOME TAX ENTITY CONCEPT IN THE CONTEXT OF SELECTED TAX LOSSES	Nebraska	74	160	Archival	Tax
Gokarn, Rajul Yoganand	AN INVESTIGATION INTO THE NEED FOR, POSSIBILITY OF, AND MEANS OF ACHIEVING INTERNATIONAL HARMONIZATION OF ACCOUNTING AND REPORTING PRACTICES	Ga St	84	145	Field Study	International
Golden, Mary Rolwing	BEHAVIORAL IMPLICATIONS OF A CHANGE FROM THE TRADITIONAL INCOME MEASUREMENT RULE TO THE GENERAL PUCHASING POWER OR CURRENT VALUE RULE.	Miss St	79	200	Experimental	Inflation
Goma, Ahmed Tawfik	EMPIRICAL INVESTIGATION OF THE INFORMATION CONTENT OF SPECIFIC PRICE CHANGE DISCLOSURES (REPLACEMENT, CURRENT COST)	NYU	85	209	FinStData-based	Inflation
Gomaa, Ismail I.	INFORMATION INDUCTANCE IN A TRANSFER PRICING SETTING	Florida	82	208	Experimental	Managerial
Goodhart, Edward S.	A MULTIPLE REGRESSION APPROACH TO COST/BENEFIT ANALYSIS IN THE MUNICIPAL FIRE DEPARTMENT	Penn St	82	142	Field Study	Not-for-profit
Goodman, Leonard	A STUDY OF THE CHAR. OF PUBLIC ACCOUNTING INTERNSHIP PROGRAMS OF MAJOR CPA FIRMS, AND THE DEVEL. OF GUIDELINES FOR THESE PROGRAMS	NYU	82	190	Field Study	Profession

Author	Title	School	Date	pp	Methodology	Topic
Gordon, Irene Malinda	UNFUNDED PAST SERVICE OBLIGATIONS: AN EFFICIENT MARKETS HYPOTHESIS TEST.	Simon Fraser	81		Market- based	Pensions
Govindarajan, V.	BEHAVIORAL EFFECTS OF AUDITS IN THE HEALTH CARE-SERVICES: A STUDY IN THE FIELD USING EXPLORATORY DATA ANALYSIS AND CLASSICAL STAT. TECHNIQUES	Harvard	78	274	Field Study	Auditing
Grabski, Severin V.	A COMPARISON OF PERCEPTUAL AND TECHNICAL SKILLS AMONG SYSTEMS ANALYSTS, INTERNAL AUDITORS, AND EDP AUDITORS	Ariz St	83	245	Field Study	Profession
Graci, Samuel P.	EFFECTS OF THE STATEMENT OF CHANGES IN FINANCIAL POSITION ON THE SHORT-TERM LOAN DECISION	Arkansas	82	119	Field Study	Statement of Ch Fin Pos
Graham, Lynford E.,Jr.	AN INVESTIGATION INTO THE ACCOUNTING PROBLEMS INVOLVED IN PRESENTING FINANCIAL STATEMENTS FOR THE U.S. BASED CO. WITH FOREIGN OPERATIONS	Penn	76	260	Field Study	Foreign Currency
Gramling, Lawrence J.	AN INVESTIGATION INTO THE IMPACT OF PEER REVIEW REPORTS ON SELECTED OUTSIDE USERS: A SERIES OF EXPERIMENTS	Maryland	82	253	Experimental	Auditing
Granger, Courtenay L.	AN ATTEMPT TO IMPROVE THE BRANCH INFORMATION SYSTEM OF AN INS. FIRM THROUGH THE INTRO. OF HUMAN RESOURCE SURROGATES: AN EMPIRICAL STUDY	Florida	75	179	Field Study	Hum.Resource Acct.
Granger, Mitchell Parker, II	AN INQUIRY INTO THE SOCIAL ACCOUNTING PRACTICES AND DISCLOSURE POLICIES OF SELECTED FIRMS IN THE PULP AND PAPER INDUSTRY OF THE SOUTHERN PINE FOREST REGION.	Arkansas	79	347	Field Study	Social
Grant, Edward B.	INTERIM INFORMATION AND THE INFORMATION CONTENT OF ANNUAL EARNINGS ANNOUNCEMENTS	Mich St	77	141	Market- based	Interim Statements
Graul, Paul R.	INTERACTION OF EXTERNAL REPORTING SYSTEMS AND MANAGEMENT DECISIONS	Berkeley	75	173	Model- based	Managerial

Author	Title	School	Date	pp	Methodology	Topic
Gray, Dahli	FOREIGN CURRENCY TRANSLATION BY UNITED STATES MULTINATIONAL CORPORATIONS: TOWARD A THEORY OF ACCOUNTING STANDARD SELECTION	Geo Wash	84	229	Experimental	Foreign Currency
Gray, O. Ronald	DIFFERENTIAL ACCOUNTING FOR CLOSELY HELD ENTERPRISES: A SURVEY OF ATTITUDES	Arkansas	80	245	Field Study	Financial
Green John L.	AN INVESTIGATION INTO THE EFFECT OF DEATH TAXES ON TRANSFER OF FARMS FROM ONE GENERATION TO ANOTHER	Houston	77	214	Archival	Tax
Green, Mitzi Chandler	AN EMPIRICAL STUDY OF EMPLOYERS' ADMINISTRATIVE COSTS AND BENEFITS OF PROVIDING A DEFINED BENEFIT PENSION PLAN IN MISSISSIPPI	Miss St	83	170	Field Study	Pensions
Greenberg, Ralph Howard	THE RELATIVE PREDICTIVE ACCURACY OF TIME SERIES PREDICTION METHODS VS. INDEXING PREDICTION METHODS: AN EMPIRICAL STUDY.	Ohio St	81	155	FinStData-based	Stochastic Properties
Greenberg, Robert R.	ESTIMATION PROCEDURES FOR REVERSED J-SHAPED TAINTING DISTRIBUTIONS IN DOLLAR-UNIT SAMPLES OF ACCOUNTS RECEIVABLE	Ariz St	81	111	Experimental	Auditing
Grief, Louis Adrian	AN EMPIRICAL STUDY OF UNSPECIFIED AND UNREPORTED INCONSISTENCIES IN CORPORATE ANNUAL REPORTS.	Kentucky	79	217	FinStData-based	Financial
Grierson, Peter Robert	AN EXAMINATION OF SELECTED POLITICAL AND TECHNICAL ASPECTS OF SETTING ACCOUNTING GUIDELINES FOR BUSINESS COMBINATIONS.	Ga St	81	207	Field Study	Business Combinations
Griffin, Paul A.	THE INFORMATIONAL CONTENT OF PUBLISHED QUARTERLY EARNIGNS AND QUARTERLY DIVIDEND ANNOUNCEMENTS: AN EMPIRICAL STUDY	Ohio St	74	210	Market- based	Quarterly Data
Griffin, Richard Bradley	A STUDY OF BUDGETING PROCEDURES AND THEIR APPLICATION BY THE UNITED METHODIST CHURCHES IN THE TENNESSEE CONFERENCE.	Miss	79	283	Field Study	Not-for-profit

Author	Title	School	Date	pp	Methodology	Topic
Grimlund, Richard A.	A FRAMEWORK FOR THE INTEGRATION OF AUDITING EVIDENCE	Wash	77	252	Model- based	Auditing
Groff, James Edward	A THEORETICAL AND EMPIRICAL ANALYSIS OF CURRENT VALUE ACCOUNTING DATA AND STOCK PRICE REACTIONS TO UNANTICIPATED INFLATION	Iowa	84	163	Model- based	Inflation
Groft, William L.	ELEMENTARY AND INTERMEDIATE ACCT. ACHIEVEMENT OF NATIVE AND TRANSFER STUDENTS IN SELECTED COLLEGES AND UNIVERSITIES IN PENN.	Iowa	78	165	Experimental	Education
Groner, Michael I.	AN ANALYSIS OF THE PROFESSIONAL ASPECTS OF PUBLIC ACCOUNTANCY	Illinois	77	242	Archival	Profession
Groomer, Stephen M.	AN ANALYSIS OF THE PREDICTIVE ABILITY OF TIME SERIES EARNINGS MODELS	Missouri	75	119	FinStData-based	Stochastic Properties
Grove, Hugh D.	IMPROVING THE USEFULNESS OF ACCOUNTING MEASUREMENT INFORMATION	S Calif	75		Experimental	Financial
Grudnitski, Gary Martin	A METHODOLOGY FOR THE DESIGN OF DECISION-MAKER ORIENTED INFORMATION SYSTEMS.	Massach	75	141	Experimental	Systems/ Computers
Guber, Quentin N.	PREDICTION OF INCOME AND STOCK PRICES OF A SEASONAL BUSINESS USING DIFFERENT CONCEPTS OF INTERIM REPORTING	Minnesota	77	236	Experimental	Interim Statements
Guithues, Denise Michele	A CRITICAL EXAMINATION OF FOREIGN CURRENCY TRANSLATION AND A SUGGESTION FOR A MORE USEFUL APPROACH	Saint Louis	83	247	FinStData-based	Foreign Currency
Gunn, Sanford Charles	THE RELATIONSHIP BETWEEN THE BUDGETARY PROCESS AND THE QUANTITY OF RESOURCES AVAILABLE TO SUBUNITS: A PRELIMINARY INVESTIGATION.	Ohio St	77	165	Field Study	Managerial

Author	Title	School	Date	pp	Methodology	Topic
Guttikonda, Ramamohana R.	A THEORETICAL STUDY FOR ANALYZING THE RELATIONSHIP BETWEEN FINANCIAL AND COST ACCOUNTING WITH AN APPLICATION TO THE ALLOCATION OF CERTAIN EXPENSES	Arkansas	84	244	Field Study	Financial
Guttmann, Paul Eston	THE DEVELOPMENT AND TESTING OF A MODEL OF STAFF TURNOVER IN PUBLIC ACCOUNTING.	Minnesota	81	174	Field Study	Profession
Habib, Abo-el-yazeed	A THEORETICAL AND EMPIRICAL INVESTIGATION INTO THE APPLICATION OF A CASH-FLOW ACCOUNTING SYSTEM	N Txs St	83	182	FinStData-based	Cash Flows
Hadley, Galen D.	A STUDY OF THE IMPACT OF ACCOUNTING RULES ON THE DECISION PROCESS OF BOND PORTFOLIO MANAGERS IN THE LIFE INSURANCE INDUSTRY	Nebraska	75	199	Field Study	Financial
Haka, Susan F.	AN INVESTIGATION OF THE RELATIONSHIP BETWEEN SOPHISTICATED CAPITAL BUDGETING TECHNIQUES AND FIRM PERFORMANCE	Kansas	83	173	Field Study	Managerial
Hale, Jack A.	AN ANALYSIS OF THE EFFICIENCY OF EX-POST INCOME MODELS AS SURROGATES FOR DIVIDEND PAYING ABILITY DURING PERIODS OF PRICE INCREASES	Cincinnati	75	167	Market- based	Inflation
Hall, James Arthur	ON THE ADEQUACY OF CURRENT AUTHORITATIVE GUIDELINES FOR THE REVIEW AND EVALUATION OF SYSTEMS DEVELOPMENT CONTROLS.	Okl St	79	195	Field Study	Auditing
Hall, Steven D.	THE EXTENT OF USE OF MANAGERIAL ACCOUNTING TECHNIQUES IN MUNICIPAL GOV. FUNDS MANAGEMENT AND PURPORTEDLY RELATED CAUSAL FACTORS	N Ill	82	339	Field Study	Not-for-profit
Hall, Thomas W.	AN EMPIRICAL TEST OF THE EFFECT OF ASSET AGGREGATION ON VALUATION ACCURACY	Okl St	80	146	Field Study	Financial
Halperin, Robert M.	THE EFFECTS OF AN INCOME TAX STRUCTURE WHICH PERMITS LIFO INVENTORY COSTING ON THE EOQ INV. POLICY: ANALYSIS AND PUBLIC POLICY IMPLICATIONS	Penn	77	169	Archival	Tax

Author	Title	School	Date	pp	Methodology	Topic
Hamamad, Ahmed-Hany B.	THE RELATIONSHIP OF ALTERNATIVE ACCOUNTING SIGNALS TO MARKET BETA AND TO CHANGES IN SECURITY PRICES	N Txs St	83	154	Market- based	Financial
Hamdallah, Ahmed El Sayed	AN INVESTIGATION OF MOTIVATION FOR VOLUNTARILY TERMINATING OVER-FUNDED PENSION PLANS	NYU	85	123	Experimental	Pensions
Hamer, John Gwenffrud	AN EMPIRICAL INVESTIGATION OF THE IMPACT OF TROUBLED DEBT RESTRUCTURING ON FIRMS IN FINANCIAL DISTRESS	Texas A&M	84	191	Experimental	Financial
Hamer, Michelle M	AN INVESTIGATION OF THE USEFULNESS OF INFORMATION THEORY DERIVED DECOMPENSATION MEASURES IN THE PREDICTION OF BUSINESS FAILURE	Wiscon	80	238	FinStData-based	Financial Distress
Hamilton, Marshall Lee	THE IMPACT OF "ACCOUNTING FOR RETAIL LAND SALES" ON FINANCIAL REPORTING BY SELECTED LAND-SALES COMPANIES 1969-1973.	Ariz St	74	304	Field Study	Real Estate
Hamilton, Robert E.	AN EXAMINATION AND CLARIFICATION OF THE ROLE FOR AUDITING IN THE PRODUCTION AND DISSEMINATION OF CAPITAL MARKET INFORMATION	S Calif	75	253	Market- based	Auditing
Hammer, Lawrence H.	THE USEFULNESS OF ALTERNATIVE ACCT. INCOME SERIES IN PREDICTING CASH FLOWS TO EQUITY INVESTORS-A SIMULATION APPROACH	Indiana	77	311	Experimental	Financial
Hanks, George F.	AN ANALYSIS CONTRASTING THE COST STRUCTURE OF THE PRESENT BURLEY TOBACCO CHANEL WITH A FEASIBLE ALTERNATIVE	Kentucky	74	194	Experimental	Managerial
Hansen, Don R	PREDICTION ERROR IN THE SYSTEMMATIC RISK OF A SECURITY AND THE VALUE OF ACCOUNTING INFORMATION TO THE INDIVIDUAL INVESTOR	Arizona	78	160	Market- based	Financial
Harbecke, Paula A.	MARKET ASSESSMENT OF DISCRETIONARY VS. NONDISCRETIONARY IRREGULAR ITEMS	Illinois	83	273	Market- based	Financial

Author	Title	School	Date	pp	Methodology	Topic
Hardman, Oswald C.	THE DEVELOPMENT AND INVESTIGATION OF A CLASSIFICATION SCHEME FOR THE DIFFERENCES BETWEEN TAX AND FINANCIAL ACCOUNTING FOR CORPORATONS	Illinois	74	275	Archival	Tax
Harkins, Jeffrey Lynn	FINANCIAL INFORMATION: DECISION MAKER PERCEPTIONS OF USEFULNESS.	Wash	80	205	Field Study	Financial
Harline, Norman L.	AN EXAM. OF THE STRUC. AND VAL.OF LEGAL AND ECON. RIGHTS OF PTNSHP. INT. OF EXT. AND GIFT TAX PURPOSES IN IMPL. A PTNSHP. CAP. FREEZE FOR FARM. ENT.	Nebraska	82	352	Archival	Tax
Harmon, Kay Poston	AN EXAMINATION OF THE RELATIONSHIP BETWEEN QUALITY COSTS AND PRODUCTIVITY IN CONJUNCTION WITH THE INTRODUCTION OF STATISTICAL PROCESS CONTROL: A CASE STUDY	Tenn	84	167	Field Study	Managerial
Harmon, William K.	AN EMP. INVEST. OF THE RELATIVE STRENGTH OF ASSO. BETWEEN MARKET REACTION AND UNCERTAIN MEASURES OF INC. AND FUNDS FLOWS TO THE ENTERPRISE	Tenn	82	118	Market- based	Financial
Harper, James C.	THE RELATIONAHIP BETWEEN DEMOGRAPHIC ATTRIBUTES AND OPINIONS OF CERTIFIED PUBLIC ACCOUNTANTS AND EDUCATION AND EXPERIENCE REQUIREMENTS CONTROVERSIES	Utah	75	243	Field Study	Profession
Harper, Robert Mitchell Jr.	INTERNAL CONTROL IN LOCAL AREA NETWORKS: CONSENSUS OF AUDITORS JUDGMENTS	Fla St	84	228	Experimental	Auditing
Harper, Thomas Robert	TAX SERVICES FOR INDIVIDUAL TAXPAYERS: AN EVALUATION.	Texas	74	181	Experimental	Tax
Harr, David James	PARTICIPATIVE BUDGETING AS A COMMUNICATION PROCESS: A MODEL AND EXPERIMENT.	Wiscon	78	233	Experimental	Managerial
Harrell, Adrian M.	ORGANIZATIONAL GOALS AND THE DECISION-MAKING OF AIR FORCE STAFF OFFICERS: A BEHAVIORAL EXPERIMENT	Texas	75	296	Experimental	Managerial

Author	Title	School	Date	pp	Methodology	Topic
Harrell, Horace W.	A CRITICAL STUDY OF A LEAD-LAG FORECASTING TECHNIQUE IN SELECTED COMPANIES	Georgia	76	153	Market- based	Financial
Harris, Robert W.	AN ANALYSIS OF SEMIPROFESSIONAL ACCOUNTANCY COMPETENCIES WITH IMPLICATIONS FOR THE OCCUPATIONAL ACCOUNTING CURRICULUM IN COMMUNITY COLLEGES	Rutgers	75	252	Field Study	Education
Harris, Trevor S.	CONSEQUENCES OF ECONOMIC CONCEPTS OF FOREIGN EXCHANGE FOR FINANCIAL ACCOUNTING	Wash	83	231	Market- based	Foreign Currency
Harris, William T.	COMMON VARIABLE COSTING SYSTEMS FOR ACHIEVING GOAL CONGRUENCE	LSU	75	154	Experimental	Managerial
Harrison, Kenneth Eugene	AN EMPIRICAL INVESTIGATION OF CONTINGENT LOSS JUDGMENTS	Texas at Austin	83	164	Field Study	Auditing
Harrison, Paul D.	AN EMPIRICAL EXAM. OF THE INFORMATION-SEEKING BEHAVIOR OF SUPERIORS AND SUBORDINATES IN COST-VARIANCE INVESTIGATIONS	Ariz St	82	171	Field Study	Managerial
Harrison, Walter T.	THE INFORMATION CONTENT OF ACCOUNTING CHANGES	Mich St	76	238	Market- based	Accounting Changes
Harsha, Phillip D.	AN EMPIRICAL INVESTIGATION OF AUDITORS' INTUITIVE STATISTICAL ABILITIES TO PERFORM TESTS OF COMPLIANCE WITH INTERNAL CONTROLS	Ga St	83	298	Experimental	Auditing
Hartgraves, Al L.	A STUDY OF THE ROLE AND RESPONSIBILITIES OF THE CPA IN THE PREPARATION OF UNAUDITED FINANCIAL STATEMENTS	Ga St	75	252	Field Study	Auditing
Hartman, Bart P.	A COMPARISON OF SELECTED FINANCIAL MEASURES USING HISTORICAL COST AND SPECIFIC PRICE INDEX ADJUSTED FINANCIAL STATEMENTS	Kentucky	75	197	FinStData-based	Inflation

Author	Title	School	Date	pp	Methodology	Topic
Harvey, Barron Henry	EXPLORING THE EFFECTS OF INCREASING EMPLOYEE SELF-CONTROL/DETERMINATION.	Nebraska	77	262	Field Study	Managerial
Haselkorn, Michael	APB OPINION NO. 8 AND FLUCTUATION IN PENSION EXPENSE: A CASE STUDY IN THE EFFECTIVENESS OF ACCOUNTING REGULATION.	Chicago	81		FinStData-based	Foreign Currency
Haskin, Daniel L.	AN INVESTIGATION OF THE USEFULNESS OF RESERVE RECOGNITION ACCOUNTING DATA	Txs Tech	82	122	Experimental	Oil & Gas
Haskins, Mark Eugene	CLIENT CONTROL ENVIRONMENT EVALUATIONS	Penn St	84	300	Field Study	Auditing
Hassanin, Badr E.	A CRITICAL EXAMINATION OF THE USE OF DETERMINISTIC MODELS IN BUDGETING PROBLEMS: A STOCHASTIC PROGRAMMING APPROACH	Illinois	74	179	Model- based	Managerial
Hasselback, James R.	AN EMPIRICAL EXAMINATION OF FINANCIAL STATEMENTS-PRESENTATION OF THE CORPORATE INCOME TAX EXPENSE	Mich St	76	150	FinStData-based	Statement Presentation
Hassell, John M.	THE EFFECTS OF SOURCES OF EARNINGS FORECASTS AND DEGREE OF SOURCE EXPERTISE ON SUBJECTS' ESTIMATES OF EPS: A FIELD EXPERIMENT	Indiana	83	156	Experimental	Forecasts
Hatami, Roben	A MANAGEMENT DECISION SUPPORT SYSTEM FOR LABOR CONTRACT EVALUATION	Texas at Austin	84	264	Field Study	Systems/Computers
Haugland, Jerry Lee	CHURCH FINANCIAL OFFICERS' ATTITUDES TOWARDS PREREQUISITES TO USING THE ATTEST FUNCTION; AN EMPIRICAL STUDY BY CHURCH CHARACTERISTICS	Okl St	75	165	Field Study	Not-for-profit
Haw, In-Mu	EMPIRICAL INVESTIGATION OF THE EFFECTS OF REPLACEMENT COST INFORMATION ON STOCK MARKET PRICES	Alabama	83	230	Market- based	Inflation

Author	Title	School	Date	pp	Methodology	Topic
Hawkins, Charles E.	A COMPARATIVE STUDY OF THE MANAGEMENT ACCOUNTING PRACTICES OF INDUSTRIAL COMPANIES IN THE UNITED STATES AND JAPAN	Nebraska	83	205	Field Study	International
Hawkins, Ennis Milton	A STUDY OF THE PROBABILISTIC NATURE OF FINANCIAL STATEMENTS.	Txs Tech	74	201	Experimental	Financial
Hayes, David C.	THE CONTINGENCY THEORY OF MANAGERIAL ACCOUNTING: AN EMPIRICAL TEST OF AN ASSESSMENT MODEL	Ohio St	75	248	Field Study	Managerial
Hayes, Randall Bryant	THE INFORMATION CONTENT OF REPLACEMENT COST DATA.	Michigan	78	190	Market- based	Inflation
Hays, Larry Lynn	THE APPLICATION OF QUANTITATIVE COST ANALYSIS OF INSTRUCTIONAL PRODUCTIVITY IN PRIVATE LIBERAL ARTS COLLEGES.	Saint Louis	81	210	Field Study	Not-for-profit
Healy, Paul M.	THE IMPACT OF BONUS SCHEMES ON ACCOUNTING CHOICES	Rochester	83	114	FinStData-based	Managerial
Heaston, Patrick H.	TOWARD A MEANINGFUL EXPERIENCE REQUIREMENT FOR THE LICENSURE OF CERTIFIED PUBLIC ACCOUNTANTS: A DELPHI APPROACH	Nebraska	82	423	Field Study	Profession
Hegstad, Larry Paul	THE INFLUENCE OF A MANAGEMENT CONTROL SYSTEM ON THE PERFORMANCE OF BRANCH BANK OFFICERS.	Wash	78	196	Field Study	Managerial
Heian, James Bernard	A STUDY OF THE DETERMINANTS OF SENIOR CERTIFIED PUBLIC ACCOUNTANT LEADERSHIP EFFECTIVENESS	Utah	85	338	Field Study	Auditing
Hein, Cheryl Donnithorne	A STUDY OF INTRA-INDUSTRY PRACTICE WITH RESPECT TO REPORTING OF RESEARCH AND DEVELOPMENT EXPENDITURES: THREE INDUSTRIES	Arkansas	83	170	Field Study	Research & Development

Author	Title	School	Date	pp	Methodology	Topic
Helal, Samir	AN APPLICATION OF RELIABILITY ENGINEERING CONCEPTS TO THE ANALYSIS OF THE ACCOUNTING CONTROL SYSTEMS	Illinois	83	244	Model- based	Systems/ Computers
Helleloid, Richard Trygve	HINDSIGHT BIAS AND JUDGMENTS BY TAX PROFESSIONALS	Minnesota	85	218	Experimental	Tax
Heller, Kenneth H.	THE IMPACT OF U.S. INC. TAX. ON THE FINANCING AND EARNINGS REMITTANCE DECISIONS OF U.S. BASED MULTINAT. FIRMS WITH CONTROLLED FOREIGN CORP.	Texas	77	406	Experimental	Tax
Helmi, Medhat A.	STEWARDSHIP RESPONSIBILITY AND FINANCIAL REPORTING, AN EMPIRICAL STUDY	Illinois	76	107	FinStData- based	Financial
Helms, Flenn Lindley	AN EXAMINATION OF THE IMPACT OF INFORMATION SYSTEM AUDITOR INVOLVEMENT IN SYSTEMS DEVELOPMENT ON THE QUALITY OF NEW APPLICATION SYSTEMS	Houston	83	276	Field Study	Systems/Com puters
Hemmingway, James R.	AN INQUIRY INTO SELECTED COMMUNICATION PROB. INHERENT WITH FIN. ST. CERTIFICATION AND INVEST./CREDITOR RESPONSE IN LIGHT OF THE RECOMMENDATIONS OF THE COMMISSION ON AUD.S' RESPONSIBILITIES	N Txs St	79	272	Field Study	Auditing
Henaidy, Hamid Mohamad	TRANSFER PRICING FOR THE MULTINATIONAL CORPORATION: A MATHEMATICAL PROGRAMMING APPROACH AND A CASE STUDY.	Missouri	80	215	Experimental	Managerial
Henderson, James Randal	CPA ADVERTISING: AN EMPIRICAL INVESTIGATION OF EXTERNAL CREDIBILITY AND MICROECONOMIC IMPACT.	Txs A&M	80	170	Field Study	Profession
Hendricks, Arthur George	ACCOUNTING RULE-MAKING IN THE PRIVATE SECTOR: AN EVALUATION OF THE SIGNIFICANCE OF FINANCIAL ACCOUNTING STANDARDS IN DETERMINING THE NET INCOME OF PUBLICLY OWNED CORPORATIONS.	Houston	77	111	FinStData- based	Standard- setting
Hendricks, James A.	HUMAN ASSET ACCOUNTING INFORMATION AND ITS RELATION TO STOCK INVESTMENT DECISIONS: AN EMPIRICAL STUDY	Illinois	74	171	Market- based	Hum.Resourc e Acct.

Author	Title	School	Date	pp	Methodology	Topic
Hennessee, Patrick Arnold	EMPLOYEE STOCK OWNERSHIP PLANS AND THE PUBLICLY HELD CORPORATION, A STUDY OF THEIR ACCOUNTING, FINANCIAL AND ECONOMIC IMPLICATIONS.	N Txs St	77	206	FinStData-based	Financial
Herrera, Fernando B.	AN EMPIRICAL ANALYSIS OF THE PREDICTIVE ABILITY OF ALTERNATIVE INCOME MEASURES	UCLA	77	148	FinStData-based	Financial
Herrera, Olga B.	INFORMATION FEEDBACK AND BUDGET-RELATED BEHAVIOR: AN INVESTIGATION OF THE BUDGETING PROCESS IN NON-PROFIT HOSPITALS	Claremont	84	308	Field Study	Not-for-Profit
Herring, Hartwell C.	AN INQUIRY INTO THE THEORY OF REPORTING FINANCIAL POSITION TO RESIDUAL EQUITY HOLDERS AND ITS IMPLICATIONS FOR FINANCIAL STATEMENT CONTENT	Alabama	74	314	Model- based	Financial
Hicks, James O., Jr.	A STUDY OF DIFFERENTIAL SUBSYSTEM PERCEPTIONS OF INNOVATIONS AND FUTURE CHANGE IN THE ACCOUNTING PROFESSION	Ga St	76	228	Field Study	Profession
Hicks, Margaret	A STUDY OF ALTERNATIVE AUDITORS' REPORTS AND LENDING BEHAVIOR	Maryland	82	155	Experimental	Auditing
Hicks, Samuel A.	THE EFFECT OF CORPORATE TAX INCENTIVES ON THE HORIZONTAL EQUITY OF THE CORPORATION INCOME TAX	Wiscon	76	258	Experimental	Tax
Hill, Robert W.	CONTINUING EDUCATION REQUIREMENTS FOR CPA LICENSE RENEWAL: CONCEPTUAL AND PRACTICAL ISSUES	S Calif	75		Field Study	Profession
Hillison, William A.	EMPIRICAL INVESTIGATION OF GENERAL PURCHASING POWER ADJUSTMENTS ON EPS AND THE MOVEMENT OF SECURITY PRICES	Florida	77	105	Market- based	Inflation
Hiltebeitel, Kenneth Merrill	THE ACCOUNTING STANDARDS OVERLOAD ISSUE: AN EMPIRICAL TEST OF THE EFFECT OF FOUR SELECTED FINANCIAL ACCOUNTING STANDARDS ON THE LENDING DECISIONS OF BANKERS	Drexel	85	262	Experimental	Standard-setting

Author	Title	School	Date	pp	Methodology	Topic
Hiltner, Arthur H.	AN INQUIRY INTO THE FUTURE OF CURRENT VALUE ACCOUNTING	Nebraska	75	246	Field Study	Inflation
Hilton, Joseph Norwood	A FOUNDATIONAL STUDY OF ACCOUNTING.	Arkansas	79	131	Archival	History
Hilton, Ronald W. \M	THE DETERMINANTS OF INFORMATION VALUE: AN INQUIRY IN THE CONTEXT OF THE COST-VOLUME-PROFIT DECISION	Ohio St	77	295	Model- based	Managerial
Hinds, John E.	AN INVESTIGATION OF THE IMPACT OF DATA AGGREGATION ON THE DECISION-MAKER PERFORMANCE AND RISK	S Calif	81		Experimental	Financial
Hines, Charles Edmund, Jr.	AN INVESTIGATION OF THE MATERIALITY DECISIONS OF FINANCIAL STATEMENT PREPARERS, AUDITORS, AND USERS IN CERTAIN ILLEGAL PAYMENT CASES.	Mich St	79	204	Field Study	Financial
Hines, Danny R	ADAPTING THE FLOW OF RESOURCES CONCEPT TO THE BUSINESS ENTERPRISE	Florida	75	185	Model- based	Systems/ Computers
Hinrichs, Anella Sue Noel	ACCOUNTING FOR STOCK DIVIDENDS AND STOCK SPLITS.	Santa Cl	74		FinStData-based	Stock Distributions
Hinton, Walter V.	THE IMIPACT OF ELECTRONIC FUNDS TRANSFER UPON THE CASH MANAGEMENT OF A PUBLIC UTILITY	Arkansas	82	177	Field Study	Managerial
Hirsch, Maurice L.	DISAGGREGATED PROBABILISTIC ACCOUNTING INFORMATION: AN EXPERIMENT TO DISCOVER SYSTEMATIC DYSFUNCTIONAL BEHAVIOR	Wash U	77	150	Experimental	Managerial
Hitzig, Neal B	SUBSTANTIVE AUDIT TESTS OF DETAILS AND THE ESTIMATION OF RARE ERRORS BY DOUBLE SAMPLING WITH PROBABILITY PROPORTIONAL TO SIZE (STATISTICS)	NYU	85	119	Experimental	Auditing

Author	Title	School	Date	pp	Methodology	Topic
Hock, Clayton Allen	EARNINGS PER SHARE FORECAST ACCURACY AND THE USE OF TWO DISCRETIONARY ACCOUNTING VARIABLES: A STUDY OF POSSIBLE INCOME MANIPULATION.	Penn St	74	181	FinStData-based	Forecasts
Hodges, Richard L.	THE EXAMINATION OF SEVERAL FACTORS THAT HINDER THE IMPLEMENTATION OF STATE GOVERNMENT ACCOUNTING PRINCIPLES	Nebraska	79	170	Field Study	Not-for-profit
Hoffman, David E.	TAX PLANNING FOR OWNER-OPERATED BUSINESSES AFTER THE 1969 TAX REFORM ACT	Texas	75	407	Experimental	Tax
Hoffman, Michael J.	AN EVAL. OF THE EFFECT OF THE PRESENTATION OF SUPPLEMENTAL CURRENT REPLACEMENT COST INFO. OF INDIVIDUAL INVEST. DEC. MAKING: A BEHAV. STUDY	Indiana	83	163	Experimental	Inflation
Hohl, Katherine J.	AN INVESTIGATION OF THE SURROGATESHIP OF THE GNP DEFLATOR FOR WHOLESALE PRICE INDICES	Okl St	77	140	FinStData-based	Inflation
Holder, William W.	THE IMPACT OF SELECTED THIRD PARTY REIMBURSEMENT POLICIES ON CAPITAL EXPENDITURE DECISIONS FOR GENERAL HOSPITALS	Oklahoma	74	184	Field Study	Not-for-profit
Holland, Michael L.	AN INVESTIGATION OF FEDERAL FARM INCOME TAXATION: ITS DEVELOPMENT WITH ATTENTION TO CONGRESSIONAL INTENT AND ITS EFFECT ON THE GEORGIA EGG IND.	Georgia	78	225	Archival	Tax
Holland, Roger G.	THE INFORMATION CONTENT OF THREE PENSION COST MEASURES: THEORETICAL AND EMPIRICAL ANALYSIS	Ohio St	81	114	Model- based	Pensions
Holley, Charles L.	AN INQUIRY INTO THE RELIABILITY OF SELECTED FORECAST FINANCIAL DATA	Tenn	76	197	FinStData-based	Forecasts
Holmen, Jay Scott	COMPARISON OF FORECASTING TECHNIQUES IN AN ANALYTICAL REVIEW BY AUDITORS.	Minnesota	81	186	Experimental	Auditing

Author	Title	School	Date	pp	Methodology	Topic
Holmes, James R.	PRICE LEVEL BUDGETING	Missouri	77	143	Experimental	Inflation
Holt, Doris L.	EVIDENCE INTEGRATION IN THE FORMATION OF RISK ASSESSMENTS BY AUDITORS AND BANK-LENDING OFFICERS	Michigan	84	285	Field Study	Auditing
Holt, Robert Nisbet, Jr.	CLASSIFICATION OF COMMERCIAL BANK LOANS: AN APPLICATION OF THE POLICY CAPTURING TECHNIQUE.	N Carol	77	177	FinStData-based	Bank Accounting
Holtfreter, Robert Eugene	TOWARD NEW INTERIM REPORTING GUIDELINES.	Nebraska	78	187	Field Study	Interim Statements
Holthausen, Robert Wood	THEORY AND EVIDENCE ON THE EFFECT OF BOND COVENANTS AND MANAGEMENT COMPENSATION CONTRACTS ON THE CHOICE OF ACCOUNTING TECHNIQUES: THE CASE OF THE DEPRECIATION SWITCH-BACK.	Rochester	80	150	Market- based	Depreciation
Holzmann, Oscar Jorge	ACCOUNTING RETURN-RISK MEASURES OF CONGLOMERATE PERFORMANCE.	Penn St	74	174	FinStData-based	Financial
Honea, James Harold	AN EMPIRICAL STUDY OF USEFULNESS AND COMMUNICATIVE ABILITY OF SEGMENT DISCLOSURES AMONG SOPHISTICATED USERS OF CORPORATE FINANCIAL STATEMENTS.	LSU	82	232	Experimental	Business Segments
Hong, Sungbin Chun	THE OUTCOME OF BANKRUPTCY: MODEL AND EMPIRICAL TEST	Berkeley	84	130	Model- based	Financial
Hooks, Karen Leah	VALUES AND VALUE SYSTEMS OF PUBLIC ACCOUNTANTS RELATING TO PROFESSIONAL SUCCESS.	Ga St	81	106	Field Study	Profession
Hooper, Herbert P.	A STUDY OF THE EVOLUTION OF THE LEGAL LIABILITY OF ACCOUNTANTS WITH IMPLICATIONS FOR THE FUTURE OF THE PROFESSION	Tulane	76	208	Archival	Profession

Author	Title	School	Date	pp	Methodology	Topic
Hopewell, Rita Jean	COST/BENEFIT ANALYSIS: SELECTION OF EDUCATIONAL MODEL FOR INTRODUCTORY ACCOUNTING.	S Calif	77		Experimental	Education
Hopkins, Albert W.	PUBLICLY DISCLOSED CORPORATE PROFIT FORECASTS AND THE EFFECT OF AUDITOR REVIEW: AN EMPIRICAL STUDY	Colorado	78	376	FinStData-based	Auditing
Hopkins, Bobbie H.	A SURVEY OF ACCT. METHODS FOR ACQUISITIONS OR CONSOLOLIDATIONS OF TELEPHONE CO. WITH EMPHASIS ON ARKANSAS TELEPHONE COMPANIES	Arkansas	75	268	Field Study	Business Combinations
Hopkins, Merle W.	THE RELATIONSHIP BETWEEN SYSTEMATIC OPERATING CASH FLOW RISK AND MARKET RETURNS TO SECURITIES: AN EMPIRICAL STUDY	Mich St	82	111	Market- based	Cash Flows
Hopkins, Raymond F.	ON THE ASSOCIATION BETWEEN FACTOR MARKET AND CAPITAL MARKET PRICES: A TEST OF THE IMPACT OF ASR 190	Okl St	82	60	Market- based	Inflation
Hopkins, W. Clyde	AN EXPLANATORY STUDY OF COMMON CHARACTERISTICS AND EXECUTIVE USES OF SUMMARY INCOME AND EXPENSE BUDGETS AMONG SOME LARGE U.S. CORP.	Miss	82	306	Field Study	Managerial
Hopwood, William S.	AN EMPIRICAL INVESTIGATION INTO THE USEFULNESS OF ACCOUNTING AND MARKET DATA IN THE FORECASTING OF ACCOUNTING EARNINGS	Florida	78	93	Model- based	Financial
Horlick, Geoffrey Richard	THE ACCOUNTANT'S ROLE IN BOX OFFICE OPERATIONS: AN INQUIRY INTO THE NECESSITY AND COMPOSITION OF BOX OFFICE AUDITS IN LEGITIMATE THEATERS.	Txs A&M	78	200	Field Study	Auditing
Horwood, Joanne Lynn	THE ROLE OF ECONOMIC PROFITS IN RISK DETERMINATION	Minnesota	84	108	Model- based	Financial
Hoshower, Leon B.	INFORMATION INDUCTANCE: ITS EFFECT ON MUTUAL FUND MGMT.: AN EMPIRICAL STUDY	Mich St	83	77	Market- based	Mutual Funds

Author	Title	School	Date	pp	Methodology	Topic
Hoskin, Robert Ellsworth	OPPORTUNITY COSTS AND BEHAVIOR.	Cornell	81	111	Experimental	Managerial
Hosseini, Ahmad	EFFECTS OF ALTERNATIVE FOREIGN CURRENCY TRANSLATION METHODS ON DIVISIONAL ROI MEASURES.	Missouri	81	296	FinStData-based	Managerial
Hoth, Gerald Blaine	TIME DIMENSIONS, FINANCIAL CONDITIONS AND THE CHOICE OF ACCOUNTING POLICY: THEIR EFFECTS ON PERFORMANCE MEASURES.	Colorado	82	199	FinStData-based	Financial
Howard, Thomas P.	ON THE USEFULNESS OF ALTERNATIVE REPORTING FORMATS FOR MUNICIPALITIES	Ariz St	78	207	Experimental	Not-for-profit
Howe, Keith R.	THE RELATIVE PERSUASIVENESS OF EVIDENTIAL MATTER.	Ariz St	79	168	Experimental	Auditing
Hreha, Karen Sue	THE IMPACT OF THE CARRYOVER BASIS AND STEPPED-UP BASIS PROVISIONS ON PROPERTY TRANSFER DECISIONS.	VPI	81	205	Experimental	Tax
Huang, Jiunn-Chang	AN EMPIRICAL INVESTIGATION INTO THE INFORMATION CONTENT OF THE REQUIRED DISCLOSURE OF OIL AND GAS RESERVE VALUES.	N Txs St	80	113	Market- based	Oil & Gas
Huber, Charles Courtland, Jr.	THE PRIVATE VALUE OF INFORMATION IN EXCHANGE MARKETS.	Stanford	78	127	Market- based	Financial
Hudson, Jean Marie Baldwin	THE INFORMATION CONTENT OF MANAGEMENT FORECASTS AS REFLECTED IN OPTION PRICES	Texas at Austin	84	161	Model- based	Forecasts
Huff, Thomas Edward	THE BOND RATER AS EXPERT JUDGE OF A NONLINEAR, NONADDITIVE STOCHASTIC DEFAULT PROCESS.	Columbia	81	247	FinStData-based	Stochastic Properties

Author	Title	School	Date	pp	Methodology	Topic
Huffman, Wilmer E.	AN EMPIRICAL TEST OF THE DEBTOR-CREDITOR HYPOTHESIS	Kansas	75	162	Market- based	Financial
Hughes, Jesse W.	EXPENDITURE PATTERNS OF LOCAL GOVERNMENTS	VPI	83	304	Field Study	Not-for-profit
Hughes, John Silver, III	OPTIMAL AUDIT PLANNING.	Purdue	74	162	Model- based	Auditing
Hughes, Marilynn L.	GUIDELINES FOR ADHERENCE TO THE GENERAL STANDARDS OF AUDITING	Alabama	75	295	Model- based	Auditing
Hull, Rita P.	AN INVESTIGATION OF THE IMPACT OF ENVIRONMENTAL DISCLOSURE ON STOCK INVESTMENT DECISIONS: A BEHAVIORAL FIELD EXPERIMENT	Okl St.	78	147	Experimental	Financial
Humma, Nancy K.	AN EXAMINATION OF THE ROLE OF ERIC LOUIS KOHLER IN THE DEVELOPMENT OF THE ACCOUNTING PROFESSION	Ga St	83	211	Archival	History
Hunt, Herbert G.	THE ECONOMIC DETERMINANTS OF CORPORATE INVENTORY COSTING DECISIONS	Colorado	82	175	FinStData-based	Managerial
Hunthausen, John Matthew	A HISTORY OF THE CPA PROFESSION IN COLORADO.	Missouri	74	342	Archival	History
Hurley, James F.	SOCIAL RESPONSIBILITY ACCOUNTING FOR BUSINESS	Nebraska	82	208	Field Study	Social
Huss, Harry F.	THE EFFECTS OF ALTERNATIVE TREATMENTS OF DEFERRED INCOME TAX CREDITS ON THE PREDICTIVE ABILITY OF FINANCIAL RATIOS IN BOND RATINGS	Tenn	82	123	FinStData-based	Deferred Taxes

Author	Title	School	Date	pp	Methodology	Topic
Hussain, Inam	INFORMATION CONTENT OF OIL AND GAS RESERVE DISCLOSURES	Missouri	84	61	Field Study	Oil & Gas
Hussein, Mohammed E.	A SOCIO-POLITICAL FRAMEWORK OF THE PROCESS OF ADOPTING GENERALLY ACCEPTED FINANCIAL ACCOUNTING STANDARDS	Pitt	77	143	Field Study	Financial
Hutchins, Ronald Earl	A TEST OF THE SEMI-STRONG FORM OF THE EFFICIENT MARKETS HYPOTHESIS USING VALUATION MODELS AND QUARTELRY INFORMATION.	Missouri	77	152	Market- based	Quarterly Data
Hyman, Ladelle M.	CONCEPTUAL FOUNDATIONS FOR COST-BENEFIT ANALYSIS IN HOMES FOR AGING-QUALIFYING RESIDENT SATISFACTION	N Txs St	75	238	Field Study	Managerial
Hyon, Yong-Ha	ASSOCIATION OF CORPORATE EARNINGS WITH STOCK PRICE: AN APPROACH BY PRINCIPAL COMPONENT ANALYSIS AND DISTRIBUTED LAG TECHNIQUES.	NYU	75	236	Market- based	Forecasts
Ibrahim, Mohamed El Hady M	AN EXAMINATION OF AN INTEGRATIVE EXPECTANCY MODEL FOR AUDITORS' PERFORMANCE BEHAVIORS UNDER TIME BUDGET PRESSURE	N Txs St	85	187	Experimental	Auditing
Icerman, Joe D.	THE PREDICTION OF CORPORATE CASH FLOWS: AN ANALYSIS OF RELEVANT MODELS AND PRESENTLY AVAILABLE FINANCIAL STATEMENT INFORMATION	N Carol	77	229	FinStData-based	Cash Flows
Icerman, Rhoda C.	DISTRIBUTIONS OF AUDITOR-INITIATED ADJUSTMENTS AND THE EFFECTIVENESS OF ANALYTICAL REVIEW PROCEDURES	Fla St	83	320	FinStData-based	Auditing
Ingram, Robert W.	THE IMPACT OF SOCIAL RESPONSIBILITY DISCLOSURES ON SECURITY RETURNS	Txs Tech	77	164	FinStData-based	Social
Iqbal, Mohammed Z.	COMPARISON OF THE ALTERNATIVES PROPOSED IN SELECTED COUNTRIES TO COPE WITH THE IMPACT OF CHANGING PRICES ON PUBLISHED FINANCIAL DATA	Nebraska	79	246	FinStData-based	Inflation

Author	Title	School	Date	pp	Methodology	Topic
Irvine, Vernon B.	PERCEIVED BUDGET INDUCED PRESSURE RELATED TO SUPERVISORY BEHAVIOR AND THE MODERATING EFFECTS OF DEPARTMENTAL VARIATION	Minnesota	76	396	Field Study	Managerial
Ismail, Badr El-Din Hassanin	A CRITICAL EXAMINATION OF THE USE OF DETERMINISTIC MODELS IN BUDGETING PROBLEMS: A STOCHASTIC PROGRAMMING APPROACH.	Illinois	74	179	Model- based	Managerial
Ismail, Hamzah B.	AN EXAM. OF THE APPLICATION OF ALTERNATIVE ACCT. MEASUREMENT ATTRIBUTES TO RATE BASE REGULATION - A SIMULATION APPROACH TO ATTRIBUTION	Indiana	78	243	Experimental	Financial
Izan, Haji Y.	AN EMPIRICAL ANALYSIS OF THE ECONOMIC EFFECTS OF MANDATORY AUDIT REGULATION	Chicago	78		Market- based	Auditing
Izard, C. Douglass	AN EMPIRICAL ANALYSIS OF THE EFFECTS OF SECTION 585 OF THE INTERNAL REVENUE CODE UPON COMMERCIAL BANKS.	Miss	81	147	FinStData-based	Tax
Izumi, Marleen M	THE EFFECTS OF EVALUATIVE ACCOUNTING INFORMATION ON PERFORMANCE: AN INVESTIGATION	Ohio St	77	213	Archival	Managerial
Jablonsky, Stephen F.	AN EXAMINATION OF THE RESOURCE ALLOCATION DECISION WITHIN UNIVERSITIES	Illinois	74	220	Field Study	Not-for-profit
Jackson, Anthony Wayne	THE INFLUENCE OF BUDGET RELATED PERFORMANCE EVALUATION MEASURES ON DECISION MAKING BEHAVIOR UNDER UNCERTAINTY (ACCOUNTING INFORMATION SYSTEMS)	Cincinnati	85	122	Experimental	Systems/Computers
Jackson, Betty R.	THE USE OF AND ALTERNATIVES TO THE GENERATION-SKIPPING TRANSFER AFTER THE TAX REFORM ACT OF 1976	Texas	82	375	Field Study	Tax
Jacobs, Frederic H.	AN APPLICATION OF STATISTICAL CONTROL MODELS TO ACCOUNTING COST VARIANCES	Illinois	76	186	Model- based	Managerial

Author	Title	School	Date	pp	Methodology	Topic
Jacobs, Frederick R.	AN EXAM. OF THE GOVERNMENTALLY ENFORCED PROFESSIONAL RESPONSIBILITIES ASSOCIATED WITH A CPA FIRM'S MGMT. ADV. SERVICES PRACTICE	Wiscon	74	299	Archival	Profession
Jacoby, Philip F.	AN EMPIRICAL DESCRIPTIVE STUDY OF SELECTED PERSONALITY CHARACTERISTICS OF PROFESSIONAL ACCOUNTANTS BASED UPON JUNGIAN TYPOLOGY.	Wash U	80	379	Field Study	Profession
Jadallah, Salih Mahmoud	PERFORMANCE AUDITING AND PROGRAM EVALUATION IN GOVERNMENT--SAUDI ARABIA AS A FIELD OF APPLICATION.	Txs Tech	78	283	Field Study	Not-for-profit
Jagolinzer, Philip	A COMPARISON OF OPINIONS OF RESIDENTS OF ARIZONA AND MAINE, REGARDING REDISTRIBUTION OF WEALTH, WITH FEDERAL ESTATE AND GIFT TAX PROVISIONS.	Arizona	78	185	Field Study	Tax
Jaikumar, Vaiyapuri	AN APPLICATION OF MATHEMATICAL CONTROL THEORY TO THE ACCOUNTING MODEL FOR MANAGEMENT CONTROL.	Columbia	79	172	Model- based	Managerial
Jain, Mahesh C.	NEW DIMENSIONS FOR REPORTING OF FINANCIAL INFORMATION IN DEVELOPING INFLATIONARY ECONOMIES-CASE OF LATIN AMERICA	N Carol	74	267	FinStData-based	Inflation
Jain, Rohit	AN EMPIRICAL INVESTIGATION OF SOME ECONOMIC CONSEQUENCES OF FASB STATEMENT NO. 8: FOREIGN CURRENCY TRANSLATION.	Florida	80	151	Market- based	Foreign Currency
Jamison, Robert Watt, Jr.	TAX PLANNING FOR THE OPERATION AND SUCCESSION OF INTEREST IN A SUBCHAPTER S CORPORATION.	Texas	80	493	Experimental	Tax
Janell, Paul Andrew	AN EMPIRICAL EVALUATION OF THE RELATIONSHIP BETWEEN ERRORS IN ANALYSTS' FORECASTS OF EARNINGS PER SHARE AND STOCK PRICES.	Mich St	74	169	FinStData-based	Forecasts
Janson, Kenneth R.	THE INTERACTION OF FIN. AND NON FIN. INFORMATION SOURCES: AN EMP. STUDY OF TIME SERIES PROPERTIES AND CAPITAL MARKET EFFECTS	Wiscon	79	315	FinStData-based	Stochastic Properties

Author	Title	School	Date	pp	Methodology	Topic
Jarnagin, Bill D.	AN EMPIRICAL INQUIRY INTO THE DESIRABILITY OF EXTENDING THE ATTEST FUNCTION TO INTERIM FINANCIAL REPORTS	Arkansas	76	168	FinStData-based	Auditing
Jenkins, David Randall	THE INCREMENTAL INFORMATION CONTENT OF THE ANNUAL REPORT TO SHAREHOLDERS AND THE TEN-K.	Arizona	81	254	Market- based	Financial
Jenne, Stanley E.	A CRITICAL EXAMINATION OF DOLLAR UNIT SAMPLING IN THE AUDIT OF ACCOUNTS RECEIVABLE	Illinois	82	186	Experimental	Auditing
Jiambolvo, James J.	PERFORMANCE EVALUATION IN CPA FIRMS: AN EMPIRICAL TEST OF AND EVALUATION MODEL OF DIRECTED JOB EFFORT	Ohio St	77	203	Field Study	Profession
Johnson, Douglas A	AN ANALYSIS OF THE FORMATION OF ACCOUNTING STUDENT EMPLOYMENT PREFERENCES	Texas	74	226	Field Study	Profession
Johnson, Johnny R.	THE ALLOWANCE FOR FUNDS USED DURING CONSTRUCTION: MARKET REACTION TO CURRENT ACCOUNTING PRACTICE	VPI	76	151	Market- based	Financial
Johnson, Kenneth L.	THE FOREIGN CORRUPT PRACTICES ACT OF 1977: AN INQUIRY INTO THE "ACCT. PROVISIONS" OF THE ACT INCLUDING A STUDY OF EXPLICIT RESPONSES BY CORP.	La Tech	81	226	Field Study	Auditing
Johnson, Raymond N.	AUDIT RISK IN INVENTORY AUDITS - AN INVESTIGATION OF ERRORS AND RELATED CLIENT CHARACTERISTICS	Oregon	81	180	Field Study	Auditing
Johnson, Sidney Bruce	AN INVESTIGATION OF THE RECOMMENDATIONS MADE BY THE COMMITTEE ON EDUCATION AND EXPERIENCE REQUIREMENTS OF THE AMERICAN INSTITUTE OF CERTIFIED PUBLIC ACCOUNTANTS.	Miss St	78	227	Field Study	Profession
Johnson, Steven B.	A NONMARKET "WILLINGNESS-TO-PAY" APPROACH TO THE SELECTION OF NORMATIVE ACCOUNTING STANDARDS	Wiscon	79	315	Model- based	Financial

Author	Title	School	Date	pp	Methodology	Topic
Johnson, Walter L.	DETERMINING GRANTEE COSTS IN FEDERAL GRANT-IN-AID PROGRAMS	Texas	74	359	Field Study	Not-for-profit
Johnson, William B.	UNCERTAINTY AND ACCOUNTING MEASURES: THE EFFECTS OF ALTERNATIVE DISCLOSURE MODES ON THE ACCURACY OF INTUITIVE PROBABILITY ESTIMATES	Ohio St	75	212	Experimental	Financial
Johnston, James G.	AN EXAMINATION OF THE CONFORMANCE OF BANK INTERNAL AUDITING STANDARDS	Missouri	82	244	Field Study	Auditing
Jolly, Stephen Alton	AN ALTERNATIVE METHOD FOR THE COMPUTATION OF EARNINGS PER SHARE.	N Carol	78	176	FinStData-based	Earnings Per Share
Jones, Richard W.	AN EXAMINATION OF THE CAPITAL FORMATION PROSPECTS OF PENN CENTRAL TRANSPORTATION COMPANY	Arkansas	75	302	Field Study	Financial
Jones, Sally Morrow	THE FEDERAL GIFT AND ESTATE TAX CONSEQUENCES OF TRANSFERS OF COMMUNITY PROPERTY.	Houston	78	206	Archival	Tax
Jopling, Samuel Haigh, Jr.	ACCOUNTING STANDARDS AND THE FINANCIAL REPORTING PRACTICES OF SECURITIES BROKER.	Penn St	75	231	FinStData-based	Financial
Jordan, William F.	AN ANALYSIS OF SELECTED CHARACTERISTICS OF THE GEORGIA PERSONAL INCOME TAX	Ga St	74	199	Archival	Tax
Joseph, Harold W.	RESEARCH AND DEVEL. COSTS AND STATEMENT OF STANDARDS #2: AN EMP. STUDY OF ACCOUNTING, DISCLOSURE AND REPORTING SIGNIFICANCE	La Tech	78	116	FinStData-based	Research & Development
Joy, Arthur C Jr.	AN EMPIRICAL INVESTIGATION INTO TRANSFER PRICING PRACTICES	Illinois	85	470	Field Study	Managerial

Author	Title	School	Date	pp	Methodology	Topic
Joy, David Walter	A MULTIPERIOD LINEAR PROGRAMMING ANALYSIS OF INCOME TAX EFFECTS OF AGRICULTURE DECISIONS	Nebraska	84	164	Archival	Tax
Joyce, Edward J.	INDIVIDUAL JUDGEMENT IN AUDIT PROGRAM PLANNING: AN EMPIRICAL STUDY	Illinois	76	107	Experimental	Auditing
Kablan, Abdelsalam Ali	MEASURING THE IMPACTS OF FASB STATEMENT NO. 8 AND THE FLUCTUATIONS IN FOREIGN CURRENCY VALUES ON MULTINATIONAL CORPORATION SECURITY PRICES.	LSU	82	177	Market- based	Foreign Currency
Kagle, Arthur Renn	THE VALUATION OF SOFT ASSETS AND SOFT LIABILITIES BY FINANCIAL MANAGERS OF EDUCATIONAL INSTITUTIONS.	Txs Tech	75	160	Field Study	Education
Kahn, Nathan	ACCOUNTING FOR THE EARLY EXTINGUISHMENT OF DEBT: AN EMPIRICAL EVALUATION OF CURRENT ACCOUNTING PRACTICE.	Columbia	80	269	Market- based	Financial
Kaliska, Burton S.	DEVELOPMENT OF AN OUTLINE FOR A TWO-YEAR COLLEGE ELEMENTARY ACCOUNTING TEXTBOOK	NYU	74	304	Field Study	Education
Kamin, Jacob Y.	INCOME SMOOTHING WITH DISCRETIONARY ITEMS: THE MANAGEMENT OF RISK-RETURN PERFORMANCE AND THE PREPARATION OF OWNERSHIP AND CONTROL IN LARGE INDUSTRIAL FIRMS	NYU	75	153	Market- based	Income Smoothing
Kamnikar, Judith A.	A STUDY OF THE EFFECTS OF FORMAT OF PRESENTATION ON USERS' UNDERSTANDING OF FINANCIAL REPORTS	Denver	82	225	Field Study	Financial
Kanaan, Georges Kaissar	THE INFORMATION CONTENT OF ALTERNATIVE INCOME MEASURES	Wiscon	84	230	Market- based	Inflation
Kandiel, El Sayed Hussein Ahmed	ACCOUNTING FOR INTERNALLY DEVELOPED SOFTWARE COSTS: A POSITIVE APPROACH	NYU	85	239	Field Study	Systems/Computers

Author	Title	School	Date	pp	Methodology	Topic
Kang, Jai S.	A STUDY OF INTERSEGMENT ALLOCATION PROBLEMS IN SEGMENTAL FINANCIAL DISCLOSURE	Txs A&M	77	178	FinStData-based	Business Segments
Kanodia, Chandra S.	ESSAYS ON THE EFECTS OF ACCOUNTING INFORMATION ON CORPORATE DECISIONS AND CAPITAL MARKET EQUILIBRIUM	Carn Mel	78	137	Market- based	Financial
Kanter, Howard Allen	A STUDY OF THE IMPORTANCE OF SELECTED COLLEGE-LEVEL AUDITING TOPICS TO THE JOB PERFORMANCE OF FIRST-YEAR STAFF AUDITORS IN CPA FIRMS IN THE CHICAGO AREA WITH IMPLICATIONS FOR AUDITING CURRICULUM DEVELOPERS	N Ill	84	336	Field Study	Education
Kaplan, Steven E.	THE EFFECTS OF CLIENT RISK, INTERNAL CONTROL EVALUATION, AND INTERNAL CONTROL STRENGTH ON AUDIT PROGRAM PLANNING: AN EMPIRICAL STUDY	Illinois	82	155	Experimental	Auditing
Karan, Vijay	OBJECTIVE EVIDENCE AND AUDITORS' EVALUATION OF AN INTERNAL ACCOUNTING CONTROL SYSTEM	Texas	83	184	Experimental	Auditing
Karbens, John P.	EDUCATION AND EXPERIENCE REQUIREMENTS FOR LISCENSING CPA'S: A SURVEY OF OPINIONS OF HAWAII CPA'S, NAA MEMBERS, AND U. OF HAWAII ACCT. GRADUATES	Hawaii	83	232	Field Study	Profession
Karlinsky, Stewart Sheldon	COMPLEXITY IN THE FEDERAL INCOME TAX LAW ATTRIBUTABLE TO THE CAPITAL GAIN AND LOSS PREFERENCE: A MEASUREMENT MODEL.	NYU	81	136	Archival	Tax
Karmon, David James	A METHODOLOGY FOR DETECTING AN IMPROVED INFORMATION SYSTEM IN AN EFFICIENT MARKET	Nebraska	84	141	Market- based	Financial
Karvel, George Raymond	AN EMPIRICAL INVESTIGATION OF AUDITOR COMMUNICATION: CONNOTATIVE MEANING OF THE AUDITOR OPINION PARAGRAPH.	Colorado	79	277	Experimental	Auditing
Kauder, William F.	THE EMPIRICAL STUDY OF THE EFFECTS OF SECTION 169 (AMORTIZATION OF POLLUTION CONTROL FACILITIES) OF THE INTERNAL REVENUE CODE	Georgia	82	253	Field Study	Tax

Author	Title	School	Date	pp	Methodology	Topic
Kaufman, Jerry M.	A CONCEPTUAL FRAMEWORK FOR COSTING DEFENSE CONTRACTS	Okl St	74	222	Model- based	Managerial
Keating, John L.	MUTUAL FUND REPORTS-PROPOSED IMPROVEMENTS BASED ON A SURVEY OF EXTANT PRACTICE	Texas	78	507	FinStData-based	Mutual Funds
Keck, John T.	THE IDENTIFICATION OF INVESTMENT DECISION MODELS FOR THE INDIVIDUAL INVESTOR AND THEIR DEPENDENCY ON FINANCIAL STATEMENT INFORMATION	Geo St	77	200	Field Study	Financial
Kee, Robert Carl	AN EMPIRICAL INVESTIGATION OF THE TIME-SERIES PROPERTIES OF QUARTERLY REVENUE AND EXPENSE DATA.	Fla St	80	205	FinStData-based	Stochastic Properties
Keith, Richard Lyman	AN EMPIRICAL INVESTIGATION INTO THE ABILITY OF CERTAIN MACROECONOMIC VARIABLES TO ENHANCE MANAGEMENT'S ANNUAL FORECASTS OF SALES AND EARNINGS.	Fla St	82	132	FinStData-based	Forecasts
Keller, Stuart B.	AN ASSESSMENT OF INDIVIDUAL INVESTOR REACTION TO CERTAIN QUALIFIED AUDIT OPINIONS: AN EMPIRICAL INVESTIGATION	N Carol	81	115	Market- based	Auditing
Kelley, Timothy Patrick	TIME-BUDGET PRESSURES AND AUDITOR BEHAVIOR	Houston	84	227	Field Study	Auditing
Kellogg, Robert Leroy	AN EMPIRICAL STUDY OF THE RULE 10B-5 BUYERS' SUITS BASED UPON ACCOUNTING DISCLOSURES.	Rochester	80	122	Market- based	Financial
Kelsy, Richard L.	FINANCIAL ANALYSTS' PERCEPTIONS OF EQUITY INVESTM. RISK AND PROFITABILITY OF MULTINATIONAL BUSINESS OPERATIONS: A BEHAV. STUDY	Wash	79	151	Experimental	Financial
Kemp, Robert S.	THE GROWTH OF EARNINGS: A PREDICTIVE MODEL USING GENERALLY AVAILABLE INFORMATION	Fla St	81	179	Model- based	Financial

Author	Title	School	Date	pp	Methodology	Topic
Kennedy, Dennis T.	AN ASSESSMENT OF THE INCREMENTAL USEFULNESS OF THE RRA SUPPLEMENTAL EARNINGS SUMMARY	Temple	83	132	Market- based	Oil & Gas
Kennedy, Helen Augusta Davis	A STUDY OF THE EFFECTS OF THE AAA-AICPA DOCTORAL FELLOWS AND VISITING SCHOLARS PROGRAM ON ACCOUNTING STUDENTS AT PREDOMINANTLY MINORITY INSTITUTIONS THAT ARE PARTICIPATING IN THE PROGRAM.	Okl St	79	114	Experimental	Education
Kennelley, Michael Dean	AUDITOR PERFORMANCE AND THE VALUE OF THE FIRM: A TEST OF ONE IMPLICATION OF AGENCY THEORY	Okl St	83	74	Experimental	Auditing
Kennett, Danny L.	AN EMPIRICAL STUDY OF THE FINANCIAL REPORTING PRACTICES OF MAYORAL CITIES AND CITY MANAGER CITIES TO DETERMINE IF THE FORM OF GOVERNMENT AFFECTS THE FINANCIAL REPORTING PRACTICES	Miss St	83	233	Field Study	Not-for-Profit
Kermis, George F.	AN EMPIRICAL STUDY OF THE EFFECTS OF TIME PRESSURE ON INTER-AUDITOR CONSISTENCY	Syracuse	82	173	Experimental	Auditing
Kessler, Lawrence F.	THE EFFECT OF DIFFERENT TYPES OF COGNITIVE FEEDBACK UPON THE PREDICTION ACHIEVEMENT OF ACCOUNTING USERS: SOME EXPERIMENTAL EVIDENCE	Texas	77	320	Experimental	Financial
Kettering, Ronald Clayton	THE EFFECT OF SELECTED VARIABLES UPON THE VALUE OF A FIRM'S BETA COEFFICIENT.	La Tech	77	127	Market- based	Financial
Ketz, John E.	A COMPARISON OF THE PREDICTABILITY OF BUSINESS FAILURE BY THE FIN. RATIOS OF GENERAL PRICE LEVEL STAEMENTS WITH THOSE OF HISTROICAL COST STATEM.	VPI	77	391	FinStData-based	Inflation
Keys, David E.	CONFIDENCE-INTERVAL FINANCIAL STATEMENTS: AN EMPIRICAL INVESTIGATION	Illinois	75	172	Experimental	Financial
Khumawala, Saleha B.	TIME SERIES PROPERTIES AND PREDICTIVE ABILITY OF QUARTERLY CASH FLOWS: AN EMPIRICAL INVESTIGATION	N Carol	78	213	FinStData-based	Stochastic Properties

Author	Title	School	Date	pp	Methodology	Topic
Kiani-Aslani, Rajabaldi	THE IMPLICATIONS OF QUANTITATIVE TOOLS OF DECISION-MAKING FOR ACCOUNTING: AN EMPIRICAL STUDY	Oklahoma	75	253	Field Study	Managerial
Kida, Thomas Edward	AN INVESTIGATION INTO AUDITORS' GOING CONCERN DECISIONS.	Massach	78	265	Experimental	Auditing
Kiddoo, Robert James	THE USE OF FINANCIAL RATIOS AS DISCRIMINANT PREDICTORS FOR CLASSIFYING BUSINESS LOAN APPLICANTS.	S Calif	78		FinStData-based	Financial Ratios
Kiel, Mark	AN EMPIRICAL INVESTIGATION OF THE EFFECTS OF REPLACEMENT COSTING ON FINANCIAL RATIOS AND THEIR DISTRIBUTION	Georgia	78	209	FinStData-based	Inflation
Kilgore, Ronald W.	MISSISSIPPI CPA'S: THEIR WORK AND ATTITUDES: A PROFILE	Miss	74	291	Field Study	Profession
Kilpatrick, Joyce	THE INTERNAL USE OF INFLATION ADJUSTED DATA	Memphis St	82	234	Field Study	Inflation
Kim, Hyo Seuk	PLANNING AND EVALUATING TWO-STAGE SAMPLES FOR MULTILOCATION AUDIT POPULATIONS	Georgia	84	412	Field Study	Auditing
Kim, Hyuk	AN EMPIRICAL STUDY OF THE MARKET REACTION TO STATEMENT OF FINANCIAL ACCOUNTING STANDARDS NO. 52: "FOREIGN CURRENCY TRANSLATION"	Indiana	85	201	Market- based	Foreign Currency
Kim, Joon Seuk	THE EFFECTS OF THE KNOWLEDGE OF THE DECISION MODEL USED BY THE DECISION MAKER ON THE EVALUATION OF INFORMATION SYSTEMS	Indiana	82	157	Experimental	Systems/ Computers
Kim, Kun Jang	AN EMPIRICAL STUDY ON THE BEHAVIOR OF THE MARKET AND THE INDIVIDUAL INVESTOR IN RESPONSE TO DIFFERING SIGNALS AND TRAITS EVOLVING FROM MANAGEMENT'S EPS FORECASTS	Kentucky	83	160	Market- based	Forecasts

Author	Title	School	Date	pp	Methodology	Topic
Kim, Kung J.	AN EMP. STUDY ON THE BEHAVIOR OF THE MARKET AND THE IND. INVESTOR IN RESPONSE TO DIFFERING SIGNALS AND TRACTS EVOLVING FROM MGMT.'S EPS FORECASTS	Kentucky	83	160	Market- based	Forecasts
Kim, Song Ki	CONTROL POLICIES FOR REPORTING AND INVESTIGATING COST VARIANCES.	Texas	79	187	Model- based	Managerial
Kim, Soon-Kee	AN EVALUATION OF ALTERNATIVE COST VARIANCE INVESTIGATION MODELS	Houston	83	148	Model- based	Managerial
Kimbrell, James A.	THE NATURE AND EXTENT OF AUDITOR LIABILITY TO THE THIRD PARTY IN THE PERFORMANCE OF THE AUDIT FUNCTION DURING THE PERIOD 1972 THROUGH 1976	La Tech	78	105	Archival	Auditing
Kimmell, Dennis L.	ACCOUNTING FOR LONG-TERM EQUITY SECURITY GAINS AND LOSSES: AN EMPIRICAL ANALYSIS	Kent St	74	170	FinStData-based	Investments
Kimura, Joseph H.	THE PREDICTIVE ACCURACY OF ACCOUNTING AND NON-ACCOUNTING INFORMATION UNDER INFLATIONARY CONDITIONS	UCLA	82	176	Field Study	Inflation
Kin, Joon S.	THE EFFECTS OF THE KNOWLEDGE OF THE DECISION MODEL USED BY THE DECISION MAKER ON THE EVALUATION OF INFORMATION SYSTEMS	Indiana	82	157	Experimental	Managerial
King, Jerry G.	ACCOUNTING AND COST CONTROLS FOR MISSISSIPPI SAW MILLS	Miss	75	234	Field Study	Managerial
King, Raymond Dean	AN EMPIRICAL EXAMINATION OF A CONTINGENT CLAIMS VALUATION MODEL APPLIED TO CONVERTIBLE BONDS.	Oregon	80	145	Market- based	Bonds
Kiringoda, Dayal	VARIABLES AFFECTING THE CHOICE OF ACCOUNTING METHODS: AN INVESTIGATION BASED ON FIRMS ADOPTING ACCOUNTING CHANGES	Nebraska	84	190	Experimental	Acconting Changes

Author	Title	School	Date	pp	Methodology	Topic
Kirkpatrick, Donald Clay	GENERAL SYSTEMS THEORY AS A FRAMEWORK FOR MANAGEMENT INFORMATION SYSTEMS.	Colorado	76	355	Field Study	Systems/ Computers
Kirkpatrick, Thomas L.	THE CASE FOR REPORTING FREE CASH FLOW IN PUBULISHED FINANCIAL STATEMENTS	N Txs St	80	287	Model- based	Cash Flows
Kirschman, Charles Frederick	A COMPUTER-BASED EVALUATION OF AN AXIOMATIC ACCOUNTING THEORY.	Kansas	74	237	Model- based	Financial
Kissinger, John N.	A STUDY OF FACTORS WHICH EFFECT AUDIT EVIDENCE ACCUMULATION	Mich St	74	339	Field Study	Auditing
Klein, Hans Emil	IMPACT OF LONG RANGE PLANNING ON PROFIT AND GROWTH IN SELECTED SEGMENTS OF COMMERCIAL BANKS	Kentucky	77	277	Field Study	Managerial
Klein, Kyle H.	SELF REGULATORY PROCESSES IN THE ACCOUNTING PROFESSION AS THEY RELATE TO THE PROFESSTIONAL COMPETENCE OF THE INDIVIDUAL	Arkansas	78	201	Field Study	Profession
Klemme, Dana K.	A STUDY OF LINE OF BUSINESS DISCLOSURES: ACCOUNTING VERSUS MARKET RISK MEASURES	Michigan	83	80	Market- based	Business Segments
Klien, Lawrence A.	THE INFLUENCE OF OUTSIDE PARTIES ON THE FASB: AN ANALYSIS OF RESPONSES TO THE EXPOSURE DRAFT ON SEGMENT REPORTING	Penn St	78	220	Field Study	Business Segments
Knapp, Michael C.	AN INTEGRATIVE EMPIRICAL ANALYSIS OF AUDITOR INDEPENDENCE	Oklahoma	82	219	Field Study	Auditing
Knauf, Janine Bernice	CONVERTIBLE DEBENTURES AND EARNINGS PER SHARE.	Columbia	81	232	FinStData-based	Earnings Per Share

Author	Title	School	Date	pp	Methodology	Topic
Knechel, Warren Robert	DEVELOPMENT OF MODELS OF THE ERROR GENERATION PROCESS IN ACCOUNTING TRANSACTION PROCESSING SYSTEMS.	N Carol	81	330	Experimental	Auditing
Kneer, Daniel Charles	AUDITING IN A DISTRIBUTED DATA PROCESSING ENVIRONMENT--A MODEL FOR THE EVALUATION OF INTERNAL CONTROL.	Missouri	81	534	Archival	Auditing
Knight, Barry Allan	OUTPUT MEASURES FOR PROFESSIONAL SCHOOLS IN HIGHER EDUCATION: A CASE STUDY.	S Calif	76		Field Study	Education
Knight, Lee Goodpaster	A DECISION-ORIENTED APPROACH TO SOCIAL PROGRAM EVALUATION.	Alabama	81	355	Field Study	Not-for-profit
Knight, Royal E.	A RATING OF TOPICS WITH IMPLICATIONS FOR FINANCIAL AND MANAGERIAL ACCOUNTING CURRICULA	N Col	76	129	Field Study	Education
Knutson, Dennis L.	AN EMPIRICAL STUDY OF PERCEPTIONS ABOUT THE IMPORTANCE OF SELECTED DISCLOSURE REQUIREMENTS FOR COMPANIES OF DIFFERENT SIZES AND TYPES	Kentucky	78	244	Field Study	Financial
Ko, Wansuk Matthew	AUDITOR'S INVENTIVE, LEGAL LIABILITY AND REPUTATION UNDER INFORMATION ASYMMETRY	Ohio St	85	107	Model- based	Auditing
Koch, Bruce S.	INCOME SMOOTHING: A LABORATORY EXPERIMENT	Ohio St	77	131	Experimental	Income Smoothing
Koeppen, David R.	AN INVESTIGATION OF THE EFFECTS OF THE FASB'S CONCEPTUAL FRAMEWORK ON AUDITORS' LIABILITY DISCLOSURE JUDGEMENTS	Wiscon	83	319	Experimental	Auditing
Koester, Robert J.	THE IMPACT OF COMPUTERS ON DECISION MAKING: A BEHAVIORAL STUDY	Nebraska	74	169	Field Study	Systems/ Computers

Author	Title	School	Date	pp	Methodology	Topic
Koogler, Paul R	COMPENSATION COSTS IMPLIED IN EXECUTIVE STOCK OPTION GRANTS	Arizona	82	239	Market- based	Financial
Kordi, Khalil Abdulfuttah Khalil	THE MAJOR CHARACTERISTICS OF THE ACCOUNTING INFORMATION SYSTEMS IN SOME SELECTED SAUDI INDUSTRIAL BUSINESSES: A CRITICAL ANALYSIS.	Arizona	79	226	Field Study	International
Kozub, Robert M.	AN EMPIRICAL INVESTIGATION OF THE RELEVANT VARIABLES IN JUDICIAL DISTINCTIONS BETWEEN ALIMONY AND PROPERTY SETTLEMENT PAYMENTS	Kentucky	83	217	Archival	Tax
Kramer, John L.	TAX AND ACCOUNTING IMPLICATIONS IN THE TERMINATION OF AN INVESTMENT IN A CONTROLLED FOREIGN CORPORATION	Michigan	75	477	Archival	Tax
Kramer, Sandra Smith	AN EXAMINATION OF THE VARIABLES AFFECTING THE VALUATION FOR TAX PURPOSES OF LARGE HOLDINGS OF PUBLICLY TRADED STOCKS.	Texas	79	313	Market- based	Tax
Krebs, Joseph F.	HISTORICAL DEVELOPMENT OF HUMAN RESOURCES AND ITS VALUE IN FINANCIAL ACCOUNTING	Miss St	74	177	Archival	History
Kreiser, Lawrence A.	APPROACHES TO MAINTAINING AND IMPROVING THE AUDIT COMPETENCE OF CPA'S: AN ANALYSIS OF CPA AND SELECTED USER REACTION	Cincinnati	75	174	Field Study	Auditing
Kreuze, Jerry Glenn	COMPREHENSIVE INCOME TAX ALLOCATION: A STUDY INVESTIGATING THE EXTENT TO WHICH THE FORM AND CONTENT OF DISCLOSURE IMPACT UPON INVESTMENT ANALYSIS	Missouri	83	229	Experimental	Deferred Tax
Krogstad, Jack L.	TOWARD THE POSTULATES OF AUDITING	Nebraska	75	207	Model- based	Auditing
Kross, William J.	AN EMP. EXAM. OF THE ABILITY OF ALTERNATIVE ACCT. INCOME NUMBERS TO PREDICT MARKET RISK MEASURES IN THE NONLIFE INSURANCE INDUSTRY	Iowa	75	130	Market- based	Financial

Author	Title	School	Date	pp	Methodology	Topic
Krueger, James M.	INFORMATION NEEDED FOR THE MGMT. OF LOCALLY ADMINISTERED MUNICIPAL PENSION FUNDS WITH INDIANA MUNICIPAL PENSION FUNDS AS A SPECIFIC CASE	Indiana	76	219	Field Study	Not-for-profit
Krueger, Lavern Eldon	THE VALUE ADDED TAX COMPARED TO THE CORPORATE INCOME TAX: EFFECTS ON CAPITAL FORMATION.	Colorado	74	216	Archival	Tax
Kucic, Anthony R.	PREDICTING ENTERPRISE EARNING POWER: REPLACEMENT VALUE ACCOUNTING VS. HISTORICAL COST ACCOUNTING: A CASE STUDY	NYU	77	214	Field Study	Inflation
Kulsrud, William Norman	TAX PLANNING FOR OWNER-OPERATED BUSINESSES AFTER THE REVENUE ACT OF 1978.	Texas	80	305	Experimental	Tax
Kunitake, Walter Kunio	AN INVESTIGATION OF THE RELATIONSHIP BETWEEN ESTABLISHMENT AND EXISTENCE OF AUDIT COMMITTEES AND SELECTION OF AUDITORS.	Arkansas	81	132	Field Study	Auditing
Kunkel, James Gregory	SOCIAL WELFARE AND PUBLIC INFORMATION IN PRODUCTION AND EXCHANGE ECONOMIES.	Berkeley	81	132	Model- based	Social
Kuo, Horng-Ching	AN EVALUATION OF ALTERNATIVE APPROACHES TO LESSEE ACCOUNTING IN THE CONTEXT OF RISK ASSESSMNENT	Miss	84	240	Field Study	Leases
Kushel, Paul Steven	THE TAXATION OF DOMESTIC OIL AND GAS PRODUCTION: AN ECONOMIC ANALYSIS.	Texas	81	345	Experimental	Tax
Kwon, Young K.	THE SOCIAL VALUE OF ACCOUNTING INFORMATION IN A TEMPORARY ECONOMIC EQUILIBRIUM	Texas	78	126	Model- based	Social
La Near, Richard E.	TESTING EFFICIENCY OF THE OPTIONS MARKET UTILIZING A MODIFIED BLACK-SCHOLES MODEL	Miss	79	150	Market- based	Financial

Author	Title	School	Date	pp	Methodology	Topic
Lacey, John M.	HUMAN CAPITAL AT PROFESSIONAL ORGANIZATIONS	UCLA	82	133	Field Study	Hum.Resource Acct.
Lacy, Melvin E.	ADVANCE RECEIPTS AND THE ACCRUAL BASIS TAXPAYER: AN EMP. INV. OF THE JUDICIALLY DETERMINED VARIABLES CONTROLLING THE RECOGNITION ISSUE	Colorado	83	182	Archival	Tax
Lake, Robert C.	IMPORTANCE OF SELECTED ACADEMIC SUBJ. AS PERCEIVED BY PRACTICING CPA'S IN THE SOUTH. STATES REGION OF THE NATL. ASSOC. OF STATE BOARDS OF ACCT.	La Tech	77	281	Field Study	Education
Lakonishok, Josef	EFFECTS OF UNANTICIPATED INFLATION ON COMMON STOCK RETURNS	Cornell	76	182	Market- based	Inflation
Lam, Wai Ping	CORPORATE AUDIT COMMITTEES IN ONTARIO, CANADA: AN EMPIRICAL STUDY	Mich St	74	269	Field Study	Auditing
Lambert, Kenneth R.	GENERAL PURCHASING POWER FINANCIAL STATMENTS: A BEHAVIORAL STUDY	Arkansas	77	144	Field Study	Inflation
Lambert, Richard A.	MANAGERIAL INCENTIVES IN MULTIPERIOD AGENCY RELATIONSHIPS	Stanford	82	193	Model- based	Managerial
Lamm, David Vincent	THE ADMINISTRATION OF COST ACCOUNTING STANDARDS	Geo Wash	76	410	Field Study	Managerial
Lammers, Lucille E.	AN EMP. STUDY OF THE VALIDITY AND RELIABILITY OF THE JOB DESCRIPTIVE INDEX FOR THE MEASUREM. OF ACCT.'S JOB SATISFACTION AND PRED. OF TURNOVER	Wiscon	75	171	Field Study	Profession
Lander, Gerald Harold	THE EMPIRICAL DEFINITION OF A COMMON BODY OF KNOWLEDGE FOR MANAGEMENT ACCOUNTING.	Kentucky	80	169	Field Study	Managerial

Author	Title	School	Date	pp	Methodology	Topic
Landsman, Wayne Robert	AN INVESTIGATION OF PENSION FUND PROPERTY RIGHTS	Stanford	84	188	Experimental	Pensions
Lane, Michael R	AN EMPIRICAL EXAMINATION OF THE EFFECT OF ASR #190 ON THE STOCK PRICES OF CERTAIN COMPANIES	Txs A&M	80	103	Market- based	Inflation
Lanen, William N.	ESTIMATING THE EFFECT OF REGULATORY ACCOUNTING RULES ON RATE-REGULATED FIRMS	Penn	83	197	FinStData-based	Financial
Langefeld, Phillip A.	AN INVESTIGATION OF CHANGES IN CORPORATE BOND RATINGS: PREDICTION AND INVESTOR REACTION	Cornell	78	193	Market- based	Financial
Langer, Russell D.	ACCOUNTING AS A VARIABLE IN MERGERS	Berkeley	76	233	Field Study	Business Combinations
Langeuin, Marcel	CORPORATE SOCIAL RESPONSIBILITY ACCOUNTING: A CANADIAN EMPIRICAL SURVEY	Syracuse	82	130	Field Study	Social
Lantz, Keith W.	AN EMPIRICAL TEST OF A CANNING-BASED THEORETICAL APPROACH FOR THE DEVELOPMENT OF ACCT. RISK SURROGATES	Iowa	75	142	Market- based	Financial
Larcker, David F.	STRATEGIC DECISION PROCESSES AND IMPLICATIONS FOR THE DESIGN OF ACCOUNTING INFORMATION SYSTEMS	Kansas	79	293	Experimental	Systems/ Computers
Larkins, Ernst R	AN INVEST. OF THE RELATIONSHIP BETWEEN THE PRESENCE OF U.S. EMPLOYEES ABROAD AND THE CHANGES IN THE TAX. OF THEIR FOREIGN EARNED INCOME	VPI	82	195	Archival	Tax
LaRue, David Wayne	CORPORATE REORGANIZATIONS UNDER THE INTERNAL REVENUE CODE OF 1954: A CRITICAL ANALYSIS OF THE LEGISLATIVE, ADMINISTRATIVE AND JUDICIAL DEVELOPMENT OF SECTION 368 (a)(1)(F) AND OF THE CAMPAIGN AGAINST "REINCORPORATION"	Houston	83	548	Archival	Tax

Author	Title	School	Date	pp	Methodology	Topic
Lasater, David B.	MANAGER INCENTIVES FOR ADVOCACY EFFORTS BEFORE ACCOUNTING STANDARD SETTING BODIES	Texas	82	134	Field Study	Profession
Lassila, Dennis Ray	TAX PLANNING FOR THE COMPENSATION OF SHAREHOLDER-EMPLOYEES OF SUBCHAPTER S CORPORATIONS.	Minnesota	81	384	Archival	Tax
Lathan, Malcolm H.	AN INVESTIGATION OF AUDIT SENIORS' UPWARD COMMUNICATION DECISIONS IN SELSCTED AUDIT CONTEXTS	N Carol	82	325	Experimental	Auditing
Lathen, William Clifford	VALUATION OF STOCK FOR CLOSELY HELD CORPORATIONS: AN EMPIRICAL TEST	Ariz St	82	220	Archival	Tax
Lau, Amy Hing-Ling	ON THE PREDICTION OF FIRMS IN FINANCIAL DISTRESS. WITH AN EVALUATION OF ALTERNATIVE FUNDS-FLOW CONCEPTS	Wash U	82	207	FinStData-based	Financial Distress
Lau, Chor Tin	ACCOUNTING INFORMATION AND PURCHASING POWER GAINS (LOSSES): AN EMPIRICAL INVESTIGATION	Oregon	76	177	FinStData-based	International
Laudeman, Max A.	SAMPLING RISKS ASSOCIATED WITH THE APPLICATION OF VARIABLE SAMPLING IN THE AUDIT ENVIRONMENT	Arkansas	76	137	Model- based	Auditing
Laverdiere, Raymond G.	AN EMPIRICAL STUDY OF THE ENVIRONMENTAL IMPACT ON INCOME SMOOTHING	Penn St	82	122	FinStData-based	Income Smoothing8:48 pm
Lavin, David	FINANCIAL STATEMENT USERS AND ACCOUNTANTS' PERCEPTIONS OF THE INDEPENDENCE OF THE AUDITOR IN SELECTED CLIENT-AUDITOR RELATIONSHIPS	Illinois	74	202	Field Study	Auditing
Lawler, William C.	EFFICIENCY MEASUREMENT IN THE REGULATED SECTOR: AN EMPIRICAL STUDY OF THE MASSACHUSETTS ELECTRIC UTILITY INDUSTRY EMPLOYING THE WILLIAMSON EXPENSE PREFERENCE THEORY IN A POOLED REGRESSION MODEL	Massach	81	176	FinStData-based	Managerial

Author	Title	School	Date	pp	Methodology	Topic
Lea, Kenneth R	AN INQUIRY INTO THE STATUS OF JURISDICTIONAL CONTINUING PROFESSIONAL EDUCATION PROGRAMS FOR CPA'S	La Tech	80	129	Field Study	Profession
Lee, Chan M.	A TRANSFER PRICING SYSTEM BASED ON OPPORTUNITY COST AND GAME THEORY	Nebraska	83	127	Model- based	Managerial
Lee, Johng Yul	A TEST OF ALTERNATIVE PRIOR PROBABILITY ELICITATION METHODS IN ASSESSING THE RELIABILITY OF INTERNAL CONTROL SYSTEMS FOR AUDIT DECISION.	LSU	79	144	Experimental	Auditing
Lee, Orland Sherer	A SYSTEM OF INVENTORY CONTROL FOR RETAIL FARM EQUIPMENT DEALERS	Okl St	78	168	Field Study	Managerial
Lee, Patsy L.	AN ANALYSIS OF AUDIT RISK IN ASSOCIATING WITH RESERVE INFORMATION OF OIL AND GAS COMPANIES	N Txs St	83	128	Experimental	Auditing
Leese, Wallace R.	MANAGEMENT'S PUBLISHED FINANCIAL FORECASTS: AN EVALUATION OF ACCURACY AND SMALL INVESTOR REACTION	Ariz St	78	241	Experimental	Forecasts
Leftwich, Richard W.	PRIVATE DETERMINATION OF ACCOUNTING METHODS IN CORPORATE BOND INDENTURES	Rochester	80	188	FinStData-based	Financial
Legault, Michel	SYSTEMATIC RISK AND ALTERNATIVE ACCOUNTING MEASURES OF PERFORMANCE	Syracuse	79	164	Market- based	Financial Ratios
Leichti, Janet Lynn Colbert	AN INVESTIGATION OF AUDITORS' JUDGMENTS OF INHERENT RISK IN INVENTORY	Georgia	84	199	Experimental	Auditing
Lemon, William Morley	DEVELOPMENT AND TESTING OF A MODEL FOR MEASURING THE MISMATCHING RISK OF FINANCIAL INTERMEDIARIES	Texas	75	186	Experimental	Financial

Author	Title	School	Date	pp	Methodology	Topic
Leong, Kenneth Kin On	THE EXISTENCE OF BONUS COMPENSATION PLANS AND THE RELATED EFFECT ON THE SIZE OF REPORTED ACCOUNTING EARNINGS	Colorado	85	131	Field Study	Financial
Lere, John C.	FIVE CHARACTERISTICS ASSOCIATED WITH USE OF VARIABLE AND ABSORPTION COSTING IN PERIODIC REPORTING	Wiscon	76	144	Field Study	Managerial
Lett, Samuel Lafayette	AN EMPIRICAL INVESTIGATION OF TRADE OR BUSINESS ATTRIBUTES OF QUASI-BUSINESS VENTURES UNDER THE INTERNAL REVENUE CODE (ACCOUNTING)	S Carol	81	158	Archival	Tax
Levine, Marc	WORK AS A CENTRAL LIFE INTEREST IN ACCOUNTANTS IN LARGE CPA FIRMS	NYU	83	174	Field Study	Profession
Levitan, Alan S.	PREDICTING FAILURE: THE GOING CONCERN ASSUMPTION	Kentucky	83	127	FinStData-based	Auditing
Lew, Albert Yee-Hong	ON THE RELATIONSHIP BETWEEN FINANCIAL (ACCOUNTING) VARIABLES AND MARKET MEASURES OF RISK AND INVESTMENT PERFORMANCE OF SELECTED U.S. MULTINATIONAL CORPORATIONS	Nebraska	84	193	Market- based	Financial
Lewis Tom Dean	ANALYSIS OF FINANCIAL AND MANAGERIAL ACCOUNTING PROCEDURES AND METHODOLOGIES UTILIZED BY INTERCOLLEGIATE ATHLETIC PROGRAMS	Nebraska	79	404	Field Study	Not-for-profit
Lewis, Barry Leroy	EXPERT JUDGMENT IN AUDITING: AN EXPECTED UTILITY FRAMEWORK	Penn St	78	145	Field Study	Auditing
Lewis, Eddie M.	FOUNDATIONS FOR THE ATTESTATION OF BUDGET DISCLOSURE	Miss St	74	211	Model- based	Auditing
Lewis, Lawrence D.	A STUDY OF THE IMPACT OF SELECTED TEACHING CREDENTIALS AND OTHER FACTORS ON THE TOPICAL CONTENT OF A ONE-SEMESTER UNDERGRADUATE MANAGERIAL ACCOUNTING COURSE	Nebraska	84	133	Field Study	Education

Author	Title	School	Date	pp	Methodology	Topic
Lewis, Stanley X.	AN ANALYSIS OF THE COSTS RELATED TO A MANUFACTURING FIRM'S SOCIAL GOALS USING GOAL PROGRAMMING	Miss St	75	245	Field Study	Social
Liao, Mawsen	A COMPARISON OF STOCHASTIC LINEAR PROGRAMMING WITH MEAN VALUE LINEAR PROGRAMMING FOR PRODUCTION AND PROFIT PLANING UNDER CONDITIONS OF UNCERTAINTY	Florida	74	141	Model- based	Managerial
Libby, Robert	PREDICTION ACHIEVEMENT AND THE USE OF SIMULATED DECISION MAKING INFORMATION EVALUATION	Illinois	74	143	Field Study	Financial
Lieberman, Arthur Z.	METHODOLOGY FOR THE AUTOMATION OF THE AUDIT PROCESS INVOLVING THE EVALUATION OF THE PLAN OF INTERNAL CONTROL	Arizona	77	237	Field Study	Auditing
Lilly, Martha S.	THE UTILITY OF CURRENT COST INFORMATION TO SELECTED USERS OF FINANCIAL STATEMENTS	Txs Tech	81	162	Experimental	Inflation
Limberg, Stephen T.	AN EVALUATION OF TAX POLICY AND INVESTMENT STRUCTURE UNCERTAINTY IN CONDOMINIUM CONVERSIONS: A SIMULATION	Ariz St	82	289	Experimental	Tax
Lin, W. Thomas	PERFORMANCE EVALUATION BASED UPON MULTIPLE OBJECTIVE PLANNING MODELS: A SIMULATION	Ohio St	75	240	Experimental	Managerial
Lindblom, Christi K.	QUALITATIVE RESEARCH INTO THE NATURE OF THE INSTITUTIONAL INVESTOR USER MODEL FOR CORPORATE SOCIAL DISCLOSURE: TOWARD A THEORY	Illinois	83	449	Field Study	Social
Lippitt, Jeffrey William	REPLACEMENT COST RETURNS IN TESTS OF THE CONCENTRATION-PROFITS HYPOTHESIS	Penn St	82	113	FinStData-based	Inflation
Lish, G. Rex	AN INVESTIGATION OF ALTERNATIVE COMMON STOCK EQUIVALENCY TESTS	Kentucky	77	244	Market- based	Earnings Per Share

Author	Title	School	Date	pp	Methodology	Topic
Listro, John P.	ACCOUNTING PRINCIPLES OF NONPROFIT ORGANIZATIONS AND THEIR STATUS IN COLLEGE ACCOUNTING PROGRAMS	Conn	76	259	Field Study	Education
Liu, Chao M.	VARIATION IN ACCOUNTING INFORMATION LOAD: THE IMPACT OF DISCLOSURE REQUIREMENTS OF FASB STATEMENT NO. 33 ON CASH FLOW PREDICTIONS OF FINANCIAL ANALYSTS	N Txs St	82	173	Experimental	Inflation
Livnat, Joshua	MARKET REACTIONS TO ACCOUNTING INFORMATION	NYU	78	92	Market- based	Financial
Lobo, Gerald Joseph	STOCK MARKET REACTION TO REVISIONS IN DISTRIBUTIONS OF SECURITY ANALYSTS' FORECASTS OF EARNINGS	Michigan	82	112	Market- based	Forecasts
Lomax, Victor William Jr.	AN EXAMINATION OF THE DETERMINANTS OF THE FINANCIAL VIABILITY OF SMALL, PRIVATE, FOUR-YEAR COLLEGES AND UNIVERSITIES	Missouri	84	250	FinStData-based	Not-for-Profit
Lookabill, Larry L.	SOME EVIDENCE OF THE RELATIONSHIP BETWEEN ACCOUNTING SIGNALS AND MARKET RETURNS IN THREE INDUSTRIES	Stanford	75	168	Market- based	Financial
Lorek, Kenneth S.	AN EMPIRICAL EXAMINATION OF THE TIME SERIES BEHAVIOR OF QUARTERLY EARNINGS	Illinois	75	140	FinStData-based	Stochastic Properties
Lovdal, Michael Lawrence	BOARDS OF DIRECTORS' AUDIT COMMITTEE: AN EXPLORATORY STUDY	Harvard	75	337	Field Study	Auditing
Lovins, W. Gene	THE EFFECT OF FEDERAL INCOME TAXES ON MARKOWITZ-TYPE PORTFOLIOS	Kentucky	76	126	Market- based	Financial
Lubell, Myron Samuel	THE SIGNIFICANCE OF ORGANIZATIONAL CONFLICT ON THE LEGISLATIVE EVOLUTION OF THE ACCOUNTING PROFESSION IN THE UNITED STATES	Maryland	78	447	Archival	History

Author	Title	School	Date	pp	Methodology	Topic
Luthy, David H.	CONFIGURAL UTILIZATION OF ACCOUNTING INFORMATION IN INVESTMENT DECISIONS: AN EMPIRICAL INVESTIGATION	Indiana	75	306	Experimental	Financial
Luzi, Andrew D	SELECTED PERFORMANCE INFORMATION SYSTEMS AND SMALL GROUP PROBLEM SOLVING BEHAVIOR	Kansas	78	224	Experimental	Managerial
Lyn, Thomas	SELECTION OF ACCT. PROCEDURES AND IMPLICATIONS OF CHANGES IN GEN.ACCEPTED ACCT. PRINCIPLES: A CASE STUDY USING OIL AND GAS ACCT.	Rochester	82	211	Market- based	Financial
Lynn, Susan A.	SEGMENTING THE MARKET FOR CPA SERVICES: AN EMPIRICAL STUDY OF THE CPA SELECTION PROCESS	Maryland	82	453	Field Study	Profession
Mac Millan, Alistair R.	STOCKHOLDER EQUITY TRANSACTIONS: SCOPE, THEORY AND PRACTICE	Missouri	77	176	FinStData-based	Financial
Mackey, James Thomas	VARIANCE CONTAMINATION DUE TO A SYSTEMS ENVIRONMENT	Illinois	81	198	Experimental	Managerial
Madeo, Silvia A.	THE ACCUMULATED EARNINGS TAX: AN EMPIRICAL ANALYSIS OF THE TAX COURT'S IMPLEMENTATION OF CONGRESSIONAL INTENT	N Txs St	77	125	Archival	Tax
Madison, Roland L.	A DESCRIPTIVE COMPARISON OF THE TRADITIONAL U.S. FINANCIAL REPORTING MODEL WITH SELECTED FOREIGN FINANCIAL REPORTING SYSTEMS	Nebraska	78	322	FinStData-based	International
Magann, Julia H.	AN EMPIRICAL INVESTIGATION OF MUNICIPAL FINANCIAL DISCLOSURES	S Carol	81	144	FinStData-based	Not-for-profit
Magee, Robert Paul	THE MARKET ASSOCIATION OF ACCOUNTING EARNINGS NUMBERS: FURTHER EVIDENCE	Cornell	74	107	Market- based	Financial

Author	Title	School	Date	pp	Methodology	Topic
Maher, John Joseph	PENSION OBLIGATIONS AND THE BOND CREDIT MARKET: AN EMPIRICAL ANALYSIS OF ACCOUNTING NUMBERS (RATINGS)	Penn St	85	168	Experimental	Pensions
Maher, Michael William	MANAGEMENT CONTROL: A STUDY OF THE INTERACTION BETWEEN FIRM GOALS AND STAFF PERFORMANCE IN SELECTED CPA FIRMS	Wash	75	277	Experimental	Managerial
Malone, Fannie Lee	ALTERNATIVE FUNDS FLOW MEASURES AS PREDICTORS OF FAILURE	Texas A&M	84	210	Model- based	Statement of Ch Fin Pos
Maloney, David Mitchell	A STUDY OF THE ASSOCIATION OF THE INVESTMENT TAX CREDIT WITH INVESTMENT SPENDING	Illinois	84	277	Archival	Tax
Maloo, Man Chand	TOWARD A THEORY OF EVOLUTION OF SELECTED ACCOUNTING IDEAS	Fla St	77	295	Model- based	Profession
Mandell, Steven Leslie	MULTINATIONAL CORPORATE COMPUTER-BASED INFORMATION SYSTEMS AND THE PARENT-SUBSIDIARY	Geo Wash	75	151	Field Study	Systems/ Computers
Manegold James G.	TIME-SERIES PROPERTIES OF THE COMPONENTS OF EARNINGS	Stanford	78	264	Market- based	Stochastic Properties
Mangold, Nancy Rueyhwa	THE EFFECT OF AUDITOR CHANGES ON EARNINGS, OPINIONS AND STOCK PRICES	Berkeley	84	174	Experimental	Auditing
Mannino, Ronald C.	THE IMPACT OF THE USE OF THE FULL COST METHOD IN THE PETROLEUM INDUSTRY ON THE MARKET PRICE OF SECURITIES	Colorado	77	162	Market- based	Oil & Gas
Mano, Ronald M.	MINORITY INTERESTS IN CONSOLIDATED BALANCE SHEETS	Nebraska	78	179	FinStData- based	Business Combinations

Author	Title	School	Date	pp	Methodology	Topic
Mansour, Fathi A.	A GENERAL FRAMEWORK FOR ANALYZING THE RELATIONSHIPS BETWEEN FIN. AND COST ACCT. WITH AN APPLICATION TO THE ALLOC. OF GEN. AND ADM. EXPENSES	Miss	76	259	Model- based	Managerial
Maples, Lawrence D.	OPERATING LOSS CARRYFORWARDS FOR FIRMS WITH DEFERRED TAX CREDITS	Miss St	76	173	FinStData-based	Tax
Mapp, Johnnie A.	A COMP. OF SIX MODELS FOR PRED. CORP. BNKRTCY.: MULT. LIN. REG. AN., MULT. LIN. DISCR. AN., STEPWISE REG. AN.,MLRA W/ RIDGE REG.,MULT.LIN. DISC. AN. W/ BIASED MIN. CHI-SQ. RULE	Georgia	81	123	Model- based	Financial
Margheim, Loren L.	AN EMPIRICAL STUDY OF EXTERNAL AUDITOR RELIANCE ON INTERNAL AUDITORS	Ariz St	84	129	Field Study	Auditing
Marks, Marcus Francis	CPA PERSONALITY PROFILES AND THEIR RELATIONSHIP TO ORGANIZATIONAL SIZE: AN EMPIRICAL STUDY	Florida	78	153	Field Study	Profession
Markwalder, Alice M.	AN EVALUATION OF THE EFFECTIVENESS OF ERISA, ASSESSED FROM THE TERMINATION OF DEFINED BENEFIT PENSION PLANS IN GEORGIA 1974-1979	Georgia	82	315	Field Study	Tax
Marquardt, John D.	INCOME TAX COMPLIANCE - AN EXAMINTAION OF CRITICAL ATTRIBUTES	Illinois	75	165	Archival	Tax
Marquette, Roberta Penny	AN INTER-TEMPORAL DISCRIMINANT MODEL FOR THE PREDICTION OF CORPORATION FINANCIAL FAILURE	Kent St	80	230	FinStData-based	Financial Ratios
Marquis, Linda M.	THE DIFFERENTIAL RISKS OF APPLYING REGRESSION ANALYSIS TO ACCOUNTING DATA	Kentucky	78	167	Experimental	Financial
Marshall, Clifford L.	AN ANALYSIS OF THE SUCCESS AND FAILURE FACTORS OF ACCT. GRAD. FROM PRED. BLACK COLLEGES AND UNIV. WHO ARE EMPLOYED BY BIG EIGHT FIRMS	N Txs St	83	69	Field Study	Profession

Author	Title	School	Date	pp	Methodology	Topic
Martin, Charles L.	AN EMPIRICAL ANALYSIS OF THE PRACTICALITY OF THE SECURITY & EXCHANGE COMMISSION'S REPLACEMENT COST DISCLOSURE REQUIREMENTS	Geo Wash	81	239	Field Study	Inflation
Martin, Dale R.	AN EXAMINATION OF THE CONGRUENCE OF VIEWPOINTS TOWARD THE BUDGETARY PROCESS AND ITS RELATIONSHIP TO PERFORMANCE	Kentucky	76	203	Field Study	Managerial
Martin, Jimmy W.	A STUDY OF PRACTICING CPA'S RISK PROFILES TO DETERMINE ATTRIBUTES RELEVANT TO THE CPA'S PERSONALITY AND PRACTICE	Alabama	78	295	Field Study	Profession
Marting, Edward D.	AN EMPIRICAL STUDY OF COMMERCIAL BANK FINANCIAL REPORTING	Ariz St	74	255	FinStData-based	Bank Accounting
Mattson, Lucretia W.	FED. AND STATE IND. INC. TAX PROV.: A COMPAR. ANALYSIS OF THE TREATMENT OF THE TWO-INCOME COUPLES WITH RESPECT TO THE "MARRIAGE PENALTY"	Kentucky	83	356	Field Study	Tax
Maupin, Rebekah J.	ANALYSIS OF JOB SATISFACTION AND PROFESSIONAL PRACTICE PATTERNS OF WOMAN CPA'S	Arkansas	82	129	Field Study	Profession
Maydew, Gary L.	A STUDY OF THE IMPACT OF CARRYOVER BASIS AND CONSTRUCTIVE REALIZATION OF CAPITAL GAINS AT DEATH; ON ESTATE PLANNING DECISIONS OF INDIVIDUALS	Illinois	78	259	Experimental	Tax
Mayer-Sommer, Alan P.	AN ASSESSMENT OF THE AWARENESS OF THE IMPLICATIONS OF THE EFFICIENT MARKETS HYPOTHESIS IN ACCOUNTING	Ga St	76	208	Field Study	Financial
Mayne, Frank Andrews	THE EFFECTS OF INFLATION AND BUSINESS INCOME TAXES ON INVESTMENT AND NATURAL RESOURCE UTILIZATION	Arizona	82	147	FinStData-based	Inflation
Mayper, Alan G.	AN INVESTIGATION OF AUDITOR'S PERCEPTIONS AND DECISION PROCESSES REGARDING EVALUATION OF MATERIAL INTERNAL ACCOUNTING CONTROL WEAKNESSES	Florida	81	230	Experimental	Auditing

Author	Title	School	Date	pp	Methodology	Topic
Mays, Robert Leland, Jr	NEGOTIATED TRANSFER PRICES AND BILATERAL MONOPOLY: AN ANALYSIS AND EXPERIMENT	Purdue	79	265	Experimental	Managerial
Mazhin, Reza	A TIME SERIES ANALYSIS OF THE PREDICTABILITY OF DISTRIBUTABLE OPERATING FLOWS	Indiana	84	155	FinStData-based	Inflation
Mboya, Fratern M.	THE IMPACT OF STATEMENT OF FIN. ACCT. STD. #14 ON THE OPERATING RISK OF MULTISEGMENT FIRMS	Arizona	81	114	Model- based	Business Segments
McAllister, John Peter	THE AUDIT IMPACT OF CLIENT BUSINESS ENVIRONMENT	Penn St	80	146	Market- based	Auditing
McAlum, Harry G.	AN ANALYSIS OF DISTRIBUTION COSTS IN THE TEXTILE INDUSTRY: A CASE STUDY	La Tech	83	160	Field Study	Managerial
McCabe, John C.	THE EFFECTS OF INFORMATION LOAD ON FINANCIAL COGNITIVE COMPLEXITY AND TASK PERFORMANCE: A LABORATORY EXPERIMENT	Indiana	82	245	Experimental	Financial
McCarthy, William E.	A RELATIONAL MODEL FOR EVENTS-BASED ACCOUNTING SYSTEMS	Massach	78	211	Model- based	Systems/ Computers
McCarty, Naomi J.	AN ANALYSIS OF SELECTED FEDERAL ESTATE TAX REFORM PROPOSALS	Arkansas	74	143	Archival	Tax
McCaslin, Thomas Eugene	AN EMPIRICAL INVESTIGATION OF THE ALLEGED TRADE-OFF BETWEEN RELEVANCE AND RELIABILITY	Tenn	82	148	Field Study	Financial
McClendon, Thurrell O.	A COMPARATIVE STUDY OF SELECTED ACCOUNTING PRINCIPLES, CONCEPTS, AND TECHNIQUES UTILIZED IN THE ADMINISTRATION OF ATHLETIC PROGRAMS IN HIGH SCHOOLS, COLLEGE OR UNIVERSITIES, AND PROFESSIONAL SPORTS	Arkansas	81	391	Field Study	Managerial

Author	Title	School	Date	pp	Methodology	Topic
McClure, Malcolm M.	ACCOUNTING AS A LANGUAGE: A LINGUISTIC APPROACH TO ACCOUNTING	Illinois	83	242	Archival	Communication
McConnell, Donald K. Jr.	AN EMPIRICAL EXAMINATION OF CERTAIN ASPECTS OF AUDITOR CHANGES IN NYSE, AMEX, AND SELECTED OTC COMPANIES	N Txs St	81	460	FinStData-based	Auditing
McCormack, Vincent Francis	OPINION LEADERSHIP AND NETWORK CENTRALITY WITH RESPECT TO TEACHING INNOVATIONS WITHIN ACCOUNTING HIGHER EDUCATION	Mich St	77	246	Field Study	Education
McEldowney, John Eugene	AN EMPIRICAL INVESTIGATION INTO THE PERCEIVED INDEPENDENCE OF AUDITORS	Miss St	84	213	Experimental	Auditing
McEnroe, John Edward	CASH FLOW FROM OPERATIONS: AN EMPIRICAL INVEST. OF TWO SELECTED USER GROUPS' ATTITUDES TOWARDS THE STATISTIC AND THE EFFECT OF EXPOSURE TO THE STATISTIC ON THEIR EVAL. OF AN ENTITY'S ECON. PERFORMANCE	Kentucky	77	139	Field Study	Cash Flows
McFerrin, William D.	SOCIAL AND BEHAVIORAL ASPECTS OF ACCOUNTING	U.S. Int. U.	76	186	Model- based	Social
McGillivray, Robert E.	INCOME CONCEPTS USED BY BANK LOAN OFFICERS IN A METROPOLITAN ENVIRONMENT	N Txs St	74	218	Field Study	Financial
McKay, Frances Ellen	A STUDY OF THE EFFECT OF THE PRESENCE OF SOCIAL RESPONSIBILITY INFORMATION IN THE INVESTMENT DECISION OF THE INDIVIDUAL INVESTOR IN CORPORATE STOCKS	Massach	81	248	Experimental	Social
McKean, Gerald William	CONGRUENCIES OF COMPUTER COMPETENCIES AS VIEWED BY ACCOUNTING PRACTITIONERS AND ACCOUNTING EDUCATORS	Illinois St	85	233	Field Study	Systems/Computers
McKee, Arnold J.	PREFERENCES FOR ACCOUNTING STANDARDS: THE USE OF DISCRIMINANT ANALYSIS IN FORECASTING CORPORATE MANAGER LOBBYING BEHAVIOR	Okl St	82	99	FinStData-based	Standard-setting

Author	Title	School	Date	pp	Methodology	Topic
McKee, Thomas F.	FINANCIAL DATA AS DISCRIMINANT PREDICTORS OF ENTERPRISE GOING CONCERN STATUS	Ga St	75	133	FinStData-based	Auditing
McKeon, Joseph M.	LOSS CONTINGENCIES RESULTING FROM LITIGATION AND FINANCIAL ACCT. STANDARDS BOARD STATEMENT NO. 5, ACCOUNTING FOR CONTINGENCIES	Kent St	79	210	FinStData-based	Loss Contingencies
McKinley, Sue H.	A COST BENEFIT APPROACH FOR THE ANALYSIS OF INTERNAL ACCOUNTING CONTROL	Georgia	82	212	Experimental	Auditing
McKinnon, Sharon M.	DISCLOSURE REQUIREMENTS OF MULTINATIONAL CORPORATIONS : AN INVESTIGATION OF COSTS AND BENEFITS	Ga St	81	271	Field Study	Financial
McKnight, Reed Harrision	MEASUREMENT ERROR AND BANKS' REPORTED EARNINGS	Oregon	81	228	FinStData-based	Bank Accounting
McMath, Herbert Kent	THE IMPACT OF MANDATED ACCOUNTING CHANGES ON MANAGEMENT DECISIONS THE STATEMENT NO. 8 EPISODE (FINANCIAL STANDARDS POLICY)	S Carol	85	232	Field Study	Foreign Currency
McMenimen, Leo Joseph	AN EXAMINIATION OF THE ACCURACY ISSUE AS AN OBSTACLE TO THE REQUIRED PUBLICAITON OF CORPORATE EARNINGS FORECASTS	Penn St	76	241	FinStData-based	Forecasts
McMickle, Peter L.	THE NATURE AND OBJECTIVE OF AUDITING: A UNIFIED RATIONALE OF PUBLIC, GOVERNMENTAL, AND INTERNAL AUDITING	Alabama	78	283	Model- based	Auditing
McNamara, James Bray	ACCOUNTING FOR EXTRAORDINARY ITEMS: A STUDY OF ADHERENCE TO APB OPINION NO. 30	Arkansas	78	118	FinStData-based	E.O.Items
Means, Kathryn M.	AN EMPIRICAL INVESTIGATION INTO THE PREDICTABILITY OF CASH FLOWS FROM OPERATIONS USING REPLACEMENT COST DATA	Ga St	79	165	FinStData-based	Inflation

Author	Title	School	Date	pp	Methodology	Topic
Meddaugh, Edsil James	THE ACCOUNTING REPORT FREQUENCY QUESTION,	Penn St	74	149	Experimental	Managerial
Meek, Gary Kenneth	FINANCIAL REPORTING IN AN INTERNATIOAL SETTING-SECURITIES PRICE RESPONSES IN THE UNITED STATES TO EARNINGS DISCLOSURES BY NON-U.S. MULTINATIONAL CORPORATIONS	Wash U	80	131	Market- based	Financial
Meixner, Wilda Furr	THE EFFECT OF THE ORGANIZATIONAL ENVIRONMENT ON JUDGMENT CONSENSUS: THE CASE FOR PROFESSIONAL GOVERNMENT AUDITORS IN THE STATE OF TEXAS	Texas A&M	85	130	Experimental	Auditing
Melcher, Trini U.	AN EMPIRICAL INVESTIGATION INTO THE EFFECTIVENESS OF ACCOUNTING PRINCIPLES BOARD OPINION NO. 20	Ariz St	77	285	Experimental	E.O.Items
Menon, Krishnagopal	FINANCIAL REPORTING BY STATE-OWNED ENTERPRISES	Penn St	82	131	FinStData-based	Not-for-profit
Mensah, Yaw Mireuk	A DATABASE APPROACH TO THE DESIGN OF MACRO-ORIENTED ENTERPRISE ACCOUNTING SYSTEMS IN DEVELOPING COUNTRIES	Illinois	79	157	Model- based	Systems/ Computers
Mensching, James Richard	FORWARD ALGORITHMS AND PLANNING HORIZONS FOR DETERMINISTIC INVENTORY PROBLEMS	Chicago	76		FinStData-based	Inventory
Merchant, Kenneth Allen	DEPARTMENTAL BUDGETTING: AN EMPIRICAL EXAMINATION OF A CONTINGENCY MODEL	Berkeley	78	135	Model- based	Managerial
Merei, Issam J.	AN ASSESSMENT OF THE NEEDS OF EXTERNAL SOPHISTICATED USERS OF FINANCIAL STATEMENTS: AN EMPIRICAL STUDY	Txs Tech	77	125	Field Study	Financial
Merino, Barbara D.	THE PROFESSIONALIZATION OF PUBLIC ACCT. IN AMERICA: A COMPARATIVE ANALYSIS OF THE CONTRIBUTIONS OF SELECTED PRACTITIONERS 1900-1925	Alabama	75	434	Archival	History

Author	Title	School	Date	pp	Methodology	Topic
Merrill, Gregory Bruce	FORECASTING INVENTORY PRICES FOR PURCHASING DECISIONS USING MULTIPLE REGRESSION TECHNIQUES	Txs A&M	81	182	FinStData-based	Managerial
Merz, Charles M.	EXTRAORDINARY LOSSES WHICH HAVE NOT BEEN REALIZED: FREQUENCY OF OCCURRENCE RELATED TO OTHER BUSINESS FACTORS	S Calif	74	185	FinStData-based	E.O.Items
Messere, Carl J.	AN EMPIRICAL INVESTIGATION OF MATERIALITY GUIDELINES AND EARNINGS TRENDS	S Carol	76	240	FinStData-based	Auditing
Messier, William Francis Jr.	AN EXAMINATION OF EXPERT JUDGMENT IN THE MATERIALITY/DISCLOSURE DECISON	Indiana	79	160	Experimental	Auditing
Messmer, Victor C.	AN EMPIRICAL INVESTIGATION OF THE EFFECTS OF STATE RATE REGULATION ON PRICE INCREASES IN ACUTE, SHORT-TERM GENERAL HOSPITALS	Kentucky	81	244	Field Study	Not-for-profit
Meyer, Kent Wyatt	A MODEL FOR USE IN EVALUATION THE EFFECT OF TAX FACTORS ON THE MANEUVERING OF LIQUID ASSETS BETWEEN MEMBERS OF A MULTINATIONAL ENTERPRISE AS ILLUSTRATED BY EVALUATION OF A BILATERAL TAX TREATY NETWORK	Texas	80	393	Experimental	Tax
Michaelson, Robert H.	A KNOWLEDGE-BASED SYSTEM FOR INDIVIDUAL INCOME AND TRANSFER TAX PLANNING	Illinois	82	387	Experimental	Tax
Michalka, William J.	THE USE OF CONCEPTS IN INCOME DETERMINATION BY MEMBERS OF THE AGRICULTURE SECTOR OF THE RAINS AREA OF TEXAS	N Txs St	76	185	Field Study	Agricultural
Middaugh, Jack Kendall II	APPLICATION OF MULTIATTRIBUTE UTILITY THEORY IN A CAPITAL BUDGETING CONTEXT	Ohio St	81	353	Experimental	Managerial
Mielke, David E.	THEORETICAL FRAMEWORK FOR PENSION COSTS	Wiscon	81	202	Model- based	Pensions

Author	Title	School	Date	pp	Methodology	Topic
Milano, Duane R.	INDEPENDENCE AND THE CERTIFIED PUBLIC ACCOUNTANT: AN EMPIRICAL ANALYSIS	Mich St	79	309	Field Study	Auditing
Milburn, John A.	INTERNATIONAL TRANSFER PRICING IN A FINANCIAL ACCOUNTING CONTEXT	Illinois	77	276	Field Study	International
Miller, James Jerome	THE UTILIZATION OF SELECTED MANAGEMENT ACCOUNTING CONCEPTS AND TECHNIQUES AMONG MEDIUM-SIZED UNITED STATES COMMERCIAL BANKS: A CRITICAL ANALYSIS	Missouri	79	132	Field Study	Managerial
Miller, Roger O	A REVIEW OF THE STATUS OF OPERATIONAL AUDITING IN STATE SUPPORTED COLLEGES AND UNIVERSITIES	Ga St	74		Field Study	Not-for-profit
Mills, John Robert	A STUDY USING THE BRUNSWIK LENS MODEL TO EVALUATE CONFLICTING CUES IN HOSPITAL BUDGET DECISIONS	Colorado	79	183	Experimental	Not-for-profit
Min, Han Ki	A THEORETICAL AND EMPIRICAL INVESTIGATION INTO PUBLICATION OF FORECASTS	Oklahoma	74	212	Field Study	Forecasts
Minmier, George S.	AN EVALUATION OF ZERO BASE BUDGETING AS A TOOL FOR PLANNING AND CONTROL OF DISCRETIONARY COSTS IN GOVERNMENTAL INSTITUTIONS	Arkansas	74	281	Field Study	Not-for-profit
Mintz, Steven M.	A COMPARISON OF ACCOUNTING STANDARDS SETTING IN THE INTERNATIONAL ENVIRONMENT AND IN THE U.S.	Geo Wash	78	340	Model- based	International
Mirghani, Mohamed Ali	THE ROLE OF ACCOUNTING IN THE ECONOMIC DEVELOPMENT OF DEVELOPING COUNTRIES: THE CASE OF THE SUDAN	Indiana	70	184	Field Study	Managerial
Misiewicz, Kevin	AN ANALYSIS OF THE DICHOTOMOUS FEDERAL INCOME TAX TREATMENT OF THE INCOME-PRODUCING EXPENSES OF INDIVIDUALS	Mich St	74	150	Archival	Tax

Author	Title	School	Date	pp	Methodology	Topic
Moffie, Robert Paul	A SIGNAL DETECTION APPROACH FOR MEASURING DATA SENSITIVITY OF AUDITORS	N Carol	78	156	Experimental	Auditing
Mohr, Rosanne Marie	AN EXAMINATION OF THE ASSOCIATION BETWEEN MARKET-BASED ESTIMATES OF BETA AND ALTERNATE ESTIMATES OF BETA WHICH INCORPORATE SEGMENTAL DATA	Wiscon	81	155	Market- based	Business Segments
Monahan, Thomas F.	PREDICTING BOND DOWNGRADING CLASSIFICATION USING HISTORICAL COST AND CONSTANT DOLLAR ACCOUNTING DATA	Temple	81	162	FinStData-based	Inflation
Moneef, Abdullah Ali	THE ATTITUDE OF THE SAUDI CITIZENS TOWARD THE IMPOSITION OF INDIVIDUAL INCOME TAX	S Carol	81	228	Field Study	Tax
Monger, Rodney Frank	RELATIONAL CHARACTERISTICS AND RESOLUTION MODES AS DETERMINANTS OF CONSTRUCTIVE AND DESTRUCTIVE CONFLICT PERCEPTIONS BETWEEN AUDIT FIRMS AND THEIR CLIENTS	Houston	81	211	Experimental	Auditing
Monroe, Gary S.	A BEHAVIORAL VIEW OF CURRENT COST ACCOUNTING INFORMATION IN PREDICTING FAILURES	Massach	78	171	Field Study	Inflation
Monroe, John E.	CASH FLOW FROM OPERATIONS.: AN EMPERICAL INVESTIGATION OF TWO SELECTED USERS' GROUP ATTITUDES TOWARDS THE STATISTIC AND THE EFFECT OF EXPOSURE TO THE STAT. ON THEIR EVAL. OF AN ENTITY'S ECONOMIC PERFORMANCE	Kentucky	77	139	Field Study	Statement of Ch Fin Pos
Moore, John Oliver	A STUDY OF MANAGEMENT CONSULTING SERVICES AND THE DECISION FACTORS USED BY FINANCIAL EXECUTIVES IN THEIR RETENTION	Houston	81	180	Field Study	Profession
Moore, John T.	THE EFFECTS OF FEDERAL INCOME TAXES ON THE CASH FLOW, OPERATING REVENUE AND NET INCOME OF ELECTRIC UTILITIES	Kentucky	82	187	FinStData-based	Tax
Moore, Phillip M.	AN EMPIRICAL STUDY OF AUDITOR INDEPENDENCE AS PERCEIVED BY SELECTED FINANCIAL STATEMENT USERS	Arkansas	83	199	Field Study	Auditing

Author	Title	School	Date	pp	Methodology	Topic
Moores, Charles T.	THE PREDICTION OF SMALL BUSINESS INSTABILITY - LOAN NONCOMPLIANCE: A DISCRIMINANT ANALYSIS APPROACH	LSU	82	187	FinStData-based	Financial Distress
Moran, Ceil Marie	LIMITED ASSURANCE ENGAGEMENTS: ENCOUNTERS OF A DIFFERENT KIND	Okl St	84	71	Experimental	Auditing
Morgan, Robert George	AN INVESTIGATION OF THE USE OF SELECTED FINANCIAL INFORMATION IN DETERMINING CONGLOMERATE MERGER STRATEGY	Ga St	74	108	FinStData-based	Business Combinations
Morris, Michael Henry	A STUDY OF THE POTENTIAL RELEVANCE OF REPLACEMENT COST ACCOUNTING DATA IN THE ASSESSMENT OF SYSTEMATIC RISK	Cincinnati	80	199	Market- based	Inflation
Morse, Dale Clayton	ASYMMETRICALLY DISTRIBUTED INFORMATION IN A MARKET SETTING: THEORETICAL AND EMPIRICAL APPROACHES	Stanford	78	153	Market- based	Financial
Morton, James R	THE COMMUNICATION EFFECTIVENESS OF FOOTNOTES IN PUBLISHED CORPORATE FINANCIAL STATEMENTS	S Calif	74	245	FinStData-based	Financial
Moseley, Owen B.	AN HISTORICAL ANALYSIS OF THE EVENTS LEADING TO THE ESTABLISHMENT OF THE COST ACCOUNTING STANDARDS BOARD	Okl St	76	324	Archival	History
Moser, Duane	A TEST FOR THE MARKET EFFECTS OF THE ACCOUNTING POLICYMAKING PROCESS: AN OIL AND GAS APPLICATION	Ohio St	84	220	Market- based	Oil & Gas
Moses, Orrin D.	ACCOUNTING CHANGE BEHAVIOR: THE RELATIONSHIP BETWEEN EARNINGS ADJUSTMENTS AND FIRM SPECIFIC EXPLANATION FACTORS: AN EMP. ANALYSIS	UCLA	83	373	FinStData-based	Accounting Changes
Moustafa, Salah	A MULTIVARIATE MODEL FOR TESTING THE INFORMATION CONTENT OF CONSTANT DOLLAR DISCL. REQUIRED BY ST. OF FIN. REP. AND CHANGING PRICES (FASB 33)	N Txs St	82	142	Market- based	Inflation

Author	Title	School	Date	pp	Methodology	Topic
Mulford, Charles W.	THE ASSOCIATION BETWEEN ACCOUNTING-BASED AND MARKET-BASED ESTIMATES OF SYSTEMATIC RISK UNDER ALTERNATIVE INCOME MEASUREMENT MODELS	Fla St	83	213	Market- based	Financial
Munter, Paul H.	THE EFFECT OF CONVERTIBLE SECURITIES ON THE ASSOCIATION BETWEEN ACCOUNTNG AND MARKET DETERMINED MEASURES OF RISK AND RETURN	Colorado	78	232	Market- based	Financial
Murdoch, Brock Gordon	THE INFORMATION CONTENT OF HISTORICAL COST AND FAS 33 RETURNS ON EQUITY	California, Irvine	84	124	FinStData-based	Inflation
Murdock, Richard J.	THE RELATIONSHIP BETWEEN ABNORMAL SECURITY RETURNS AND UNEXPECTED CHANGES IN PUBLICLY AVAILABLE DATA: AN EMPIRICAL TEST	Cornell	77	139	Market- based	Financial
Murphy, Kevin E.	A SIMULATION ANALYSIS OF THE EFFECTIVENESS OF POLLUTION CONTROL TAX INCENTIVES IN ENCOURAGING COMPLIANCE WITH POLLUTION STANDARDS	Wiscon	83	180	Experimental	Tax
Murray, Dennis Francis	DIFFERENTIAL MARKET REACTION TO SELECTED ACCOUNTING CHANGES	Massach	81	157	Market- based	Accounting Changes
Mutchler, Jane F.	A MULTIVARIATE ANALYSIS OF AUDITOR DECISION MAKING IN THE PRESENCE OF GOING-CONCERN UNCERTAINTIES	Illinois	83	228	Field Study	Auditing
Mykelburst, Harold N.	A COMPAR. STUDY OF HUMAN RESOURCE PERFORM.: TESTING A MULTI-VALUE ACCT. MODEL AND LIKERT'S THEORY OF RESOURCE MEAS. IN EVAL. EMPL. AND VOL. SERVICES IN HOSP.	American	75	367	Field Study	Not-for-profit
Nagarajan, Nandu Jaishankar	AUDITOR CONTRACTS AND REGULATORY STANDARDS: AN APPROACH TO INVESTIGATING THE EFFECTIVENESS OF LEGAL LIABILITY IN REGULATING AUDITOR PERFORMANCE	Northwest ern	84	163	Field Study	Auditing
Naggar, Ali K	AN EMPIRICAL STUDY OF EVALUATING "SUCCESSFUL EFFORTS" AND "FULL COST" METHODS OF ACCOUNTING FOR FINDING COSTS OF OIL AND GAS INDUSTRY FROM THE INVESTOR'S POINT OF VIEW	Okl St	75	227	Field Study	Oil & Gas

Author	Title	School	Date	pp	Methodology	Topic
Nagoda, Robert John, II	PRIVATE ANNUITIES AND INSTALLMENT SALES FOR ESTATE PLANNING: AN ANALYTICAL COMPARISON	Ariz St	82	164	Archival	Tax
Nair, Raghavan D.	THE SENSITIVITY OF TESTS OF CORPORATE INVESTMENT MODELS TO ACCT. METHODS OF INVENTORY VALUATION AND DEPR.: AN EMPIRICAL ANALYSIS	Michigan	77	171	Experimental	Financial
Naloo, Man C.	TOWARD A THEORY OF EVOLUTION OF SELECTED ACCOUNTING IDEAS	Fla St	77	245	Model- based	Financial
Namazi, Mohammed	ACCOUNTING INFORMATION AND OPTIMAL INCENTIVE CONTRACTS IN A MULTI-OBJECTIVE SETTING	Nebraska	83	144	Model- based	Managerial
Nance, Jon Roland	A STUDY OF THE FOREIGN CURRENCY TRANSLATION PROBLEM IN ACCOUNTING	Georgia	81	172	FinStData-based	Foreign Currency
Nanni, Alfred John Jr.	THE AUDITOR'S EVALUATION OF INTERNAL ACCOUNTING CONTROL: A SYSTEMS VIEW OF PROFESSIONAL JUDGMENT	Massach	81	271	Experimental	Auditing
Naoum, Christos	STOCK MARKET REACTION TO MANAGEMENT EARNINGS FORECAST	Penn St	77	178	Market- based	Forecasts
Naser-Tavauolian, Mohsen	STOCKHOLDERS' EQUITY PER SHARE: MEASUREMENT AND EVALUATION	Missouri	80	247	Market- based	Financial
Nathan, Edward C.	AN EXAMINATION OF AUDITOR DECISION-MAKING BEHAVIOR IN THE PREPARATION OF AUDIT TIME ESTIMATES	Texas	81	205	Field Study	Auditing
Nathan, Kevin Stuart	AN EMPIRICAL STUDY OF THE ECONOMIC CONSEQUENCES OF ALTERNATIVE ACCOUNTING AND OTHER FACTORS ON MERGER AND TENDER OFFER PREMIUMS	Oregon	84	128	Experimental	Business Combinations

Author	Title	School	Date	pp	Methodology	Topic
Ndubizu, Gordian Anumudu	AN EMPIRICAL INVESTIGATION OF THE SECURITY MARKET REACTION TO MULTINATIONAL ACCOUNTING CHANGES: STATEMENT OF FINANCIAL ACCOUNTING STANDARD NUMBER 52, FOREIGN CURRENCY TRANSLATION	Temple	85	176	Market- based	Foreign Currency
Neidermeyer, Adolph A.	A DETERMINATION OF THE BEHAVIORAL EFFECTS OF ANTICIPATION OF AN EXTERNAL AUDIT	Iowa	74	116	Experimental	Auditing
Neilson, Denis Peter	AN EVALUATION OF COMPUTER-INSTRUCTION IN UNDERGRADUATE ACCOUNTING CURRICULA	Berkeley	74		Experimental	Education
Neimark, Marilyn	THE SOCIAL CONSTRUCTION OF ANNUAL REPORTS: A RADICAL APPROACH TO CORPORATE CONTROL	NYU	83	516	Field Study	Social
Neumann, Bruce Richard	A MULTIVARIATE ANALYSIS AND CLASSIFICATION OF LARGE COMMUNITY HOSPITALS	Illinois	75	162	FinStData-based	Not-for-profit
Neumann, Reuben	AN INQUIRY INTO THE PREFERRED CONTENT AND FORMAT OF PUBLISHED FINANCIAL FORECASTS	Ariz St	74	196	Field Study	Forecasts
Newhouse, Benjamin	CASH RECOVERY RATE, CORPORATE CONTROL, AND CORPORATE PERFORMANCE	Michigan	82	132	FinStData-based	Managerial
Newman, Bruce R.	A MULTIVARIATE ANALYSIS OF CLASSIFICATION OF LARGE COMMUNITY HOSPITALS	Illinois	75	162	Field Study	Not-for-profit
Newman, Donald Paul	TOWARD AN INTEGRATIVE THEORY OF ACCOUNTING INFORMATION PRODUCTION AND UTILIZATION	Texas	77	200	Model- based	Financial
Newton, Grant W.	BANKRUPTCY AND INSOLVENCY: ACCOUNTING PRACTICE AND PROCEDURE	NYU	74	646	Field Study	Profession

Author	Title	School	Date	pp	Methodology	Topic
Newton, Lauren K.	THE CPA'S ATTITUDE TOWARD RISK AND MATERIALITY DECISIONS	Alabama	76	406	Field Study	Auditing
Ng, David Siu Po	ESSAYS ON THE EFFECTS OF INFORMATION IN FINANCIAL MARKETS	Berkeley	75		Market- based	Financial
Nichols, David Lloyd	WEALTH ESTIMATION: DEVELOPMENT OF A METHODOLOGY FOR ESTIMATING GROSS STOCKS OF MANUFACTURERS' PLANT AND EQUIPMENT AT A COUNTY LEVEL.	Arkansas	78	165	FinStData-based	Financial
Nichols, Richard L.	AN EVALUATION OF THE NEED FOR AND DESIRABILITY OF ESTABLISHNG A SET OF ACCT. PRINCIPLES AND STANDARDIZED REPORTING PRACTICES FOR CHURCHES	Arkansas	80	165	Field Study	Not-for-profit
Nichols, William Donald	AN EMPIRICAL STUDY OF STOCK SPLITS AND STOCK DIVIDENDS, THEIR ACCOUNTING TREATMENTS AND THE MARKET'S PERCEPTION OF THEIR ECONOMIC VALUE	Fla St	78	138	Market- based	Stock Distributions
Niemeyer, Ronald Duane	THE DEVELOPMENT OF INFORMATION SYSTEMS FOR PLANNING CONTROLLING THE LARGE DAIRY FARM	Miss St	74	507	Field Study	Agricultural
Nieminsky, Arthur C.	AN EMPIRICALLY DEVELOPED MODEL TO PRICE-LEVEL ADJUST FIXED ASSET PORTFOLIOS	UCLA	75	87	FinStData-based	Inflation
Ninsuvannakul, Prawit	AN INQUIRY INTO THE CONCEPTUAL RELATIONSHIP BETWEEN BUSINESS ACCOUNTING AND MACRO ACCOUNTING	Illinois	74	264	Model- based	Financial
Nissing, Burton J.	AN ANALYSIS OF THE USE OF THE PRIVATE FOUNDATION IN ESTATE PLANNING	Saint Louis	76	323	Archival	Tax
Nitterhouse, Denise	EFFECTS OF REPORTING REQUIREMENTS ON THE BEHAVIOR OF INFORMATION SENDERS	Harvard	81	269	Experimental	Managerial

Author	Title	School	Date	pp	Methodology	Topic
Nix, Paul E.	AN EMPIRICAL STUDY OF THE RELATIONSHIP BETWEEN FINANCIAL ACCT. MEASUREMENTS AND RESEARCH AND DEVELOPMENT EXPEND. IN PUBLIC CORP.	N Txs St	77	162	FinStData-based	Research & Development
Noe, Joann M.	AN INVESTIGATION INTO REPLACEMENT COST SURROGATES	Illinois	81	72	FinStData-based	Inflation
Noel, James Carl	AGENCY COSTS AND THE DEMAND AND SUPPLY OF AUDITING	Ohio St	81	182	Field Study	Auditing
Nordhauser, Susan Litt	AN EXAMINATION TO DETERMINE WHETHER CHANGES IN THE U.S. TAX LAWS MIGHT PROMPT CHANGES IN THE CORPORATE STRUCTURE OF MULTINATIONAL ENTERPRISES	Texas	78	235	Model- based	Tax
Noreen, Eric W.	EXECUTIVE STOCK OPTIONS: AN ECONOMIC AND ACCOUNTING ANALYSIS	Stanford	77	203	Model- based	Stock Options
Norris, Daniel M.	MINICOMPUTER CONTROL EVALUATION: AN EMPIRICAL STUDY OF AUDITORS' JUDGEMENTS OF COMPENSATING CONTROLS	Missouri	82	169	Experimental	Systems/ Computers
Norton, Curtis L.	A COMPARISON OF THE ABILITIES OF GENERAL PRICE LEVEL AND CONVENTIONAL FINANCIAL RATIOS TO PREDICT BANKRUPTCY	Ariz St	76	169	FinStData-based	Inflation
Nosari, John Stanley	EDUCATIONAL REQUIREMENTS OF INTERNAL AUDITORS	Saint Louis	84	513	Field Study	Education
Novin, Adele M.	AN EMPIRICAL INVESTIGATION OF THE INFORMATION CONTENT OF DISCLOSURES ON THE VALUE OF OIL AND GAS RESERVES	Georgia	82	163	Market- based	Oil & Gas
Nunamaker, Thomas R.	EFFICIENCY MEASUREMENT AND MEDICARE REIMBURSEMENT IN NONPROFIT HOSPITALS: AN INVEST. OF THE USEFULNESS OF DATA ENVELOPMENT ANALYSIS	Wiscon	83	197	Field Study	Not-for-profit

Author	Title	School	Date	pp	Methodology	Topic
Nunley, Terry J.	CAN DISCLOSURES OF THE EFFECTS OF CHANGING PRICES BE AUDITED?: A CASE STUDY	Alabama	83	158	Field Study	Auditing
Nutter, David E.	AN INQUIRY INTO THE DESIREABILITY AND FEASIBILITY OF CONTINOUS AUDITING OF LISTED COMPANIES	S Calif	74	143	Field Study	Auditing
Nyadroh, Emmanuel Mawuenyega Kwaku	CORPORATE DIVERSIFICATION, INFORMATION DISCLOSURE AND THE RISK-RETURN CHARACTERISTICS OF FIRMS	Northwest ern	81	444	Market- based	Financial
O'Brien, Francis James	THE ASSOCIATION BETWEEN MARKET DETERMINED AND ACCOUNTING DETERMINED RISK MEASURES IN THE IRISH ECONOMY 1966-1976	Pitt	79	320	Market- based	Financial
O'Connor, Walter Francis	AN INQUIRY INTO THE FOREIGN TAX BURDENS OF U. S. BASED MULTINATIONAL CORPORATIONS	NYU	76	473	Archival	Tax
O'Dell, Michael Arthur	AN EXAMINATION OF THE TAX ASPECTS OF FOREIGN INVESTMENT IN U. S. FARMLAND	Texas	80	207	Experimental	Tax
O'Doherty, Brian A.	MODERN ACCOUNTING APPROACHES TO CAPITAL MAINTENANCE AND VALUATIONS	Florida	78	163	Model- based	Financial
O'Keefe, Hubert A.	PERFORMANCE ACCOUNTABILITY AND AUDITING OF FEDERAL GRANTS-IN-AID TO STATE AND LOCAL GOVERNMENTS	Ga St	74	183	Model- based	Auditing
O'Keefe, William T.	USING OPINION RELATED EFFECTS ON CAPITAL MARKET EQUILIBRIUM TO MEASURE THE SOCIAL COST OF AN INAPPRO. AUDIT OPINION ABOUT GOING CONCERN STATUS	Fla St	78	218	Market- based	Auditing
O'Neil, Cherie Jeanne	THE IMPACT OF THE TARGETED JOBS CREDIT ON THE EMPLOYMENT DECISION PROCESS	Colorado	80	229	Field Study	Tax

Author	Title	School	Date	pp	Methodology	Topic
O'Rourke, Vincent	THE USEFULNESS OF FINANCIAL RATIO ANALYSIS FOR DISCRIMINATION OF SMALL BUSINESS CREDIT RISKS	Utah	82	252	FinStData-based	Financial Ratios
Oatsvall, Rebecca Johnson	CAPITAL GAIN/ORDINARY INCOME TREATMENT OF REAL ESTATE SALES	S Carol	78	135	Archival	Tax
Oestreich, Nathan Alan	REAL PROPERTY RENTALS AND THE "TRADE OR BUSINESS" DETERMINATION FOR FEDERAL INCOME TAX PURPOSES	Houston	81	209	Archival	Tax
Ogan, Pekin	A HUMAN RESOURCE VALUE MODEL AND ITS OPERATIONALIZATION IN A CPA FIRM	N Carol	74	321	Field Study	Hum.Resource Acct.
Ogunjimi, Emmanuel O.	CAPITAL MARKETS' RESPONSE TO CHANGES IN ACCT. METHODS: AN EMPIRICAL INVESTIGATION OF CHANGES TO LIFO	Arkansas	80	154	FinStData-based	Accounting Changes
Oien, M. Burton	A COMPARISON OF COST AND MARKET BASED ACCOUNTING MODELS FOR A MAJOR PETROLEUM COMPANY	Oklahoma	76	127	Field Study	Oil & Gas
Okpechi, Simeon O.	INTERDIVISIONAL TRANSFER-PRICING: A CONFLICT RESOLUTION APPROACH	Ohio St	76	191	Field Study	Managerial
Olds, Philip R.	AN INVESTIGATION TO EVALUATE THE LONG RANGE OBJECTIVES OF SELECTED ACCOUNTING ORGANIZATIONS	Ga St	82	281	Field Study	Profession
Oliver, Janice B.	THE EFFECTS OF PRESENTATION FORM AND TASK VARIABLES ON THE SALIENCY OF INFORMATION IN EVALUATIONS OF COMPANY PERFORMANCE	UCLA	79	214	Experimental	Financial
Oliver, Joseph Robert	AN INVESTIGATION INITO THE FEASIBILITY AND USEFULNESS FOR ACCOUNTING OF A MICROECONOMIC PRICE INDEX: A CASE STUDY	Missouri	76	129	Field Study	Inflation

Author	Title	School	Date	pp	Methodology	Topic
Oliver, Thomas W.	AN EMPIRICAL INVESTIGATION OF THE ECONOMIC IMPACT OF ACCOUNTING STANDARDS FOR LEASE DISCLOSURE	Massach	83	188	Market- based	Leases
Olivera, Herbert Ernest	A CRITICAL ANALYSIS AND EVALUATION OF SOME OF THE INEQUITIES OF THE UNITED STATES FEDERAL INCOME TAX SYSTEM WITH SOME RECOMMENDATIONS FOR REFORM	Ariz	75	258	Archival	Tax
Olsen, Ronnie Gary	PROFESSIONAL CORPORATIONS IN MEDICINE, LAW AND ACCOUNTING	Ariz	74	265	Field Study	Profession
Olson, Stevan K.	INDIVIDUAL INVESTORS' PERCEPTIONS OF THE CREDIBILITY OF CORPORATE FORECAST COMMUNICATIONS	Wiscon	74	242	Field Study	Forecasts
Oppong, Andrews	CROSS-SECTIONAL DIFFERENCES IN THE INFORMATION CONTENT OF ANNUAL EARNINGS ANNOUNCEMENTS	Iowa	76	147	Market- based	Financial
Orbach, Kenneth Ned	ACCOUNTING AS A MATHEMATICAL MEASUREMENT THEORETIC DISCIPLINE	Texas A&M	78	103	Model- based	Financial
Ormsby, Susan Y.	BY PRODUCT ACCOUNTING IN THE EXTRACTIVE INDUSTRIES: A HISTORY AND SURVEY OF CURRENT PRACTICE	Arkansas	82	143	Field Study	Managerial
Osborn, John Paul	THE COURT-DETERMINED ISSUES RELEVANT IN DECIDING THE VALIDITY OF OWNERSHIP INTERESTS IN FAMILY PARTNERSHIPS	Georgia	81	261	Archival	Tax
Ostrowski, Barbara A.	ALTERNATIVE INDEXING SCHEMES FOR NEW BUSINESS INCOME TAXATION: DISTRIBUTION AND REVENUE EFFECTS	Illinois	83	314	Experimental	Tax
Ou, Jane Ai Jiuan	THE INFORMATION CONTENT OF NON-EARNINGS ACCOUNTING NUMBERS AS EARNINGS PREDICTORS	Berkeley	84	148	FinStData-based	Financial

Author	Title	School	Date	pp	Methodology	Topic
Outslay, Edmund	INDIVIDUAL EQUITY CONSIDERATIONS OF THE CURRENT AND PROPOSED SOCIAL SECURITY BENEFIT PROVISIONS	Michigan	81	340	Archival	Tax
Ovadia, Arie	INVENTORY HOLDING AND EXPECTED INFLATION- AN EMPIRICAL STUDY OF THREE INDUSTRIES	Penn	78	174	Field Study	Inflation
Overbey, John T.	UNDERGRADUATE PREPARATION IN INFORMATION SYSTEMS FOR ACCOUNTANTS	Texas	76	234	Field Study	Education
Owens, Robert Willis	AN EXPLORATORY STUDY OF THE PERFORMANCE EVALUATION PHASE OF THE CAPITAL BUDGETING CYCLE	Wash U	78		Field Study	Managerial
Owings, Guy W.	AN INQUIRY INTO DIFFERENTIAL DISCLOSURE STANDARDS FOR SMALLER AND/OR CLOSELY HELD BUSINESSES	Missouri	80	150	Field Study	Financial
Oxner, Thomas H.	AN EVALUATION OF THE PREDICTIVE ABILITY OF ENTITY VS. SUB-ENTITY DATA	Georgia	77	204	FinStData-based	Financial
Palmon, Dan	THE MANIPULABILITY VS TIMELINESS OF REPORTED INCOME: THE LAND DEVELOPMENT CASE	NYU	74	224	Field Study	Financial
Palmrose, Zoe-Vonna	QUALITY-DIFFERENTIATION, SURROGATES, AND THE PRICING OF AUDIT SERVICES: AN EMPIRICAL INVESTIGATION	Wash	82	181	Field Study	Auditing
Pan, Sheng-Der	AN EMPIRICAL STUDY OF INVESTORS' UTILIZATION OF ACCOUNTING INFORMATION-AN APPLICATION OF THE STRUCTURAL THEORY OF ACCOUNTING	Illinois	74	195	Experimental	Financial
Panich, Richard Louis	AN EXAMINATION OF STRUCTURAL INCOME TAX REVISION FROM A PERSONAL WEALTH REDISTRIBUTION PERSPECTIVE	Ariz St	85	399	Archival	Tax

Author	Title	School	Date	pp	Methodology	Topic
Pannell, Richard L.	AN INQUIRY INTO THE MEANING OF STEWARDSHIP IN FINANCIAL ACCOUNTING	NYU	78	100	Archival	Financial
Pany, Kurt J.	QUARTERLY FINANCIAL REPORTING: A TEST OF VARYING FORMS OF AUDITOR ASSOCIATION	Illinois	78	187	Experimental	Auditing
Paolasini, Arnold L.	AN EMPIRICAL TEST REGARDING CONSISTENT DISCLOSURE OF FINANCIAL STATEMENT VARIABLES AMONG THE DIVERSE SECTIONS OF ANNUAL REPORTS	Illinois	76	249	FinStData-based	Financial
Paperman, Jacob B.	THE ACCOUNTANTS' PERCEPTION OF THE USEFULNESS OF HUMAN RESOURCE ACCOUNTING INFORMATION IN PUBLISHED FINANCIAL STATEMENTS	Cincinnati	76	199	Field Study	Hum.Resource Acct.
Pare, Paul-Victor	AN EMPIRICAL EVALUATION OF COMPOSITE PREDICTORS OF ACCOUNTING DATA	Michigan	83	103	FinStData-based	Financial Ratios
Parikh, Rajeev N.	ACCOUNTING PRINCIPLES BOARD OPINION 15 AND INFORMATION CONTENT OF EARNINGS PER SHARE	SUNY-Buf	82	198	Market-based	Earnings Per Share
Park, Hai G.	AN EMPIRICAL EVALUATION OF TWO JOINT COST ALLOCATION SCHEMES: A LABORATORY EXPERIMENT	Oklahoma	83	152	Experimental	Managerial
Park, Joengdae	AN EMPIRICAL INVESTIGATION OF A BANKRUPTCY PREDICTION MODEL WHICH COMBINES CHANGES IN RATIOS AND INFORMATION MEASURES	Fla St	84	174	Model-based	Financial Ratios
Park, Soong H.	A MODEL OF AUDIT PROCESS WITH EXPLICIT CONSIDERATION OF THE INTERRELATIONSHIPS AMONG ACCOUNT BALANCES	Iowa	77	163	Model-based	Auditing
Parker, Hugh J.	PREDICTION OF LIQUIDATION OR REORGANIZATION FOR FIRMS FILING UNDER CHAPTER X OF THE BANKRUPTCY ACT OF 1898	Okl St	82	71	FinStData-based	Financial Distress

Author	Title	School	Date	pp	Methodology	Topic
Parker, Larry M.	COGNITIVE DISSONANCE, SELECTIVE PERCEPTION AND THE SELF-FULFILLING PROPHECY IN THE EXAMINATION OF AUDIT EVIDENCE	Houston	81	201	Experimental	Auditing
Parker, Mary V.	POPULATION DYNAMICS AND BENEFIT ALLOCATION PATTERNS FOR DEFINED BENEFIT PENSION PLANS SUBJECT TO FASB STATEMENT 35 REQUIREMENTS	Colorado	82	174	Model- based	Pensions
Parker, Seth K.	A VALUE-ADDED TAX: ITS COMPLIANCE COSTS FOR INDIVIDUAL US NON-RETAIL BUSINESS FIRMS	Mich St	74	323	Field Study	Tax
Parmley, William K.	A CASE STUDY INVESTIGATION OF THE APPLICATION OF SELECTED MANAGERIAL TECHNIQUES AND USE OF ACCT. BASED INFORMATION IN DECISION-MAKING PROCESSES FOR A MUNICIPALITY	Okl St	78	188	Field Study	Not-for-profit
Parrish, Lillian C.	A PRELIMINARY EVALUATION OF THE EFFECTIVENESS OF ACCT. CONTROL FOR MGMT PURPOSES IN SMALL STATE-SUPPORTED COLLEGES AND UNIV. BRANCHES IN ARK.	Miss	77	340	Field Study	Not-for-profit
Parry, Robert W.	THE EFFECTS OF LEASE CAPITALIZATION ON THE DEBT RATIOS OF SELECTED PENNSYLVANIA CITIES	Lehigh	79	166	FinStData-based	Leases
Parsons, Gregory L.	FORMAL LANGUAGE MODELS FOR ACCOUNTING INFORMATION	Purdue	80	237	Model- based	Financial
Pastena, Victor S.	AN EVALUATION OF COMPLIANCE WITH AND THE EFFICIENCY OF ASR 138	NYU	76	212	FinStData-based	Financial
Patell, James M.	CORPORATE EARNINGS FORECASTS: EMPIRICAL TESTS AND A CONSUMPTION-INVESTMENT MODEL	Carn Mel	77	268	Market- based	Forecasts
Patterson, Jeffrey L.	THE ROLE OF EFFICIENCY AND PHYSICAL MEASURES IN EXPLAINING BETA AND BOND RISK PREMIUM IN THE AMERICAN RAILROAD INDUSTRY	Penn St	83	168	Market- based	Financial

Author	Title	School	Date	pp	Methodology	Topic
Pattison, Diane D.	THE EFFECTS OF PRICE CHANGES ON A FIRM'S INVESTMENT DECISIONS	Wash	81	96	Field Study	Inflation
Patton, James M.	USEFULNESS OF MUNICIPAL FINANCIAL REPORTS	Wash U	75	196	Field Study	Not-for-profit
Patz, Dennis H.	A GENERAL THEORY FOR THE TRANSLATION AND CONSOLIDATION OF FOREIGN ACCOUNTS	Texas	75	266	Model- based	International
Paul, John W.	THE FEASIBILITY OF EMPLOYING A SYSTEM SURVEILANCE MECHANISM IN A CONTINUOUS AUDITING FRAMEWORK	Lehigh	78	213	Experimental	Auditing
Pawliczek, Ronald B.	A STUDY OF THE EFFECTS OF DIFFERENT SCORING PLANS OF STUDENT PERFORMANCE IN AN ELEMENTARY ACCOUNTING COURSE	Massach	75	153	Experimental	Education
Paxton, William E.	A PRIORI EVALUATION OF THE IMPACT OF ACCOUNTING ALTERNATIVES ON FINANCIAL STATEMENTS	Kent St	83	286	Field Study	Financial
Peacock, Kenneth E.	MUNICIPAL BOND RATINGS: A MULTIPLE DISCRIMINANT ANALYSIS	LSU	79	92	FinStData-based	Not-for-profit
Pearson, Della A.	THE FEDERAL INCOME TAX SYSTEM: A COMPARATIVE STUDY OF DIFFERENCES BETWEEN PERCEPTIONS AND ATTITUDES OF TAX ACCOUNTANTS AND THE GENERAL PUBLIC	Txs A&M	78	223	Field Study	Tax
Pearson, Michael A.	AN EXAMINATION OF THE INDEPENDENCE CONSTRUCT AS IT RELATES TO EXTERNAL AUDITING IN GENERAL AND THE "BIG EIGHT" INDEPENDENT EXTERNAL AUDITORS IN PARTICULAR	Kent St	79	237	Field Study	Auditing
Pelz, Ulrich	THE INFLUENCE OF QUARTERLY EARNINGS ANNOUNCEMENTS ON STOCK MARKET BEHAVIOR	Colorado	76	301	Market- based	Quarterly Data

Author	Title	School	Date	pp	Methodology	Topic
Penman, Stephen H.	CORPORATE FORECAST DISCLOSURE, SUBSTITUTE INFORMATION AND THE MARKET FOR INFORMATION	Chicago	78		Market- based	Forecasts
Penno, Mark C.	ISSUES OF ASYMMETRIC INFORMATION IN MANAGERIAL ACCOUNTING	Northwest ern	83	144	Model- based	Managerial
Peters, Richard M.	A COMPARISON OF METHODOLOGIES FOR LEASE-PURCHASE DECISIONS	Penn St	76	171	Field Study	Managerial
Petro, Louis W.	THE EFFECTS OF REGULATORY AND TAX ACCOUNTING POLICIES ON INVESTOR-OWNED PUBLIC UTILITY LEASE-BUY DECISION	Michigan	74	205	Model- based	Managerial
Peyvandi, Ali Agha	ACCOUNTING AND REPORTING FOR INVESTMENT IN JOINT VENTURE ARRANGEMENTS	Missouri	80	248	FinStData-based	Financial
Pffeiffer, Glenn M.	ACCOUNTING FOR LONG TERM FINANCIAL COMMITMENTS: AN INVESTIGATION INTO THE ECONOMIC EFFECTS OF LEASE ACCOUNTING CHANGES	Cornell	80	168	Market- based	Leases
Philipich, Kirk Lynn	THE EFFECT OF THREE FACTORS ON THE ACCURACY OF UNIVARIATE TIME-SERIES FORECASTS OF QUARTERLY EARNINGS	Indiana	84	83	Field Study	Forecasts
Phillips, Mary	STOCK MARKET EFFECTS OF FOURTH QUARTER EARNINGS REPORTS LAGS	N Carol	83	151	Market- based	Quarterly Data
Phillips, Thomas E.	AN INQUIRY INTO THE INFORMATIONAL REQUIREMENTS OF MEDIUM SIZED INDUSTRIAL FIRMS IN REGARDS TO OBSOLETE MAINTENANCE INVENTORY	Nebraska	74	206	Field Study	Managerial
Phillips, Thomas James Jr.	AN EMPIRICAL INVESTIGATION AND ANALYSIS OF THE USEFULNESS OF SELECTED REVISIONS IN CONCEPT, FORM, AND CONTENT OF THE STATEMENT OF CHANGES IN FINANCIAL POSITION (FUNDS)	Ga St	84	184	Experimental	Statement of Ch Fin Pos

Author	Title	School	Date	pp	Methodology	Topic
Pincus, Karen Vandermause	FRAUD DETECTION ABILITY: INDIVIDUAL DIFFERENCES AND THEIR RELATIONSHIP TO COGNITIVE STYLE DIFFERENCES	Maryland	84	379	Field Study	Auditing
Pincus, Morton P.	INFORMATION CHARACTERISTICS OF ACCT. EARNINGS ANNOUNCEMENTS AND STOCK MARKET BEHAVIOR: EMPIRICAL TESTS	Wash U	82	110	Market- based	Financial
Pitman, Marshall K.	AN EMPIRICAL ANALYSIS OF THE IMPACT OF FASB STATEMENT NO. 34, CAPITALIZATION OF INTEREST COST, ON STOCK PRICES	Miss	83	138	Market- based	Interest Capitalization
Pitre, Richard	AN INVESTIGATION OF THE RELATIONSHIP BETWEEN HOSPITAL MANAGEMENT INFORMATION SYSTEM AND HOSPITAL EFFECTIVESNESS	Houston	78	138	Field Study	Managerial
Pitt, Harold R.	AN EMPIRICAL INVESTIGATION OF INVESTOR REACTIONS TO CHANGES IN TOP MANAGEMENT PERSONNEL	Okl St.	78	66	Market- based	Managerial
Plewa, Franklin J.	AN EMPIRICAL INVESTIGATION OF THE EXTENT OF DISCLOSURE IN MUNICIPAL ANNUAL REPORTS	LSU	83	243	Field Study	Not-for-profit
Plumlee, Roy D.	THE STANDARD OF OBJECTIVITY FOR INTERNAL AUDITORS: A LABORATORY EXPERIMENT	Florida	82	121	Experimental	Auditing
Pocano, Thomas M.	USERS' PREDICTIONS UNDER DISCLOSURE VS. NON-DISCLOSURE OF SEGMENT DATA: AN EMPIRICAL INVESTIGATION	Indiana	76	175	Experimental	Business Segments
Pollard, William B.	AN EMPIRICAL MODEL OF JUDICIAL INTERPRETATIONS OF INTERNAL REVENUE CODE SECTION 162(A) (2): THE LOCATION OF A TAX HOME	S Carol	81	219	Archival	Tax
Pope, Thomas R	REVENUE EFFECTS OF SUBSTANTIAL CONFORMITY WITH THE INTERNAL REV. CODE BY THE COMMONWEALTH OF KY. FOR PERSONAL INC. TAXATION	Kentucky	76	243	Archival	Tax

Author	Title	School	Date	pp	Methodology	Topic
Porcano, Thomas M.	USER'S PREDICTIONS UNDER DISCLOSURE VS. NONDISCLOSURE OF SEGMENT DATA: AN EMPIRICAL INVESTIGATION	Indiana	76	175	Experimental	Business Segments
Porter, Gary A.	AN EMPIRICAL EXAMINATION INTO THE DETERMINANTS OF THE ACCURACY OF MANAGEMENT FORECASTS OF EARNINGS	Colorado	77	153	Market- based	Forecasts
Porter, Leslie R	COMPUTER-BASED MODEL FOR EVALUATING EDP CONTROL STRATEGIES	UCLA	81	231	Experimental	Auditing
Porter, Mattie C.	THE ROLE OF CONSTITUENCY RESPONSES IN SETTING ACCOUNTING STANDARDS	Txs A&M	79	263	Field Study	Standard-setting
Posey, Clyde L.	AN HISTORICAL ANALYSIS OF THE EVENTS LEADING TO THE ESTABLISHMENT OF THE INVESTMENT TAX CREDIT AND ITS MODIFICATION THROUGH JUNE 30, 1977	Okl St	78	335	Archival	Tax
Posey, Roderick B.	AN INVESTIGATION OF THE DIFFERENCES IN BOND DISCLOSURES MADE BY PUBLIC AND PRIVATE COLLEGES	Okl St	80	153	FinStData-based	Not-for-profit
Potts, A. J.	A STUDY OF THE SUCCESS AND FAILURE RATES OF SMALL BUSINESS AND THE USE OR NON-USE OF ACCOUNTING INFORMATION	Geo Wash	77	131	Field Study	Financial
Potts, James H.	AN ANALYSIS OF THE EVOLUTION OF MUNICIPAL ACCT. TO 1935 WITH PRIMARY EMPHASIS ON DEVELOPMENTS IN THE U.S.	Alabama	76	258	Archival	History
Powell, Norma C.	THE RELIABILITY OF SELECTED INCOME PRODUCING REAL ESTATE APPRAISAL MODELS: AN EMPIRICAL STUDY	Txs A&M	82	151	FinStData-based	Real Estate
Powers, Marian	AN EXAMINATION OF THE USEFULNESS OF SEGMENT INFORMATION FOR ASSESSING THE OPERATING RISK OF THE FIRM	Illinois	82	112	FinStData-based	Business Segments

Author	Title	School	Date	pp	Methodology	Topic
Powers, Marian	AN EXAMINATION OF THE USEFULNESS OF SEGMENT INFORMATION FOR ASSESSING THE OPERATING RISK OF THE FIRM	Illinois	82	112	Market- based	Business Segments
Pratt, James H.	THE ASSOCIATION BETWEEN FINANCIAL REPORT COMPLEXITY AND USER FINANCIAL INFORMATION CONCEPTUAL LEVELS: AN ANALYSIS UNDER EXPER. CONDITIONS	Indiana	77	197	Experimental	Financial
Preis, Nancy J.	CORPORATE BANKRUPTCY: FROM ECONOMIC FAILURE TO REORGANIZATION OR LIQUIDATION	Michigan	82	253	FinStData-based	Financial
Prober, Larry M.	A COMPARISON OF HISTORICAL COST AND GENERAL PRICE-LEVEL ADJUSTED MEASURES IN THE PREDICTION OF DIVIDEND CHANGES.	Temple	85	179	FinStData-based	Inflation
Pulliam, Dale R.	A MODEL FOR OPTIMAL INTERSPOUSAL TRANSFERS IN ESTATE PLANNING	N Txs St	79	150	Experimental	Tax
Pumhrey, Lela Dale	AUDIT COMMITTEES IN NONGOVERNMENT NOT-FOR-PROFIT SHORT-TERM GENERAL HOSPITALS: AN EMPIRICAL STUDY	Missouri	84	271	Field Study	Not-for-Profit
Puro, Marsha B.	AUDIT FIRM LOBBYING ON FINANCIAL ACCOUNTING STANDARDS: AN EMPIRICAL STUDY	Wash U	83	173	FinStData-based	Standard-setting
Purvis, S.E.C.	THE AUDITOR'S PRELIMINARY EVALUATION OF INTERNAL ACCOUNTING CONTROL: A BEHAVIORAL ANALYSIS	Columbia	85	408	Field Study	Auditing
Pushkin, Ann B.	AN INVESTIGATION OF THE VALIDITY OF AUDITING PROCEDURES USED IN MEAN-PER-UNIT SAMPLING PLANS	VPI	78	365	Experimental	Auditing
Putnam, Donald F.	DISCLOSURE CRITERIA FOR BUSINESS ENTERPRISES	Claremont	76	262	Model- based	Financial

Author	Title	School	Date	pp	Methodology	Topic
Putnam, Karl B.	AN EMPIR. EVAL. OF THE ASSOC. OF RECENT CHANGES IN THE SECURITIES' REGULATORY ENVIRON. WITH THE PREDICTIVE ABILITY OF QUARTERLY EARNINGS	Okl St	80	106	Market- based	Quarterly Data
Raabe, William A.	INCOME TAX SIMPLICITY: AN EXAMINATION OF AN ELECTIVE FILING SYSTEM	Illinois	79	253	Experimental	Tax
Raiborn, Cecily A.	EMPIRICAL FORECASTING EXPERIENCE AND FORMULATION OF RELATED AUDIT STANDARDS	LSU	75	245	Experimental	Auditing
Raiborn, Debra D.	AN EMPIRICAL STUDY OF AUDIT PROBLEMS ENCOUNTERED WITH SMALL BUSINESS ENGAGEMENTS	Txs Tech	81	258	Field Study	Auditing
Ramakrishnan Ram T. S.	INFORMATION, CONTROL AND RESOURCE ALLOCATION ISSUES IN ORGANIZATIONS	Northwestern	81	294	Model- based	Financial
Raman, Krishnamurthy K.	AN EMPIRICAL INVESTIGATION INTO THE DESIRABILITY OF APPLYING COMMERCIAL ACCOUNTING PRINCIPLES TO MUNICIPAL REPORTING	Indiana	79	181	Field Study	Not-for-profit
Ramsey, Louis P.	AN EMPIRICAL STUDY OF INCOME ALLOCATION METHODS FOR COMMON STOCK PORTFOLIOS OF P-L INSURANCE COMPANIES	Kent St	75	139	FinStData-based	Financial
Rankin, Larry J.	A STUDY OF THE EFFECTS OF COMPILATION AND REVIEW REPORTS ON CPAS' AND BANKERS' PERCEPTIONS OF THE RELIABILITY OF FINANCIAL STATEMENTS	Mich St	82	251	Field Study	Auditing
Rans, Donald L.	FEDERAL COLLECTION OF STATE INDIVIDUAL INCOME TAXES: AN EMPIRICAL EVALUATION	Indiana	72	361	Field Study	Tax
Ransom, Charles R.	THE EXPECTED INFORMATION CONTENT OF ALTERNATIVE ACCOUNTING INFORMATION SYSTEMS: AN EMPIRICAL INVESTIGATION	Wiscon	83	134	Model- based	Systems/ Computers

Author	Title	School	Date	pp	Methodology	Topic
Rao, Honnudike V.	AN ANALYSIS OF ACCOUNTING INFORMATION NEEDS OF SELECTED USERS OF FINANCIAL STATEMENTS	Txs A&M	74	227	Field Study	Financial
Rao, Kailas J.	AN EVALUATION AND EMPIRICAL STUDY OF THE DISCLOSURE OF ACCOUNTING POLICIES IN PUBLISHED FINANCIAL STATEMENTS	Oklahoma	74	125	Field Study	Financial
Rasch, Ronald H.	AN ANALYSIS OF INFORMATION STRUCTURE AND OPTIMAL TRANSFER PRICING DECISION RULES FOR DECENTRALIZED FORMS	Texas	80	139	Model- based	Managerial
Raslan, Maher Mahmoud	EMPIRICAL STUDY OF THE EFFECTS OF FOREIGN INVESTMENTS ON PROJECT EVALUATION TECHNIQUES USED BY MULTINATIONAL FIRMS	Arkansas	83	131	Experimental	Managerial
Ratcliffe, Thomas H.	A SIMULATION OF CHANGES IN THE SOCIAL CONTRACT: A STEP TOWARD A SOCIAL ACCOUNTING MODEL	Alabama	77	151	Experimental	Social
Ratliff, Richard L.	A STUDY OF SELECTED CONGRESSIONAL ATTITUDES REGARDING PUBLIC ACCOUNTING ISSUES	N Carol	79	151	Field Study	Profession
Raval, Vasant H.	CERTAIN ASPECTS OF BUDGET RELATED BEHAVIOR AS MODERATED BY LOCUS OF CONTROL AND ENVIRONMENTAL UNCERTAINTY	Indiana	76	194	Field Study	Managerial
Rayburn, Frank R.	A STUDY OF THE EFFECT OF ACCT. PRIN. STD.OP. 16 ON THE USE OF POOLING OF INTEREST ACCT. FOR BUS. COMB. AND OF INST. ENFORCEMENT OF POOLING CRITERIA OF OP. NO. 16	Alabama	74	240	FinStData-based	Business Combinations
Read, William Joseph	MODELING AUDITOR JUDGMENT IN NONSTATISTICAL SAMPLING	VPI	84	250	Model- based	Auditing
Rebele, James Edward	AN INVESTIGATION OF THE IMPACT OF SOURCE EXPERTISE IN THE AUDITOR-CLIENT RELATIONSHIP	Indiana	84	249	Experimental	Auditing

Author	Title	School	Date	pp	Methodology	Topic
Reber, Dennis L.	A COMPARISON OF ATTITUDES TOWARD THE ROLE OF COLLEGES AND UNIVERSITIES IN ACCT. CONTINUING PROF. ED. AMONG MEMBERS OF STATE BOARDS OF ACCT., PRACTICING ACCTS. AND ACCT. PROFESSORS	S Carol	79	116	Field Study	Education
Reckers, Philip M.	AN EXAMINATION OF THE CHOICE-SHIFT PHENOMENON IN AN AUDITING FRAMEWORK	Illinois	78	216	Experimental	Auditing
Redding, Rodney J.	EVALUATING CAPITAL EXPENDITURE DECISION CRITERIA: AN EXTENDED CORPORATE FINANCIAL PLANNING MODEL APPROACH	Penn St	79	376	Experimental	Managerial
Reed, Barbara L.	RELATIONSHIP BETWEEN INFORMATION CONTENT OF MANAGERIAL FORECASTS AND FORECAST ATTRIBUTES	Ariz St	82	117	Market- based	Forecasts
Reed, Ira M.	AN EMPIRICAL INVESTIGATION OF THE EFFECT OF APB OP.#16 AND APB OP.#17 ON THE ACCOUNTING FOR BUSINESS COMBINATIONS	Missouri	76	238	FinStData-based	Business Combinations
Reed, Ronald O.	A STUDY OF ACCOUNTANTS' PROCEDURES PERFORMED AND BANKERS' PERCEPTION OF PROCEDURES PERFORMED IN COMPILATIONS AND REVIEWS OF FINANCIAL STATEMENTS	Txs Tech	81	244	Field Study	Auditing
Reed, Sarah Auman	THE IMPACT OF NON-MONETARY PERFORMANCE MEASURES UPON BUDGETARY DECISION MAKING IN THE PUBLIC SECTOR	N Txs St	84	400	Field Study	Not-for-Profit
Reeder, David B.	AN ANALYSIS OF THE EFFECT OF ASSET ACQ. METHODS-PURCHASE OR LEASE-& ACCT. METH. ON THE FIN. STRUCTURE OF SELECTED PRIVATELY OWNED ELEC. UTIL.	Kentucky	80	262	FinStData-based	Financial
Reeder, Janis R.	THE CHILD CARE DEDUCTION: ISSUES IN HORIZONTAL EQUITY	S Carol	78	187	Archival	Tax
Rees, David A.	USER-ORIENTED MUNICIPAL FOOTNOTE REPORTING MODELS: IDEAL AND PRACTICAL	Txs Tech	82	230	Field Study	Not-for-profit

Author	Title	School	Date	pp	Methodology	Topic
Reese, Craig E.	THE USE OF TAX POLICY TO CONTROL POLLUTION: A COMPARATIVE ANALYSIS OF THE MAJOR INDUSTRIALIZED COUNTRIES IN NORTH AMERICA AND WESTERN EUROPE	Texas	79	449	Archival	Tax
Reeve, James M.	AN INVESTIGATION OF GROUP VS INDIVIDUAL PROCESSING OF ACCOUNTING INFORMATION	Okl St	80	129	Experimental	Financial
Reid, George R.	AN ANALYSIS OF THE ROLE OF DEPRECIATION ACCOUNTING IN MUNICIPAL ENTERPRISES IN RELATION TO MANAGEMENT FINANCIAL POLICIES	Missouri	83	261	Model- based	Not-for-profit
Reinstein, Alan	A CONCEPTUAL FRAMEWORK FOR AUDIT COMMITTEES	Kentucky	80	202	Field Study	Auditing
Remmele, David Alan	COURT-DETERMINED MATERIALITY: AN EMPIRICAL ANALYSIS OF THE CRITERIA COURTS USE AND THE IMPLICATIONS FOR ACCOUNTANTS	Wiscon	85	252	Field Study	Auditing
Reneau, James H.	AN APPLICATION OF ANNUAL TIME SERIES MODELS TO THE POTENTIAL AUDIT PROBLEM OF DETERMINING THE REASONABLENESS OF CORPORATE SALES FORECASTS	Missouri	75	226	FinStData-based	Auditing
Renfer, Karin	THE IMPACT OF ETHICS ON DECISION MAKING IN TAX PRACTICE: AN EXAMINATION OF STRATEGIES AND TRADEOFFS	Michigan	82	272	Field Study	Tax
Reveley, Thomas R.	INVENTORY UNCERTAINTY: A STUDY OF ITS NATURE AND CAUSES AND A SIMULATION OF ITS BEHAVIOR	Houston	78	122	Experimental	Managerial
Rexroad, William M.	AN INVEST. OF THE EFFECTS OF CERTAN ENVIRON. VARIABLES OF ILLINOIS MUN. FIN. ST. WITH RESPECT TO THEIR COMPLIANCE WITH GAAP AND GAAS OF REPORTING	Illinois	78		FinStData-based	Not-for-profit
Reynolds, Ruthie	RESOURCE PROVIDERS' AND PRACTICING ACCOUNTANTS' PERCEPTIONS OF THE IMPORTANCE AND QUALITY OF ACCT. INF. ON VOL. HEALTH AND WELFARE AGENCIES	Ga St	81	204	Field Study	Not-for-profit

Author	Title	School	Date	pp	Methodology	Topic
Rezac, Reginald N.	A COURSE OF STUDY IN INDIVIDUAL INCOME TAX FOR THE NON-ACCOUNTANT	N Colo	74	112	Archival	Education
Rhee, Thomas A.	CORPORATION INCOME TAX AND CAPITAL STRUCTURE	Wayne St	82	126	Field Study	Tax
Ricchiute, David N.	THE ENTITY-PROPRIETARY DEBATE: AN ANLYSIS OF THE VIEWPOINTS OF SELECTED AUTHORITATIVE ACCOUNTING BODIES AND CPA'S	Kentucky	77	171	Field Study	Financial
Rice, Steven J.	A STUDY OF THE INFORMATION PROVIDED BY FULLY DILUTED EPS	Texas	74	132	Market- based	Earnings Per Share
Rich, Anne J.	INFORMATION AND BEHAVIORAL CONSIDERATIONS OF BANKERS IN THE SMALL BUSINESS LOAN DECISION	Massach	78	216	Experimental	Financial
Richards, Evan W.	COST CONTROL OF EDP SERVICES: A COST ACCOUNTING MODEL AND EXAMINATION OF CURRENT PRACTICES	Mich St	76	235	Field Study	Managerial
Richardson, Frederick M.	THE SENSITIVITY OF STATISTICAL DECISION MODELS TO ACCOUNTING NUMBER INPUTS: AN EXPLORATION	N Carol	80	197	Experimental	Financial
Richardson, Gordon D.	A THEORETICAL AND EMPIRICAL INVESTIGATION OF THE INFORMATION CONTENT OF ANNUAL EARNINGS ANNOUNCEMENTS	Cornell	83	167	Market- based	Financial
Richardson, Willie	AN EMP. ANAL. OF RELATIONSHIPS BETWEEN THREE TAXPAYER GROUPS AND TAX RETURN PREPAYERS: SUPPORTED BY SELECTED OPINIONS OF TAXPAYERS OR RETURN PREPARERS	Georgia	78	213	Field Study	Tax
Ricks, William E.	THE MARKET'S RESPONSE TO THE 1974 LIFO SWITCH	Berkeley	80	136	Market- based	Accounting Changes

Author	Title	School	Date	pp	Methodology	Topic
Riise, Arne J.	AN INQUIRY INTO COST ACCOUNTING MODELS AS A SOURCE FOR INFORMATION FOR MANAGERIAL DECISION MAKING	Illinois	78	2809	Archival	Managerial
Rittenberg, Larry E.	THE IMPACT OF INTERNAL AUDITING DURING THE EDP APPLICATION DESIGN PROCESS ON PERCEPTIONS OF INTERNAL AUDIT INDEPENDENCE	Minnesota	75	253	Field Study	Auditing
Rivera Fernandez, Juan Manuel	A CRITICAL STUDY OF THE ACCOUNTING AND ECONOMIC EVALUATION OF MEXICAN PUBLIC INVESTMENT PROJECTS IN ROADS AND IRRIGATION	Illinois	75	196	Field Study	Financial
Rivers, Richard A.	A NETWORK THEORETIC APPROACH TO FORECASTING AND BUDGETING	Kent St	76	113	Model- based	Managerial
Ro, Byung-Tak	THE DISCLOSURE OF CAPITALIZED LEASE INFORMATION AND STOCK PRICE	Mich St	76	151	Market- based	Leases
Robbins, Walter A.	THE IMPORTANCE OF SELECTED INFORMATION ITEMS TO MUNICIPAL BOND ANALYSIS AND THEIR DISCLOSURE IN MUNICIPAL ANNUAL REPORTS: AN EMPIRICAL ASSESSMENT	Tenn	82	154	Field Study	Not-for-profit
Roberts, Martin B.	AN INVESTIGATION OF GUIDELINES FOR REVIEW AND EVALUATION OF ACCOUNTING CONTROLS IN DATA BASE MANAGEMENT SYSTEMS	Ga St	80	268	Field Study	Systems/ Computers
Roberts, Ray	EVOLUTION OF FINANCIAL AUDIT CRITERIA WITH EMPHASIS ON SELECTED LEGAL AND REGULATORY INFLUENCES 1917-1972	Santa Cl	78	373	Archival	Auditing
Robinson, Christopher Michael	AN EMPIRICAL INVESTIGATION OF ERROR CORRECTION DECISIONS MADE BY AUDITORS IN PRACTICE	Toronto	85		Experimental	Auditing
Robinson, John R.	THE INFLUENCE OF SELECTED TAX VARIABLES ON PREMIUMS PAID UPON CORPORATE COMBINATION	Michigan	81	112	FinStData-based	Tax

Author	Title	School	Date	pp	Methodology	Topic
Robinson, Michael A.	AN INTEGER GOAL PROGRAMMING METHODOLOGY FOR MULTIPLE OBJECTIVE COST/BENEFIT ANALYSIS OF INTERNAL ACCOUNTING CONTROL SYSTEMS	Illinois	81	112	Experimental	Managerial
Robison, John C.	TAX COURT CLASSIFICATION OF ACTIVITIES NOT ENGAGED IN FOR PROFIT: SOME EMPIRICAL EVIDENCE	Arizona	82	143	Archival	Tax
Rodgers, Fay H.	ACCOUNTING FOR THE EFFECTS OF PRICE LEVEL FLUCTUATIONS: A PROPOSAL	Ga St	76	251	Field Study	Inflation
Rodgers, Waymond	USEFULNESS OF DECISION MAKERS' COGNITIVE PROCESSES IN A COVARIANCE STRUCTURAL MODEL USING FINANCIAL STATEMENT INFORMATION	S Calif	84		Model- based	Financial
Roemmich, Roger A.	STATISTICAL ANALYSIS OF ALTERNATIVE COST ACCOUNTING METHODS	Mich St	75	156	Field Study	Managerial
Rogers, Richard L.	THE PERCEIVED VALUE OF AUDITING CURRENT COST FINANCIAL INFORMATION: AN EMPIRICAL INVESTIGATION	Penn St	81	134	Field Study	Inflation
Rogow, Robert B.	AN ANALYSIS OF THE IMPACT OF PROPERTY TAX CREDIT/REBATE PROGRAMS ON STATE REVENUES AND TAX EQUITY	Arkansas	76	451	Experimental	Tax
Rohrbach, Kermit J.	MONETARY UNIT ACCEPTANCE SAMPLING: SEQUENTIAL AND FIXED SAMPLE SIZE PLANS FOR SUBSTANTIVE TESTS IN AUDITING	Illinois	83	209	Experimental	Auditing
Rolfe, Robert J.	AN EMPIRICAL INVESTIGATION INTO THE JUDICIAL CLASSIFICATION OF TRANSACTIONS AS SALES OR LEASES FOR FEDERAL INCOME TAX PURPOSES	Oklahoma	83	172	Archival	Tax
Romney, Marshall B.	THE ELICITATION OF AUDITORS' PRIOR PROBABILITY DISTRIBUTIONS FOR VARIABLES ESTIMATION	Texas	77	203	Experimental	Auditing

Author	Title	School	Date	pp	Methodology	Topic
Rosanas, Josep M.	CHOICE OF INFORMATION STRUCTURES: ITS EFFECTS ON BELIEFS, EQUILIBRIUM PRICES, AND RESOURCE ALLOCATION IN EXCHANGE AND PRODUCTION ECONOMICS	Northwestern	77	155	Model- based	Financial
Rosen, Louis I.	THE LEGAL PROCESS INVOLVES A DESCRIPTION OF THE ACCOUNTANTS' DISCLOSURE OBLIGATION-AN IN-DEPTH ANALYSIS OF THE CONTINENTAL VENDING MACHINE CO. CASE	Maryland	74	404	Field Study	Profession
Rosenzweig, Kenneth Y.	EFFECTS OF COMPANY ORGANIZATION STRUCTURE ON THE ACCOUNTING SYSTEM	Mich St	77	319	Field Study	Managerial
Roser, Sherman R.	RELEVANCY OF SOCIAL ACCOUNTING INFORMATION FOR DECISION MAKERS: AN EMPIRICAL STUDY	Nebraska	79	167	Field Study	Social
Ross, Ronald S.	AN ANALYSIS OF DISC LEGISLATION AND COMPARISON WITH EXPORT INCENTIVES OF SELECTED FOREIGN COUNTRIES	Texas	78	512	Archival	Tax
Roth, Harold P.	AN EMPIRICAL INVESTIGATION OF A SOCIAL ACCT. ISSUE: A STUDY OF THE ASSOCIATION BETWEEN ENERGY USAGE AND BUSINESS RISK	VPI	80	208	Market- based	Social
Rouse, Robert W.	AN EVALUATION OF THE EFFECTS OF THE FEDERAL TRADE COMMISSION MERGER GUIDELINES UPON THE TEXTILE MILL PRODUCTS INDUSTRY	S Carol	74	154	Field Study	Financial
Rowe, Thomas Milton	AN EMPIRICAL ANALYSIS OF THE QUALITY OF DIOCESAN FINANCIAL DISCLOSURE (AUDITING, CATHOLIC CHURCH, FULL DISCLOSURE, DEPRECIATION)	Texas A&M	85	241	Field Study	Not-for-Profit
Roy, Stephen P.	THE INFORMATION CONTENT OF ANNUAL DIVIDEND ANNOUNCEMENTS	Iowa	79	187	Market- based	Financial
Rozanski, Eugene R.	INVESTOR REACTION TO THE ANNOUNCEMENT OF DISCRETIONARY LOSSES	LSU	75	227	Market- based	Financial

Author	Title	School	Date	pp	Methodology	Topic
Rue, Joseph C.	A STUDY OF ALTERNATIVE COMMON STOCK EQUIVALENCE RULES AS PREDICTORS OF CONVERSION	Penn St	79	135	FinStData-based	Earnings Per Share
Rueschhoff, Donald S.	AN EXPLORATORY STUDY OF SOCIAL PERFORMANCE ACCOUNTING AND THE REACTION OF INDIANA BANKS	Nebraska	79	251	Field Study	Social
Ruffner, Roy A.	RELEVANT ACCT. MEAS. OF INSTRUCTIONAL INPUT/OUTPUT RELATIONSHIPS FOR BUDGETARY AND CONTROL PURPOSE IN PRIVATE LIBERAL ARTS COLLEGES	Missouri	74	178	Field Study	Not-for-profit
Ruland, Robert G.	ETHICS AND ACCOUNTING POLICYMAKING: THE ECONOMIC CONSEQUENCES ISSUE	Illinois	82	231	Archival	Ethics
Ruland, William J.	THE ACCURACY AND INFORMATIONAL CONTENT OF EPS FORECASTS REPORTS BY FIRMS	SUNY-Buf	76	156	FinStData-based	Earnings Per Share
Rupp, Galen L.	A SIMULATION STUDY OF ALTERNATIVE METHODS FOR TRANSLATING FINANCIAL STATEMENTS OF AUTONOMOUS FOREIGN ENTITIES	Okl St.	82	90	Experimental	Foreign Currency
Russell, Keith A.	THE ATTITUDES OF SELECTED ACCT. ED. ABOUT THE INTERACTION BETWEEN THE BIG 8 FIRMS AND ACCT. PROG./ED. ON SELECTED AREAS OF CURRENT INTEREST	Arkansas	81	129	Field Study	Education
Rwegasiru, Kami	THE APPLICATION OF A CREDIT STRENGTH INDEX TO IMPROVE FINANCIAL ANALYSIS IN TANZANIAN COMMERCIAL BANK LENDING	Columbia	79	235	Field Study	Managerial
Ryerson, Frank E.	AN EMPIRICAL EVALUATION OF THE IMPACT OF FINANCIAL ACCT. STDS. BOARD STATEMENT NO. 34 ON THE BEHAVIOR OF SECURITY PRICES	Alabama	83	236	Market- based	Interest Capitalization
Rymer, Victoria Sharp	AN EXPLORATORY STUDY TO EXAMINE THE PRACTICING PUBLIC ACCOUNTANTS' AND COMMERCIAL BANK LOAN OFFICERS' RESISTANCE TO ACCOUNTING INNOVATION AND THE INDIVIDUAL BARRIERS WHICH MAY SERVE TO ENTRENCH THE RESISTANCE	Maryland	83	189	Experimental	Profession

Author	Title	School	Date	pp	Methodology	Topic
Saftner, Donald V.	THE INFORMATION CONTENT OF ASR 190 REPLACEMENT COST DISCLOSURES: AN EFFICIENT MARKET STUDY	Penn St	80	174	Market- based	Inflation
Sage, Lloyd George	RECOGNITION OF THE IMPACT OF CHANGING PRICES ON CONVENTIONAL HISTORICAL COST FINANCIAL STATEMENTS OF HOSPITALS	Nebraska	84	216	FinStData-based	Not-for-profit
Sager, Clayton R.	MARKET BASED RISK MEASURES AND THE ECONOMIC EFFECT OF CAPITAL LEASES	Iowa	81	136	Market- based	Leases
Saghafi, Ali	ACCOUNTING FOR STOCK APPRECIATION RIGHTS	Missouri	79	348	FinStData-based	Financial
Salatka, William Kenneth	A STUDY OF THE CAPITAL MARKET REACTION TO THE ACCOUNTING POLICY DECISION PROCESS RELATING TO FOREIGN CURRENCY ACCOUNTING	Iowa	84	135	Field Study	Foreign Currency
Saldana, Cesar G.	BUDGETARY CONTROL SYSTEMS UNDER UNCERTAINTY, MORAL HAZARD AND MULTI-PERIOD SETTINGS	Northwestern	82	187	Field Study	Managerial
Salimi, Anwar Yazdani	ADJUSTMENTS BY INVESTORS TO ACCOUNTING INCOME FIGURES	UCLA	84	148	Model- based	Financial
Salter, John H.	AN APPLICATION OF SELECTED COMMUNICATION THEORY CONCEPTS TO ACCOUNTING EDUCATION	LSU	75	154	Model- based	Education
Sami, Heibatollah	A COMPARISON OF SFAS 33 DISCLOSURES AND HISTORICAL COST INFORMATION IN PREDICTING STOCK PRICES (INFLATION, CHANGING PRICES)	LSU	84	154	FinStData-based	Inflation
Samson, William D.	CONFORMING THE NO. CAROLINA INDIVIDUAL INCOME TAX TO THE FEDERAL INCOME TAX: AN EMPIRICAL EXAMINATION OF THE SHIFTS IN TAX BURDENS	N Carol	81	329	Archival	Tax

Author	Title	School	Date	pp	Methodology	Topic
Samuelson, Bruce A.	MEASUREMENT THEORY APPLIED TO THE UNCERTAINTY IN ACCOUNTING NUMBERS: A STUDY OF PENDING LITIGATION	S Calif	78		Field Study	Financial
Sanborn, Robert H.	A MULTI DIMENSIONAL MODEL OF BUSINESS COMBINATIONS	Georgia	82	108	FinStData-based	Business Combinations
Sanderson, George Norman	CONTINUING PROFESSIONAL EDUCATION FOR CERTIFIED PUBLIC ACCOUNTANTS: STATE OF THE ART AND PREDICTIONS FOR CHANGE	Nebraska	85	188	Field Study	Profession
Sandretto, Michael J.	THE RELATIVE EFFICIENCY OF SMALLER VERSUS LARGER FIRMS	Illinois	79	154	Market- based	Financial
Sangeladji, Mohamad	A THEORETICAL AND EMPIRICAL INVESTIGATION OF HUMAN RESOURCE ACCOUNTING	Oklahoma	75	239	Field Study	Hum.Resourc e Acct.
Sannella, Alexander	SEGMENT REPORTING: THE COST ALLOCATION ISSUE	NYU	84	224	Field Study	Business Segments
Santos, Dante E.	ASSET STRUCTURE OF MANUFACTURING CORPORATIONS	Santa Cl	76	223	FinStData-based	Financial
Sap, Richard W.	AN EMPIRICAL INVESTIGATION INTO THE RELATIONSHIP BETWEEN LONG-RANGE PLANNING AND BANK PERFORMANCE	Houston	78	182	Field Study	Managerial
Sardians, Joseph L.	COMPUTER SECURITY AND THE AUDITOR'S RESPONSIBILITY	Penn St	75	231	Field Study	Auditing
Sardinha, Jose C.	A LABORATORY STUDY OF THE EFFECTS OF ACCOUNTING VALUATION METHODS ON MANAGER PERFORMANCE UNDER DIFFERENT INFLATION ENVIRONMENTS	S Calif	81		Experimental	Managerial

Author	Title	School	Date	pp	Methodology	Topic
Sarhan, Mostafa H.	AN EMPIRICAL STUDY OF THE EFFECT OF DIVISIONALIZATION ON RISK MEASUREMENT	Arkansas	83	161	Field Study	Managerial
Saubert, Lynn K.	FURTHER EMPIRICAL RESEARCH ON THE PREDICTIVE POTENTIAL OF INTERIM REPORTS	Wiscon	77	315	Field Study	Interim Statements
Saul, William E.	AN EXPER. STUDY OF THE EFFECT OF COMPUTER AUGMENTED INSTRUCTION ON ACHIEVEMENT AND ATTRIBUTION OF BEGIN. ACCT. AT MIAMI-DADE COUNTY COLLEGE, N. CAMPUS	Tenn	74	145	Experimental	Education
Saunders, Gary J.	FROM THE ACCOUNTING PRINCIPLES BOARD TO THE FASB: A CPA'S OPINION SURVEY	Kentucky	77	189	Field Study	Profession
Savage, Linda J.	THE FINANCIAL PREORTING AND DISCLOSURE EFFECTS OF APB OPINION NO. 30	Florida	76	141	FinStData-based	E.O.Items
Sayre, Julian R.	EQUITY IN THE FEDERAL TAXATION OF INDIVIDUALS' GAINS AND LOSSES FROM TRANSACTIONS IN ASSETS DURING A PERIOD OF INFLATION	Arizona	80	275	Experimental	Tax
Sbrocchi, Frank L.	A SURVEY OF REGISTERED INDUSTRIAL ACCOUNTANTS ON THE IMPORTANCE OF SELECTED MANAGEMENT ACCOUNTING TOPICS	Concord	82		Field Study	Education
Schaefer, Thomas F.	THE INFORMATION EFFECTS OF CURRENT COST INCOME AS COMPARED TO DIVIDENDS AND HISTORICAL COST INCOME	Illinois	83	94	Market- based	Inflation
Scheiner, James H.	ACCOUNTING POLICY DETERMINATION: A DECISION MODEL APPROACH	Ohio St	75	238	Model- based	Profession
Schell, Wayne Morris	AN ANALYSIS OF CERTAIN TAX AVOIDANCE TECHNIQUES AVAILABLE UNDER VIRGINIA LAW TO MULTISTATE CORPORATE BUSINESSES	VPI	84	247	Archival	Tax

Author	Title	School	Date	pp	Methodology	Topic
Schepanski, Albert A.	COGNITIVE INFORMATION PROCESSING CREDIT JUDGEMENT	Illinois	78	202	Experimental	Financial
Schilit, Howard M.	AN EMPIRICAL STUDY OF AUDITOR INDEPENDENCE	Maryland	81	183	Field Study	Auditing
Schipper, Katherine	AN ANALYSIS OF THE FINANCIAL CONDITION OF PRIVATE COLLEGES	Chicago	77		Field Study	Not-for-profit
Schmidgall, Raymond S.	AN EMP. INV. OF THE ATTITUDES OF FIN. ST. PREPARERS, AUDITORS, AND USERS REGARDING THE INT. ACCT. CONTROL PROV. OF THE FOR. COR. PRAC. ACT OF 1977	Mich St	80	263	Field Study	Auditing
Schmidt, Richard J.	CURRENT REPLACEMENT COST ACCT. OBJECTIVES: REPLACEMENT COST CONCEPTS AND THE MEASUREMENT OF REPLACEMENT COSTS	Santa Cl	79	163	Model- based	Inflation
Schmutte, James L.	AN EMPIRICAL INVESTIGATION OF THE FIDELITY OF ACCOUNTING COMMUNICATION	Kentucky	83	197	Experimental	Financial
Schneider, Arnold	EXTERNAL AUDITOR'S EVALUATIONS OF INTERNAL AUDITING: A CONJOINT MEASUREMENT APPROACH	Ohio St	82	217	Experimental	Auditing
Schneider, Harold C.	AN EMPIRICAL INVESTIGATION OF DIFFERENT APPROACHES TO ACCOUNTING FOR CHANGING PRICES	Missouri	81	189	FinStData-based	Inflation
Schoch, Hubert P.	A COMPARATIVE STUDY OF SELECTED REPORTING PRACTICES IN FOUR COUNTRIES	American	74	482	FinStData-based	International
Schreiner, Paul W.	STOCK MARKET REACTION TO MANAGEMENT EPS FORECASTS	Illinois	76	103	Market- based	Forecasts

Author	Title	School	Date	pp	Methodology	Topic
Schroeder, Douglas A.	EXPECTATIONS DATA AND THE STOCHASTIC PROPERTIES OF ACCOUNTING NUMBERS: A MULTIPLE TIME SERIES METHODOLOGY	Kansas	80	203	FinStData-based	Stochastic Properties
Schroeder, Jack D.	POTENTIAL SIMPLIFICATION OF THE FEDERAL INCOME TAX LAW BY ELIMINATING SPECIAL TREATMENT OF CAPITAL GAINS AND LOSSES	Mich St	75	172	Archival	Tax
Schroeder, Mary S.	AN EMPIRICAL INVESTIGATION OF AUDIT COMMITTEE MEMBERS' PERCEPTION OF AUDIT QUALITY	Arizona	83	178	Field Study	Auditing
Schroeder, Nicholas Waldo	THE ASSOCIATION OF EARNINGS MANAGEMENT AND DEGREE OF SEPARATION OF OWNERSHIP AND CONTROL	Colorado	84	213	Field Study	Financial
Schroeder, Richard G.	THE EFFECTS OF LOCALISM-COSMOPOLITANISM AND PERCEIVED BUREAUCRATIC STRUCTURE ON SELECTED ATTITUDES OF CERTIFIED PUBLIC ACCOUNTANTS	Ariz St	74	189	Field Study	Profession
Schueller, Robert H.	USEFUL INFORMATION IN PUBLIC SCHOOL ADMINISTRATION	Missouri	74	409	Field Study	Not-for-profit
Schugart, Gary L.	A DISCRIMINANT ANALYSIS OF EXCEPTIONAL EARNINGS GROWTH	Kansas	74	120	FinStData-based	Financial
Schultq, Joseph J.	THE INDEPENDENT AUDITOR AND ROLE CONFLICT RESOLUTION	Texas	74	292	Field Study	Auditing
Schultz, Norman O.	MICROCOMPUTER ACQUISITION AND USAGE STRATEGIES IN ORGANIZATIONS: AN EMPIRICAL INVESTIGATION	Utah	83	153	Field Study	Systems/ Computers
Schwartz, Bill N.	ESTIMATING DEFERRED TAXES USING PARTIAL TAX ALLOCATION AND DETERMINING ITS IMPACT ON THE FINANCIAL STATEMENTS: AN EMPIRICAL STUDY	UCLA	78	262	Experimental	Tax

Author	Title	School	Date	pp	Methodology	Topic
Schwartz, Kenneth B.	ACCOUNTING RESPONSE TO FINANCIAL LIQUIDITY CONSTRAINTS	Syracuse	82	114	FinStData-based	Auditing
Schwarzbach, Henry R.	AUDITING MGMT. INFORMATION SYSTEMS: AN EMPIRICAL INVESTIGATION OF THE IMPORTANCE OF MGMT. INFORMATION SYSTEMS AUDITS	Colorado	76	420	Field Study	Auditing
Schweikart, James	THE VALUE OF MANAGERIAL ACCOUNTING INFORMATION TO U.S. MANUFACTURING FIRMS ABROAD	Indiana	84	137	Field Study	Managerial
Scott, Edward R.	AN EMPIRICAL TEST OF THE STOCK MARKET RESPONSE TO THE CONSISTENCY EXCEPTION IN AUDITORS' REPORTS	Illinois	74	129	Market- based	Auditing
Seamans, Dana Gerald	AN ANALYSIS OF THE FEDERAL TAX RAMIFICATIONS OF GOODWILL	Texas Tech	85		Archival	Tax
Seat, Donald L.	A LOGICAL AND EMPIRICAL INVESTIGATION OF THE RELEVANT DECISION VARIABLES IN SUPREME COURT ESTATE AND GIFT TAX CASES	Kentucky	80	218	Archival	Tax
Sefcik, Stephen E.	THE INFORMATION CONTENT OF DIVIDENDS: AN EMPIRICAL ANALYSIS OF WARRANTS CONDUCTED BY EXAM. OF THE IMPLIED VARIABILITY OF STOCK PRICES	Illinois	83	173	Market- based	Financial
Selama, Yehia A.	AN EMP. INV. OF THE INFORMATION CONTENT OF THE STATEMENT OF FIN. ACCT. STDS. NO.34 CAPITALIZATION OF INTEREST COSTS	Alabama	83	147	Market- based	Interest Capitalization
Selin, John R.	A CRITICAL ANALYSIS OF THE FINANCIAL ACCOUNTING AND REPORTING PRACTICES IN THE INSTITUTIONALLY-OPERATED BOOKSTORES OF FOUR SELECTED UNIVERSITIES IN WISCONSIN	Minnesota	74	349	Field Study	Not-for-profit
Sellers, Fred Evans	ZERO-BASE BUDGETING: IMPLICATIONS FOR THE DESIGN OF ACCOUNTING SYSTEMS (ORGANIZATIONAL BEHAVIOR, ENVIRONMENTAL SCARCITY)	Kansas	84	244	Field Study	Managerial

Author	Title	School	Date	pp	Methodology	Topic
Selling, Thomas I.	COGNITIVE PROCESSES IN INFORMATION SYSTEM CHOICE	Ohio St	82	277	Experimental	Systems/ Computers
Selph, Carl J.	FINANCIAL RATIOS AS INDICATORS OF REPAYMENT OR DEFAULT OF BANK LOANS TO SMALL BUSINESSES: A MULTIVARIATE DISCRIMINANT ANALYSIS	Fla St	79	207	FinStData- based	Financial Ratios
Selto, Frank H.	INFORMATION AND DECISION MODEL EVALUATION FOR WILDERNESS MANAGEMENT	Wash	77	167	Experimental	Managerial
Senatra, Phillip T.	AUDITORS' PERCEPTIONS OF ROLE CONFLICT AND ROLE AMBIGUITY IN PUBLIC ACCT. FIRMS: AN EMPIRICAL STUDY	Iowa	76	260	Field Study	Profession
Sepe, James F.	THE IMPACT OF THE FASB'S PROPOSAL FOR GENERAL PRICE-LEVEL ADJUSTED FINANCIAL INFORMATION ON THE SECURITY PRICE STRUCTURE	Wash	80	123	Market- based	Inflation
Seville, Mary Alice	USER AND PROVIDER PERCEIVED IMPORTANCE OF INFORMATION ABOUT VOLUNTARY HEALTH AND WELFARE ORGANIZATIONS	Illinois	83	241	Field Study	Not-for-Profit
Shaaban, Hamed A.	A NORMATIVE CAPITAL MAINTENANCE MODEL FOR DEPRECIABLE ASSETS PURCHASED FROM A FOREIGN COUNTRY DURING A TIME OF INFLATION	Nebraska	82	164	Model- based	Inflation
Shalchi, Hossein	A COMP. STUDY OF TIME SERIES BEHAVIOR AND PREDICTIVE ABILITY OF HIST. COST EARN. AND GEN. PURCH. POWER ADJUSTED EARN.: AN EMPIRICAL INVESTIGATION	Indiana	81	153	FinStData- based	Inflation
Shaltout, Mohanned K.	AN INVESTIGATION OF DIFFERENT ACCT. PRIN. AND CONCEPTS AMONG ACCOUNTANTS IN EGYPT: A COMMUNICATION APPROACH	Miss St	83	278	Field Study	International
Shane, Philip B.	INTERNALIZATION OF SOCIAL COSTS AND THE VALUE OF THE FIRM: A DESCRIPTIVE EMPIRICAL STUDY	Oregon	82	202	Field Study	Social

Author	Title	School	Date	pp	Methodology	Topic
Sharifi Fardi, Moshen	A PRAGMATIC APPROACH TO DEVELOPMENT AND APPLICATION OF TOTAL INFORMATION SYSTEMS	LSU	75	350	Model- based	Systems/ Computers
Sharp, Durwin L.	CONSISTENCY BASED ACCOUNTING POLICY: A MULTIDIMENSIONAL PERSPECTIVE	UCLA	79	293	Field Study	Financial
Sharp, Florence C.	LEASE VS PURCHASE: A FIELD STUDY OF ASSET ACQUISITION DECISIONS IN MUNICIPAL GOVERNMENT	Illinois	82	182	Field Study	Not-for-profit
Sharp, Robert F.	INVESTIGATING RELIABILITY AND COMPARABILITY OF ALTERNATIVE ACCOUNTING MODELS IN ESTIMATING AND PREDICTING DISTRIBUTABLE CAPITAL	Texas	78	307	FinStData-based	Financial
Sheldahl, Terry K.	DEVELOPMENT OF A CODE OF PROFESSIONAL ETHICS FOR MANAGEMENT ACCOUNTANTS	Alabama	79	578	Field Study	Ethics
Sheldon, Debra	THE CONCEPTUAL PROBLEMS OF FORECASTED EPS FOR PUBLISHED FIN. ST. FROM THE PERSPECTIVE OF THE PUBLIC AUDITOR'S ATTEST FUNCTION	Geo Wash	81	297	FinStData-based	Auditing
Shelton, Fred A.	TIME SERIES ASSOCIATION OF EARNINGS FORECAST ERRORS AND ABNORMAL SECURITY RETURNS	Iowa	78	176	Market- based	Forecasts
Sheriff, Jimmy D.	AN EMPIRICAL INVESTIGATION OF ATTITUDES TOWARD CURRENT VALUES AMONG ACCT. GROUPS IN SOUTH CAROLINA	Georgia	76	197	Field Study	Inflation
Sherman, H. David	MEASUREMENT OF HOSPITAL TECHNICAL EFFICIENCY: A COMPARATIVE EVALUATION OF DATA ENVELOPMENT ANALYSIS AND OTHER EFFICIENCY MEASUREMENT TECHNIQUES FOR MEASURING AND LOCATING INEFFICIENCY IN HEALTH CARE ORGANIZATIONS	Harvard	81	382	Field Study	Not-for-profit
Sheteini, Idris A.	A VALUE-ADDED APPROACH TO CORPORATE FINANCIAL REPORTING	Missouri	81	272	Model- based	Financial

Author	Title	School	Date	pp	Methodology	Topic
Shields, Michael D.	AN EMPIRICAL INQUIRY INTO THE EFFECTS OF INFORMATION LOAD ON PERFORMANCE REPORT ANALYSIS PROCESSES	Pitt	78	214	Experimental	Managerial
Shields, Paul D.	THE CPA FIRM REFERRAL BEHAVIOR OF ATTORNEYS AND BANKERS FOR A TYPICAL SMALL BUSINESS	Michigan	80	221	Field Study	Profession
Shimerda, Thomas A.	FINANCIAL RATIOS AS PREDICTORS OF PROFITABILITY	Nebraska	78	241	FinStData-based	Financial Ratios
Shin, Joon Y.	INCOMPLETE INFO., MORAL HAZARD, AND HIERARCHIAL STRUC., ACCT. INF. SYS. AS AN INCOMPLETE MONITORING DEVICE IN THE CONTEXT OF THE THEORY OF THE FIRM	Minnesota	83	72	Model- based	Managerial
Shook, Charles H.	BEHAVIORAL OBJECTIVES AS A COMMUNICATIONS LINK BETWEEN ACCOUNTING PRACTICE AND ACADEMIC PREPARATION	Okl St	79	171	Experimental	Education
Short, Daniel G.	THE USEFULNESS OF PRICE-LEVEL ADJUSTED ACCOUNTING NUMBERS IN THE CONTEXT OF RISK ASSESSMENT	Michigan	77	142	Market- based	Inflation
Shoulders, Craig D.	CRITERIA FOR IDENTIFYING THE MUNICIPAL ORGANIZATIONAL REPORTING ENTITY	Txs Tech	82	201	Field Study	Not-for-profit
Shriver, Keith Alva	ALTERNATIVE CURRENT COST MEASUREMENTS OF INDUSTRIAL MACHINERY AND EQUIPMENT	Texas at Austin	83	250	Field Study	Inflation
Siegel, Gary H.	SEGMENTATION IN THE ACCOUNTING PROFESSION	Illinois	77	151	Field Study	Profession
Siegel, Joel G.	THE CONCEPT OF THE QUALITY OF EARNINGS: ANALYSIS AND EVALUATION	CUNY-Bar	78	389	Field Study	Financial

Author	Title	School	Date	pp	Methodology	Topic
Sil, Amar Nath	VALUATION OF A CORPORATE PENSION PUT OPTION AND ITS EFFECT ON PENSION LIABILITY	Columbia	84	84	Experimental	Pensions
Silhan, Peter A.	THE PREDICTIVE ABILITY OF ENTITY VERSUS SUB-ENTITY EARNINGS: A TEST USING SIMULATED MERGERS OF EXISTENT AUTONOMOUS FIRMS	Tenn	80	134	Experimental	Financial
Silvester, Wilfred H.	ANALYSIS OF FRAUD CASES-AIDS TO THE AUDITOR	Missouri	78	241	Archival	Auditing
Simiar, Farhad	APPLICATION OF DISCOUNTED CASH FLOW TECHNIQUES IN VALUATION OF OIL AND GAS RESERVES	S Calif	75		FinStData-based	Oil & Gas
Simkins, Allen F.	AN EMPIRICAL STUDY INTO THE IMPORTANCE OF THE THIRD MOMENT IN INVESTMENT SELECTION	Ariz St	76	172	Experimental	Financial
Simon, Daniel T.	COMPENSATION EFFECTS AND ACCOUNTING CHANGES: AN EMPIRICAL EXAMINATION	Northwestern	83	173	FinStData-based	Managerial
Simon, John R.	STANDARDS FOR THE EVALUATION OF INTERNAL CONTROL-AN EMPIRICAL TEST IN THE PUBLIC SECTOR	Illinois	74	238	Field Study	Auditing
Singh, Dan	THE IMPACT OF IMPROVED FINANCIAL DISCLOSURE ON THE COST OF EQUITY CAPITAL	Arizona	77		FinStData-based	Financial
Singleton, William R.	AN EMPIRICAL STUDY OF THE EFFECTS OF TAXATION ON INVESTMENT EXPENDITURES BY SELECTED FIRMS IN THE FORREST PRODUCTS INDUSTRY	Hawaii	83	246	FinStData-based	Tax
Sinning, Kathleen E.	AN EVALUATION OF THE INFORMATION CONTENT OF STATEMENT OF FINANCIAL ACCOUNTING STANDARDS NO. 2	Mich St	78	105	Market- based	Research & Development

Author	Title	School	Date	pp	Methodology	Topic
Skantz, Tereance R.	A SYNTACTICAL AND SEMANTICAL ANALYSIS OF ACCOUNTING EXPLANATION	Okl St.	79	199	Model- based	Financial
Skeith, Arlette W.	FORECASTING TECHNIQUES FOR ANALYTICAL REVIEWS: AN EMPIRICAL INVESTIGATION OF LINEAR REGRESSION AND ARIMA	Arkansas	83	188	Experimental	Auditing
Skekel, Ted D.	AN EMPIRICAL INVESTIGATION OF RELATIONSHIPS OF SELECTED FIRM ATTRIBUTES AND PERFORMANCE VARIABLES TO VOLUNTARY ACCOUNTING CHANGES	Oregon	77	143	FinStData-based	Accounting Changes
Skousen, Clifford R.	THE ACCOUNTING PROFESSION AND PUBLIC SERVICE ACTIVITIES	Gold Gate	79	201	Field Study	Profession
Slavin, Nathan S.	ROLE AMBIGUITY AND CONFLICT IN AN ALIEN AUDIT ENVIRONMENT	CUNY-Bar	80	411	Experimental	Auditing
Slaymaker, Adrianne Lee Einfeldt	THE LEASE: A DEDUCTIVE ANALYSIS OF THE ACCOUNTING REQUIREMENTS OF SFAS NO. 13 AS AMMENDED WITH A NORMATIVE MODLE OF THE ECONOMIC SUBSTANCE	Kentucky	84	344	Field Study	Leases
Smieliauskas, Waldemar J.	SIMULATION ANALYSIS OF THE STATISTICAL VALIDITY OF THE INTERNAL CONTROL HYPOTHESIS OF AUDITING WITH IMPLICATIONS FOR SUBSTANTIVE TESTING METHODS AND LINKAGE RULES	Wiscon	80	448	Experimental	Auditing
Smith, Abbie Jean	AN EMPIRICAL INVESTIGATION OF THE INFORMATION EFFECTS OF A CHANGE IN THE FINANCIAL REPORTING STANDARDS FOR OIL AND GAS PRODUCERS: THE PROPOSED ELIMINATION AND SUBSEQUENT RETENTION OF FULL COST ACCOUNTING	Cornell	81	245	Market- based	Oil & Gas
Smith, Alvin G.	THE ORGANIZATIONAL STRUCTURES OF SELECTED LARGE PUBLIC ACCOUNTING FIRMS	Oklahoma	74	203	Field Study	Profession
Smith, David B.	AN EXAMINATION OF THE RISK DETERMINANTS OF NONCONVERTIBLE CUMULATIVE PREFERRED STOCK	Illinois	79	218	Market- based	Financial

Author	Title	School	Date	pp	Methodology	Topic
Smith, Emmett D.	THE EFFECT OF THE SEPARATION OF OWNERSHIP FROM CONTROL ON ACCOUNTING POLICY DECISIONS	Ohio St	74	129	FinStData-based	Managerial
Smith, George S.	AN INVESTIGATION INTO ACCOUNTANT-CLIENT PRIVELEDGED COMMUNICATIONS IN THE COURTROOM	Arkansas	78	297	Archival	Profession
Smith, Howard Gromel	THE STUDY OF THE IMPLICATIONS OF SFAS 33 TO THE SMALL BUSINESS ENTERPRISE: USEFULNESS IN LONG-TERM LOAN APPLICATIONS	Texas Tech	85		FinStData-based	Inflation
Smith, James D.	AN ANALYSIS OF OVERLAP AND CONFLICT BETWEEN THE ACCOUNTING RULES OF THE CASB, FASB, AND SEC	Nebraska	79	154	Field Study	Profession
Smith, James F.	A CONTINGENCY MODEL FOR THE SELECTION OF DECISION STRATEGIES: SOME EXTENSIONS AND EMPIRICAL TESTS	Wash	80	244	Experimental	Managerial
Smith, Janice A.	THE MEASUREMENT OF INVESTMENT CENTER MANAGERIAL PERFORMANCE WITHIN SELECTED DIVERSIFIED FIRMS: AN INQUIRY	LSU	75	237	Field Study	Managerial
Smith, Julian D.	A THEORETICAL STUDY OF THE EFFECT OF VARIOUS ASSUMPTIONS REGARDING THE USE OF WARRANT PROCEEDS ON EPS COMPUTATIONS	LSU	75	349	FinStData-based	Earnings Per Share
Smith, Lawrence M.	AN INQUIRY INTO FACTORS AFFECTING FEES OF LOUISIANA CPA FIRMS	La Tech	83	125	Field Study	Profession
Smith, Maureen H.	THE EFFECTS OF VARIATIONS IN ACCT. SEGMENT REPORTING LEVELS ON THE EARNINGS PROJECTIONS OF FINANCIAL ANALYSTS	Ohio St	79	214	Field Study	Business Segments
Smith, Roy	THE EXTENT OF USE OF MANAGERIAL ACCT. TECHNIQUE IN MUNICIPAL GOV'T FUNDS MGMT. AND PURPORTEDLY RELATED CAUSAL FACTORS	N Col	82	411	Field Study	Not-for-profit

Author	Title	School	Date	pp	Methodology	Topic
Smith, Wilbur Irvin	DECISION AIDS FOR THE INDEPENDENT AUDITOR'S PRELIMINARY EVALUATION OF INTERNAL ACCOUNTING CONTROL: AN EMPIRICAL ANALYSIS OF CHERNOFF FACES AND DYADIC AUDIT TEAMS	Wiscon	84	343	Experimental	Auditing
Sneed, Florence Richwood	A STUDY OF THE EFFECTS OF CONVERSATION ON THE EVIDENTIAL SAMPLE-SIZE DECISIONS MADE BY AUDITORS.	N Txs St	79	131	Experimental	Auditing
Snow, Charles J.	CHARACTERISTICS OF FIRMS WHICH MAKE DISCRETIONARY ACCOUNTING CHANGES	NYU	80	151	FinStData-based	Accounting Changes
Snowball, Douglas Alexander Thomas	ACCOUNTING AND HUMAN INFORMATION PROCESSING SYSTEMS.	Wash	75	429	Experimental	Financial
Snyder, Andrew G.	THE ECONOMIC IMPLICATIONS OF A DECOMPOSITION ANALYSIS OF THE RISK CHAR. OF SELECTED PROPERTIES OF EARNING FORECASTS AND FORECAST ERRORS	Purdue	81	269	FinStData-based	Forecasts
Soliman, Soliman Youssef	A STATISTICAL ANALYSIS OF THE RELIABILITY OF INTERNAL CONTROL SYSTEMS.	Georgia	79	187	Model- based	Managerial
Soloman, Lanny M.	COMPUTER-ASSISTED INSTRUCTION IN UNDERGRADUATE ACCOUNTING EDUCATION	Case Wes	74	222	Field Study	Education
Solomon, Ira	AGGREGATING PRIOR PROBABILITY DISTRIBUTIONS FOR AUDIT DECISION MAKING.	Texas	79	374	Experimental	Auditing
Sorkin, Horton L.	AN EMPIRICAL STUDY OF THREE CONFIRMATION TECHNIQUES: DESIREABLILITY OF EXPANDING THE RESPONDENTS' DECISION FIELD	Minnesota	77	210	Experimental	Auditing
Soroosh Joo, Jalaleddin	AN EMPIRICAL INVESTIGATION OF THE INFORMATIONAL CONTENT OF THE SUPPLEMENTARY DATA REQUIRED BY THE FASB STATEMENT NO. 33, FINANCIAL REPORTING AND CHANGING PRICES.	Miss	81	183	Market- based	Inflation

Author	Title	School	Date	pp	Methodology	Topic
Spede, Edward C.	THE ROLE OF ACCOUNTANTS IN THE FEDERAL TAX PROCESS: AN EMPIRICAL INVESTIGATION	VPI	82	230	Field Study	Tax
Spero, Abba V.	FINANCIAL PROFILE OF FIRMS REPURCHASING THEIR OWN STOCK	NYU	76	110	Market- based	Financial
Spero, Leslie Lawrence	THE EXTENT AND CAUSES OF VOLUNTARY DISCLOSURE OF FINANCIAL INFORMATION IN THREE EUROPEAN CAPITAL MARKETS: AN EXPLORATORY STUDY.	Harvard	79	355	FinStData-based	Financial
Spiceland, J. David	AN EMPIRICAL INVESTIGATION OF PUBLISHED RISK MEASURES AS DETERMINANTS OF DEBENTURE YIELD DIFFERENTIALS	Arkansas	76	183	Market- based	Bonds
Spicer, Barry H.	INVESTORS, ENVIRONMENTAL PROTECTION, AND THE CAPITAL MARKET: AN EMPIRICAL INVESTIGATION	Wash	76	103	Market- based	Social
Srinidhi, Bindiganavale Narayan	PROBABILITY MODELING OF INTERNAL CONTROL SYSTEMS IN AUDIT DECISION MAKING	Columbia	84	169	Model- based	Auditing
Srivasteva, Rajendre P.	THE RELIABILITY OF INTERNAL ACCOUNTING CONTROL SYSTEMS; DESIGN AND ANALYSIS	Oklahoma	82	197	Model- based	Systems/ Computers
St. Pierre, Kent Edgar	AUDITOR RISK AND LEGAL LIABILITY.	Wash U	81	174	Archival	Auditing
Stagliano, Anthony J.	FEDREAL CORPORATE TAXATION OF LIFE INSURANCE COMPANIES: AN EMPIRICAL INVESTIGATION OF SHORTRUN SHIFTING BEHAVIOR	Illinois	77	254	FinStData-based	Tax
Stambaugh, Clyde T.	THE EFFECTS OF ERRORS ON SAMPLE SIZE FOR SAMPLE RANDOM STRATIFIED, AND DUS ESTIMATION, AND IMPLICATIONS FOR AUDITORS	Kentucky	81	221	Experimental	Auditing

Author	Title	School	Date	pp	Methodology	Topic
Stanga, Keith G.	AN EMPIRICAL STUDY OF THE EXTENT OF DISCLOSURE IN THE PUBLISHED ANNUAL REPORTS OF LARGE INDUSTRIAL CORPORATIONS	LSU	74	211	Field Study	Financial
Starr, Douglas Alan	A SENSITIVITY ANALYSIS OF THE RISK-ADJUSTED AND CERTAINTY-EQUIVALENT INVESTMENT EVALUATION TECHNIQUES: A SIMULATION.	Penn St	78	296	Experimental	Managerial
Steed, Steve Alan	AN EMPIRICAL STUDY OF THE EFFECTIVENESS OF INDEPENDENCE DISCRIMINATION RESULTING FROM THE APPLICATION OF AICPA ETHICAL INTERPRETATION 101-3--ACCOUNTING SERVICES	N Txs St	85	177	Field Study	Ethics
Steedle, Lamont F.	EVALUATING CAPITAL EXPENDITURE DECISION CRITERIA: A CORPORATE FINANCIAL PLANNING MODEL APPROACH	Penn St	78	132	Experimental	Financial
Steinbart, Paul John	THE CONSTRUCTION OF AN EXPERT SYSTEM TO MAKE MATERIALITY JUDGMENTS	Mich St	85	158	Archival	Auditing
Stephens, Lynn M.	AN EMP. INVEST. OF THE CONNECTION BETWEEN FINANCIAL RATIOS AND OPERATING CHARACTERISTICS OF HOMOGENEOUS GROUPS OF MANUFACTURING FIRMS	Nebraska	83	339	FinStData-based	Financial Ratios
Stephens, Ray G.	USES OF FINANCIAL INFORMATION IN STRUCTURING AND IMPROVING DECISION PROCESSES FOR BANK LENDING OFFICERS	Harvard	78	365	Experimental	Financial
Stern, Myles S.	ACCOUNTING INFORMATION FOR ENVIRONMENTAL DECISIONS	Mich St	74	280	Field Study	Social
Sterner, Julia Ann	AN ANALYSIS OF THE COMMON STOCK EQUIV. TEST FOR CONVERTIBLE BONDS AS USED IN APB OP. #15 AND THE SELECTION OF VARIABLES TO PREDICT CONVERSION	Saint Louis	82	265	Market- based	Earnings Per Share
Stevens, William Patrick	MARKET REACTION TO CORPORATE SOCIAL PERFORMANCE.	Illinois	80	229	Market- based	Social

Author	Title	School	Date	pp	Methodology	Topic
Stevenson, Francis Liddell Jr.	AN EMPIRICAL TEST OF THE FIFO/LIFO CHANGE (DISCRETIONARY QUARTERLY, UNEXPECTED)	Oregon	84	170	FinStData-based	Inventory
Stewart, Dave Nelson	EMPLOYEE OR INDEPENDENT CONTRACTOR: AN EXAMINATION OF THE RELEVANT VARIABLES EMPLOYED BY THE FEDERAL COURTS IN DECIDING THE QUESTION.	Florida	80	198	Archival	Tax
Stewart, John Ray	THE EFFECT ON ACHIEVEMENT IN ELEMENTARY ACCOUNTING OF DIAGNOSTIC TESTING AND REMEDIAL INDIVIDUALIZED INSTRUCTION USING AUDIOVISUAL MATERIALS.	N Colo	77	153	Experimental	Education
Stillabower, Linda May	UNITED STATES TAXATION OF FOREIGN DIRECT INVESTMENT OF UNITED STATES CORPORATIONS: AN ANALYSIS OF SELECTED PROPOSALS FOR REFORM.	Case Wes	82	245	Archival	Tax
Stiner, Frederic M.	THE ATTITUDES OF CPA'S TOWARDS SOCIAL ACCT.: A SURVEY OF NATIONAL AND NEBRASKA OPINION	Nebraska	76	198	Field Study	Social
Stivers, Bonnie La Von Philbrook	CONTROL AND AUDITABILITY FEATURES OF SELECTED SMALL BUSINESS COMPUTER ACCOUNTING SYSTEMS	Ga St	83	262	Experimental	Systems/Computers
Stocks, Kevin Dayna	AN ANALYSIS OF PERFORMANCE EVALUATION USING SINGLE AND MULTIPLE ATTRIBUTES IN A SHORT-RUN AND A LONG-RUN SETTING.	Okl St	81	159	Experimental	Managerial
Stolar, Robert W.	A PROPOSED FLOW OF RESOURCES MODEL WITH PARTICULAR REFERENCE TO THE NATIONAL ACCOUNTS OF THE UNITED STATES AND CANADA	Florida	78	169	Model- based	Financial
Stone, Kenneth E.	ACCOUNTING FOR ISSUANCE OF STOCK DIVIDENDS: AN EVALUATION OF THE 20-25% GUIDELINE	Missouri	76	109	Market- based	Stock Distributions
Stone, Mary Sheetz	AN EXAMINATION OF THE EFFECT OF DISCLOSURES CONCERNING UNFUNDED PENSION BENEFITS ON MARKET RISK MEASURES.	Illinois	81	251	Market- based	Pensions

Author	Title	School	Date	pp	Methodology	Topic
Stone, Ronald Summer	THE INFLUENCE OF ORDER OF PRESENTATION OF FINANCIAL AND NON-FINANCIAL INFORMATION ON EVALUATIONS OF FIRM PERFORMANCE: AN EMPIRICAL STUDY	Berkeley	83	277	Experimental	Statement Presentation
Stout, David E.	EMPIRICAL TESTS OF THE EQUITY VALUATION MODEL	Pitt	82	236	FinStData-based	Financial
Stout, Gary Raymond	TAX POLICY AND CAPITAL FORMATION: AN EMPIRICAL ANALYSIS OF THE POTENTIAL DIFFERENTIAL IMPACT OF THE ITC	S Calif	77		Field Study	Tax
Stratton, William O.	ACCOUNTING INTERNAL CONTROL SYSTEMS: THEIR RELIABILITY AND DICHOTOMINIC STRUCTURE FUNCTIONS	Claremnt	77	199	Field Study	Systems/ Computers
Strecker, Mary F.	ACCOUNTING CURRICULUM DESIGN FACTORS	Missouri	74	457	Archival	Education
Streer, Paul J.	AN EMPIRICAL AND ANALYTICAL INVESTIGATION OF ORDINARY AND NECESSARY BUSINESS EXPENSES FOR FEDERAL INCOME TAX PURPOSES	Illinois	78	167	Archival	Tax
Streffeler, John M.	THE IMPACT OF THE TAX REFORM ACT OF 1969 UPON CHARITABLE CONTRIBUTIONS OF ORDINARY INCOME PROPERTY	Arizona	77	205	Field Study	Tax
Strickland, Sherre Geane	DISCRETIONARY ACCOUNTING CHANGES IN RELATION TO INCOME SMOOTHING, FIRM CHARACTERISTICS AND BANKRUPTCY PREDICTION MODELS.	Txs A&M	81	146	FinStData-based	Accounting Changes
Strobel, Caroline D.	THE MARITAL DEDUCTION AFTER THE TAX REFORM ACT OF 1976	Georgia	78	215	Experimental	Tax
Stryker, Judson P.	THE EFFECTS OF SUPPLEMENTAL INFLATION ACCOUNTING INFORMATION ON THE INVESTMENT DECISION PROCESS: AN EMPIRICAL STUDY	Miss St	81	212	Experimental	Inflation

Author	Title	School	Date	pp	Methodology	Topic
Stumbaugh, Charles C.	THE EFFECT OF COLLEGE ALGEBRA AND HIGH SCHOOL BOOKKEEPING ON ACHIEVEMENT IN THE SECOND COURSE OF ELEMENTARY ACCOUNTING.	Oklahoma	75	100	Field Study	Education
Suadi, Arief	SECURITY PRICE MOVEMENTS IN RESPONSE TO FASB STATEMENT NO. 13.	Missouri	81	144	Market- based	Leases
Suleiman, Nader A.	MUNICIPAL FISCAL STRESS: AN ANALYSIS OF CLASSIFICATION METHODS	S Carol	81	195	Field Study	Not-for-profit
Sullens, Robert T.	EVALUATION OF CURRENT PENSION REPORTING PRACTICES	Kent St	74	242	FinStData-based	Pensions
Sullivan, Mark James	AN INVESTIGATION OF THE ADEQUACY OF THE UNITED STATES' INCOME TAX CAPITAL ALLOWANCE SYSTEM.	Wiscon	79	202	FinStData-based	Tax
Sumners, Glenn Earl	AN EMPIRICAL INVESTIGATION OF THE IMPACT OF THE SENSITIVE PAYMENTS ISSUE AND THE FOREIGN CORRUPT PRACTICES ACT OF 1977 ON THE INTERNAL AUDIT FUNCTION.	Tenn	81	327	Field Study	Auditing
Sunby, Lawrence C.	AN INQUIRY INTO THE RELATIONSHIP BETWEEN PERCEPTIONS OF INDUSTRIAL ENGINEERING AND MANAGEMENT ACCOUNTING IN SELECTED AREAS OF MUTUAL INVOLVEMENT	Nebraska	75	187	Field Study	Managerial
Sunder, Shyam	AN EMPIRICAL STUDY OF STOCK PRICE AND RISK AS THEY RELATE TO ACCOUNTING CHANGES IN INVENTORY VALUATION METHODS.	Carn Mel	74	211	Market- based	Accounting Changes
Sutton, Timothy G.	CORPORATE MANAGEMENT'S ROLE IN THE SETTING OF ACCOUNTING STANDARDS: AN ANALYSIS WITH EMPIRICAL TESTS	Wash	80	237	Field Study	Financial
Swad, Randy Gene	ESOPS AND TAX POLICY: AN EMPIRICAL INVESTIGATION OF THE IMPACT OF ESOPS ON COMPANY OPERATING PERFORMANCE.	LSU	79	163	Field Study	Tax

Author	Title	School	Date	pp	Methodology	Topic
Swanson, Edward P.	THE ABILITY OF ALTERNATIVE REPORTING METHODS TO PREDICT THE SUBSEQUENT PERIOD'S CASH FLOW	Wiscon	77	179	FinStData-based	Cash Flows
Swanson, Gale A.	A LIVING SYSTEMS GENERAL THEORY OF ACCOUNTING	Ga St	82	251	Model- based	Financial
Swanson, Robert Dean	FAMILY FARM EFFICIENCY: IMPLICATIONS FOR THE ESTATE TAXATION OF FARMERS.	Iowa	78	178	Archival	Tax
Swearingen, James G.	INVESTIGATION OF ERROR BEHAVIOR IN ACCOUNTS RECEIVABLE	Wash	82	181	Field Study	Auditing
Sweeney, Janet Ann Lawson	SETTING MATERIALITY GUIDELINES--A MULTI-METHOD APPROACH.	Cornell	77	334	FinStData-based	Auditing
Swenson, Charles William	SOME ALTERNATIVE APPROACHES TO MITIGATING INFLATIONARY EFFECTS ON CORPORATE TAXATION	S Calif	84		Archival	Tax
Swindle, Charles B.	ACCOUNTING RATIOS AS MEASURES OF BENEFITS TO COMPANIES INITIATING PENSION PLANS	LSU	79	106	FinStData-based	Pensions
Swingen, Judyth	THE ALLOCATION AND APPORTIONMENT OF DEDUCTIONS BY MULTINATIONAL ENTERPRISES: AN ANALYSIS OF TREASURY REGULATIONS	Wiscon	84	270	Archival	Tax
Syck, Lawrence J.	PRESENT AND PROPOSED METH. OF TREATM. OF PREPAID INC.-AN ATTEMPT TO EXPAND THE ALLOW. OF DEFERRALS FOR INC. DETERM. IN ACCORD. WITH SEC. 446 AND 451 OF THE 1954 INT. REV. CODE	Arizona	76	288	Archival	Tax
Tabor, John George	THE ROLE OF THE ACCOUNTANT IN THE DETECTION AND PREVENTION OF INFORMATION ABUSES IN SOCIAL PROGRAMS.	Northwestern	78	540	Model- based	Auditing

Author	Title	School	Date	pp	Methodology	Topic
Tabor, Richard Herbert	INTERNAL CONTROL INFORMATION AND AUDIT PROGRAM REVISION: AN EMPIRICAL STUDY OF HUMAN JUDGMENT.	Florida	80	186	Experimental	Auditing
Tackett, James A.	THE IMPACT OF QUALIFIED AUDIT REPORTS ON THE SUBS. AUDIT REPORTS: A TEST CORRELATING LITIGATION AND ASSET REAL. "SUBJECT TO" OPIN. ACROSS TIME	Ohio St	83	103	FinStData-based	Auditing
Tai, Benjamin Yuk-Kwong	POLLUTION CONTROL INVESTMENTS AND TAX INCENTIVES: AN ADAPTATION OF CAPITAL INVESTMENT DECISION MODELS FOR USE BY NOT-FOR-PROFIT INSTITUTIONS.	Missouri	81	339	Field Study	Not-for-profit
Talbott, John Cotton	NORMATIVE HEALTH CARE PROVIDER FINANCING VIA THE BLUE CROSS REIMBURSEMENT FORMULA AND THE MEMBER-HOSPITAL CONTRACT.	Kentucky	74	272	Field Study	Not-for-profit
Talib, Moechtar	A CRITICAL EVALUATION OF THE INDONESIAN CENTRAL GOVERNMENT ACCOUNTING SYSTEM	Illinois	75	330	Field Study	Not-for-profit
Tang, Roger Y.	AN EMPIRICAL INVEST. OF THE TRANSFER PRICING PRACTICES OF LARGE INDUSTRIAL CORP. IN THE U.S. AND JAPAN	Nebraska	77	193	Field Study	International
Tanju, Murat N.	AN EMPIRICAL INVESTIGATION OF THE INFORMATION CONTENT OF SEGMENT DATA	Georgia	77	131	Market- based	Business Segments
Tantral, Panadda	ACCOUNTING LITERATURE IN NON-ACCOUNTING PERIODICALS: AN ASSESSMENT AND ANNOTATED BIBLIOGRAPHY	NYU	83	417	Archival	Profession
Tarabzune, Muhiadin Rashad	AN ANALYSIS OF THE EFFECT OF CAPITALIZING EXPLORATION AND DEVELOPMENT COSTS IN THE PETROLEUM INDUSTRY-WITH EMPHASIS ON POSSIBLE ECONOMIC CONSEQUENCES IN SAUDI ARABIA.	Arkansas	75	367	FinStData-based	Oil & Gas
Tassin, Maurice F.	COMPULSORY CONTINUING EDUCATION FOR CPA'S: A MODEL PROGRAM FOR THE STATE OF LOUISIANA	LSU	75	273	Field Study	Profession

Author	Title	School	Date	pp	Methodology	Topic
Tawfik, Mohamed Sherif	AN OPTIMAL INTERNATIONAL TRANSFER PRICING SYSTEM: A NONLINEAR MULTI-OBJECTIVE APPROACH.	Penn St	82	253	Model- based	Managerial
Taylor, Barbara	THE POTENTIAL IMPACT OF GRAPHIC FORMATTING ON THE RELIABILITY OF FINANCIAL REPORTS	Txs Tech	83	194	Experimental	Financial
Taylor, Martin E.	THE EVALUATION OF ACCOUNTING STANDARDS-A COMPARISON OF SIX COUNTRIES	Texas	74	257	FinStData-based	International
Taylor, Robert D.	MATERIALITY DECISIONS IN ACCOUNTING: A STUDY OF DEFINITIONS, DECISIONS, AND DECISION CRITERIA	Colorado	74	131	Field Study	Auditing
Taylor, Robert Earl	THE EFFECTS OF CERTAIN ENVIRONMENTAL, ORGANIZATIONAL, AND PSYCHOLOGICAL VARIABLES UPON THE FILTERING OF INFORMATION INPUTS BY BOUNDARY ROLE PERSONS.	N Carol	74	203	Experimental	Managerial
Taylor, Ronald Leslie	DEFINING CAPITAL GAINS IN REAL ESTATE ANALYSIS TO DEFINITIONAL ELEMENTS.	Tenn	78	119	Field Study	Tax
Taylor, William J.	PUBLICLY DISCLOSED MANAGEMENT FORECASTS: AN EVALUATION OF THE RELEVANCY, IMPLICATIONS, AND ACCURACY OF SUCH DISCLOSURES	Ga St	74	266	FinStData-based	Forecasts
Techavichit, Joseph Virachai	EVALUATION OF INTERNAL CONTROL IN A DATABASE SYSTEM ENVIRONMENT.	Missouri	79	386	Model- based	Systems/ Computers
Teichman, Ronald J.	DEVELOPMENT OF INFORMATION SYSTEMS ACTIVITIES AND INTERFACES TO SUPPORT TOP MANAGEMENT FUNCTIONS.	Northwestern	77	449	Archival	Systems/ Computers
Tennyson, Barney Mack, III	THE USEFULNESS OF NARRATIVE DISCLOSURES IN THE PREDICTION OF BANKRUPTCY.	S Carol	82	120	FinStData-based	Financial Distress

Author	Title	School	Date	pp	Methodology	Topic
Thakkar, Rashmi Bhanuchandra	PORTFOLIO MODELS WITH STOCHASTIC CASH DEMAND.	NYU	77	219	Market- based	Financial
Thibadoux, Gregory Maurice	THE DEVELOPMENT OF HOSPITAL COST REGRESSION MODELS FOR USE AS ANALYTICAL REVIEW TOOLS BY CPAs	Houston	84	152	Model- based	Auditing
Thomas, Charles William	A COMPARISON OF INVESTOR AND AUDITOR PERCEPTIONS OF MATERIALITY WITH RESPECT TO THE ACCOUNTING CHANGE.	Texas	78	258	Market- based	Auditing
Thomas, Lynn R	THE INFORMATION CONTENT OF REPLACEMENT COST DATA.	Kansas	80	119	Market- based	Inflation
Thomas, Michael Francis	AN APPLICATION OF SOCIO-TECHNICAL SYSTEMS ANALYSIS TO ACCOUNTING VARIANCE CONTROL THEORY	Wiscon	85	546	Field Study	Managerial
Thomas, Phyllis L.	THE EFFECTS OF CHANGES OF INFORMATIONAL FEEDBACK ON DECISIONS MADE IN AUTOMATIC ORDERING SYSTEMS	Txs A&M	83	115	Experimental	Managerial
Thompson, Billy D.	A STUDY OF THE UNIVERSITY OF ARKANSAS ACCOUNTING GRADUATES AND ACCOUNTING EDUCATION	Arkansas	74	303	Field Study	Education
Thompson, Carolyn L.	OPINIONS OF SELECTED PROFESSIONALS CONCERNING ACCOUNTING FOR LISTED CALL STOCK OPTIONS	Arkansas	80	149	Field Study	Financial
Thompson, Forrest	A STUDY OF THE MARKET REACTION TO THE FORMULATION OF SFAS NO. 14.	Txs A&M	78	118	Market- based	Business Segments
Thompson, James H.	ESTATBLISHING ALPHA AND BETA RISK LEVELS IN THE EVALUATION OF SUBSTANTIVE STATISTICAL AUDITING TESTS THAT EMPLOY HYPOTHESIS TESTING	Oklahoma	82	119	Experimental	Auditing

Author	Title	School	Date	pp	Methodology	Topic
Thompson, Joel E.	ALTERNATIVE ECONOMETRIC MODELS FOR DETECTING THE EFFECTS OF ACCOUNTING POLICY DECISIONS	Mich St	82	162	Market- based	Financial
Thompson, John A.	AN INQUIRY INTO THE NATURE OF EPS WITH EMPHASIS ON THE USEFULNESS AND PREDICTIVE ABILITY OF PRIMARY AND FULLY DILUTED EPS CONCEPTS	Arkansas	74	151	Field Study	Earnings Per Share
Thompson, Robert B.	AN EXAMINATION OF SHARE PRICE BEHAVIOR DURING THE 1973-1976 LESSEE ACCOUNTING STANDARD-SETTING PROCESS	Florida	84	235	Field Study	Leases
Thompson, Steven Craig	THE ASSIGNMENT OF INCOME: EFFECTIVE METHODS FOR THE REDUCTION OF TAXES	Houston	84	243	Archival	Tax
Tiessen, Peter	AN INVESTIGATION OF SOME EFFECTS OF DATA AGGREGATION AND COGNITIVE STYLE ON DECISION MAKING PERFORMANCE	Minnesota	76	337	Experimental	Managerial
Tiller, Mikel Glen	A MODEL FOR GOAL SETTING IN A PARTICIPATIVE BUDGETING CONTEXT: AN EMPIRICAL INVESTIGATION OF THE EFFECTS OF COGNITIVE DISSONANCE ON BUDGET COMMITMENT AND PERFORMANCE	Indiana	80	195	Experimental	Managerial
Tillery, Jean Dupree	FINANCIAL STATEMENT USERS' PREFERENCES FOR DESCRIPTIVE VERSUS TECHNICAL ACCOUNTING TERMINOLOGY.	Ga St	82	134	Field Study	Financial
Tipgos, Manuel A.	THE ACCOUNTING ASPECTS OF CORPORATE SOCIAL RESPONSE	LSU	74	338	Model- based	Social
Tishlias, Dennis P.	THE INFLUENCE OF ALTERNATIVE COST ALLOCATIONS ON THE NEW PRODUCT PRICING DECISION: AN EMPIRICAL INVESTIGATION	Cincinnati	84	208	Experimental	Managerial
Tolouian, Pouran	THE EFFECT OF HUMAN RESOURCE ACCOUNTING ON THE VALUE OF STOCK AS MEASURED BY FINANCIAL ANALYSTS.	Alabama	81	166	Experimental	Hum.Resource Acct.

Author	Title	School	Date	pp	Methodology	Topic
Tomassini, Lawrence A.	HUMAN RESOURCE ACCOUNTING AND MANAGERIAL DECISION BEHAVIOR: AN EXPERIMENTAL STUDY	UCLA	74	191	Experimental	Hum.Resource Acct.
Tomczyk, Stephen H.	FINANCIAL RATIOS AND THE ABILITY TO PAY WAGE INCREASES	Kentucky	75	140	FinStData-based	Managerial
Tondkar, Rasoul H.	AN EMP. INV. OF THE POTENTIAL USE OF DATA REQUIRED BY FASB ST. 33 BY FINANCIAL ANALYSTS IN THE DALLAS/FORT WORTH AND HOUSTON REGIONS	N Txs St	80	130	Field Study	Inflation
Toole, Howard R.	PREDICTING SALES IN MULTI-OUTLET BUSINESSES	Iowa	76	141	FinStData-based	Managerial
Tosanguan, Prayoon	THE PREDICTIVE ABILITY OF PARSIMONIOUS QUARTERLY TIME-SERIES MODELS AND ANALYSTS' FORECAST	Indiana	83	221	FinStData-based	Forecasts
Tosh, David Edward	AN EMPIRICAL EVALUATION OF ALTERNATIVE ACCOUNTING MEASURES OF DEFINED BENEFIT PENSION PLAN LIABILITIES	Penn St	85	209	Experimental	Pensions
Tower, Ralph Burnett, Jr.	A STUDY OF THE CONFORMITY OF AUDITED FINANCIAL STATEMENTS WITH INDUSTRY ACCOUNTING STANDARDS.	N Carol	78	210	FinStData-based	Financial
Tranter, Terry L.	THE EFECT OF ALTERNATIVE METHODS OF ACCOUNTING FOR RESEARCH AND DEVELOPMENT EXPEND. ON THE AMOUNT OF R & D EXPENDITURES	Wash	78	177	FinStData-based	Research & Development
Trapnell, Jerry E.	AN EMPIRICAL STUDY OF THE DESCRIPTIVE NATURE OF FINANCIAL RATIOS RELATIVE TO INDUSTRY SPECIFIC CHARACTERISTICS	Georgia	77	276	FinStData-based	Financial Ratios
Traub, Jack	REPORTING PRACTICES OF PRIVATE FOUNDATIONS	CUNY-Bar	76	428	Field Study	Not-for-profit

Author	Title	School	Date	pp	Methodology	Topic
Traugh, Helen M	A STUDY OF INDIRECT COSTS IMPOSED BY REQUIREMENTS FOR SUPPLEMENTAL INFORMATION DISCLOSURE	Okl St.	81	101	Model- based	Financial
Trebby, James P.	AN INVESTIGATION OF THE ABILITY OF DIFFERING ACCOUNTING FRAMEWORKS ON THE PREDICTION OF CASH FLOWS TO TO EQUITY INVESTORS	Kentucky	82	84	FinStData-based	Cash Flows
Trigg, Rodger R	AN ANALYSIS OF WHY COMPANIES USE OR DO NOT USE THE LIFO METHOD OF INVENTORY VALUATION	Arkansas	82	116	Field Study	Inventories
Tripp, John Cassius	TOWARD QUANTIFYING LEGAL REASONING: A CASE STUDY OF JUDICIAL DECISIONS WHEN THE EXISTENCE OF A PARTNERSHIP IS IN QUESTION FOR FEDERAL INCOME TAX PURPOSES.	Houston	80	283	Archival	Tax
Troberg, Pontus Henrik	ACCOUNTING RESOURCE (CURRENCY) TRANSLATION: A COMPARATIVE ANALYSIS OF APPROACHES.	Oklahoma	82	188	FinStData-based	Foreign Currency
Troxel, Terri E.	LIFE INSURANCE COMPANY INCOME MEASUREMENTS: AN ANALYSIS OF THE INCOME SMOOTHING CAPABILITIES OF SELECTED POLICY RESERVING METHODS	Penn	77	645	Experimental	Income Smoothing
Truitt, Jack F.	INCOME SMOOTHING AND THE INVESTMENT DECISION: A LABORATORY EXPERIMENT	Illinois	75	251	Experimental	Income Smoothing8:4 8 pm
Tse, Senyo Yawo	SECURITY VALUATION, ACCOUNTING INFORMATION AND THE USEFULNESS OF SEGMENT DATA	Berkeley	83	224	Model- based	Business Segments
Tucker, James Joseph III	STOCK DIVIDENDS: HISTORICAL, CONCEPTUAL AND REPORTING PERSPECTIVES	Penn St	85	108	Archival	Stock Distributions
Tucker, Michael James	AN EMPIRICAL STUDY OF THE ATTITUDES OF THE ACCOUNTING PROFESSION CONCERNING THE PRACTICE OF TAX ACCOUNTING.	Houston	80	299	Field Study	Tax

Author	Title	School	Date	pp	Methodology	Topic
Tull, Guy L.	A STUDY OF MORAL DEVELOPMENT OF SELECTED EMPLOYEES IN CERTAIN PUBLIC ACCOUNTING FIRMS	LSU	82	162	Field Study	Ethics
Tully, Gregory John	CHARACTERISTIC INFORMATION STRUCTURES FOR FINANCIAL ACCOUNTING DATA	Berkeley	83	247	Field Study	Systems/Computers
Turki, Hedi	A STUDY OF MANAGEMENT'S BUDGET-ORIENTED BEHAVIOR IN TUNISIAN BUSINESS ENTERPRISES.	UCLA	76	218	Field Study	Managerial
Twombly, John Roger	THE INFORMATION CONTENT OF SEGMENT REPORTS.	Chicago	80		Market- based	Business Segments
Tyler, June Diane	ACCOUNTING FOR THE TIME DIMENSION OF DEPARTMENTAL PERFORMANCE VIA A SCHEDULING VARIANCE.	Indiana	79	200	Experimental	Managerial
Tzur, Joseph	THE AGENCY MODEL WITH SEARCH FOR ALTERNATIVES	Columbia	83	111	Model- based	Managerial
Uddin, M. Jamir	A COMPARISON OF OPININIONS OF PUB. H.S. ACCT. TEACH., 2-YR. COLL. ACCT. TEACH., AND 4-YR. ACCT. TEACH. OF THE N.CEN. REGION OF THE U.S. CONCERNING THE OBJ. AND METH/TECH USED IN TEACH. THE ELEM. ACCT. COURSE	N Ill	77	714	Field Study	Education
Ugault, Michel	SYSTEMATIC RISK AND ALTERNATIVE ACCOUNTING MEASURES OF PERFORMANCE	Syracuse	79	164	FinStData-based	Financial
Umapathy, Srinivasan	THE PROCESS OF BUDGETING IN DECENTRALIZED FIRMS.	Harvard	80	259	Field Study	Managerial
Urbancic, Frank Robert	A DETERMINATION OF THE REPORTING EXPERIENCE UNDER FINANCIAL ACCOUNTING STANDARDS BOARD STATEMENT NO. 8.	Kent St	77	214	FinStData-based	Foreign Currency

Author	Title	School	Date	pp	Methodology	Topic
Uruwink, David R.	AN EMP. INV. OF THE INFO. CONTENT OF SFAS NO. 33'S PROCEDURES FOR CALCULATING PRICE-LEVEL ADJUSTED EARNINGS OF ELECTRIC UTILITIES	Arkansas	82	138	Market- based	Inflation
Ushman, Neal L.	AN EXAMINATION OF THE TIME SERIES PROPERTIES OF BETA	Cornell	83	146	Market- based	Stochastic Properties
Van Breda, Michael F.	THE PREDICTION OF CORPORATE EARNINGS	Stanford	79	170	Model- based	Financial
Van Dongen, William Orson	A STUDY OF THE UNDERLYING VALUES THAT MOTIVATE ELEMENTARY AND ADVANCED ACCOUNTING STUDENTS.	N Txs St	81	157	Field Study	Education
Van Zante, Neal R.	A SURVEY OF THE PERCEPTIONS OF INDUSTRIAL CMA'S ON THE IMPORTANCE OF SELECTED MANAGEMENT ACCOUNTING TOPICS	Okl St	76	120	Field Study	Education
Vanecek, Michael Thomas	BAYESIAN DOLLAR UNIT SAMPLING IN AUDITING.	Texas	78	424	Model- based	Auditing
Vawter, Charles L.	ACCUMULATED EARNINGS TAX: A COMPARISON OF CHARACTERISTICS OF LITIGATED AND NONLITIGATED CASES	Ariz St	75	170	Field Study	Tax
Veazey, Richard E.	THE SELECTION OF FINANCIAL ACCT. RATIOS TO MEASURE HIGHLY SUCCESSFUL MANUFACTURING FIRMS: A DISCRIMINENT ANALYSIS	Saint Louis	81	210	Model- based	Financial
Vent, Glenn A.	A SIMULATION STUDY OF THE FULL COST AND SUCCESSFUL EFFORTS METHODS OF ACCOUNTING IN THE PETROLEUM INDUSTRY	Arizona	83	213	Experimental	Oil & Gas
Verreault, Daniel Arthur	A CONTINGENCY THEORY OF INTERUNIT RELATIONS OF THE INTERNAL AUDIT FUNCTION	Texas A&M	84	216	Field Study	Auditing

Author	Title	School	Date	pp	Methodology	Topic
Verreault, Kathryn M.	AUDIT PARTNERS' PERCEPTIONS OF THE VARIABLES ASSO. WITH THE DECISIONS TO WITHDRAW FROM AUDIT ENGAGEMENTS	Txs A&M	82	168	Archival	Auditing
Verrecchia, Robert Ernest	THE IMPACT OF PUBLICLY DISCLOSED INFORMATION.	Stanford	76	133	Model- based	Financial
Verschoor, Curtis C.	A STUDY OF THE IMPORT. OF COMPUTER-RELATED COMPETENCIES FOR GEN. STAFF AUDITORS IN LARGE CPA FIRMS IN THE U.S. AND LARGE CORP. IN THE CHICAGO AREA	N Ill	77	211	Field Study	Systems/ Computers
Vickery, Don W.	AN ANALYSIS OF THE MAJOR NUMERICAL ARGUMENTS OF THREE FREQUENTLY-ADVOCATED ACCOUNTING SYSTEMS FROM THE PERSPECTIVE OF THE THEORY OF FUNDAMENTAL MEASUREMENT	Texas	75	264	Model- based	Financial
Vicknair, David B.	AN INVESTIGATION OF USERS' PERCEPTIONS CONCERNING CORPORATE FUNDS FLOW INFORMATION	Tenn	83	188	Field Study	Statement of Ch Fin Pos
Vidulich, Barbara Bader	THE INTERACTION OF OPEN- AND CLOSED-MINDEDNESS WITH PARTICIPATION IN BUDGETING.	Colorado	79	145	Experimental	Managerial
Vigeland, Robert L.	STATEMENT OF FINANCIAL ACCOUNTING STANDARDS NO. 2 AND MARKET EQUILIBRIUM	Columbia	77	179	Market- based	Research & Development
Visse, Richard H.	THE EFFECT OF REWARD MOTIVATION FEEDBACK FREQUENCY ON ASPIRATION LEVELS AND PERFORMANCE OF INDIVIDUALS OPERATING UNDER A CONTROL BUDGET	Ariz St	74	180	Experimental	Managerial
Vives, Antonio	CLOSED-END FUNDS: DISCOUNTS, PREMIUMS, MARKET EFFICIENCY AND RISK ADJUSTMENT.	Carn Mel	75	179	Market- based	Financial
Volkan, Ara G.	A FINANCIAL REPORTING MODEL FOR MACROECONOMIC DECISION MAKERS	Alabama	79	429	Model- based	Financial

Author	Title	School	Date	pp	Methodology	Topic
Volkert, James F.	A COMPARISON OF ACCOUNTING AND INTERNAL RATES OF RETURN FOR THE FIRM IN A DYNAMIC SETTING	Illinois	81	169	Experimental	Financial
Vorherr, Phillip H.	CONTINGENT PAYMENTS IN THE BUSINESS COMBINATION: A CRITICAL ANALYSIS AND A PROPOSED THEORY	Cincinnati	75	200	Model- based	Business Combinations
Vruwink, David R.	AN EMPIRICAL INVESTIGATION OF THE INFORMATION CONTENT OF SFAS NO. 33'S PROCEDURES FOR CALCULATING PRICE-LEVEL ADJUSTED EARNINGS OF ELECTRIC UTILITIES	Arkansas	82	138	Market- based	Inflation
Wade, Charles Murray	A CAPITAL EQUIPMENT BUDGETING SYSTEM APPLICABLE TO SELECTED MIDSOUTH NOT-FOR-PROFIT COMMUNITY HOSPITALS.	Miss	77	251	Field Study	Not-for-profit
Wade, Daniel Eugene	A STUDY OF THE LONG-RUN NATURE AND USEFULNESS OF ZERO-BASE BUDGETING.	Kentucky	81	135	Field Study	Managerial
Waegelein, James F.	THE IMPACT OF EXECUTIVE COMPENSATION ON MANAGERIAL DECISIONS: AN EMPIRICAL INVESTIGATION	Penn St	82	169	FinStData-based	Managerial
Wagner, Charles R.	THE CPA'S RESPONSIBILITY FOR THE PREVENTION AND DETECTION OF COMPUTER FRAUD	Nebraska	76	288	Archival	Auditing
Wagner, Robin M	A DESCRIPTIVE THEORY OF ACCOUNTING NUMBERS IN COMPLETE MARKETS	Berkeley	82	156	Model- based	Financial
Walker, John P.	HUMAN RESOURCE ACCOUNTING FOR MANAGERIAL PLANNING AND CONTROL: A GENERAL AND SOCAL SYSTEMS APPROACH	Cincinnati	76	180	Model- based	Hum.Resource Acct.
Wallace, Wanda A.	THE IMPACT OF SELECTED FINANCIAL REPORTING PRACTICES AND THE NATURE OF THE AUDIT OPINION UPON MUNICIPAL INTEREST COST AND BOND RATING	Florida	78	192	Field Study	Not-for-profit

Author	Title	School	Date	pp	Methodology	Topic
Wallace, William Duane	AN INVESTIGATION OF THE EFFECTS OF PRICE LEVEL ADJUSTED TAXABLE INCOME UPON THE ALLOCATION OF CASH TAX PAYMENTS.	Okl St	78	154	FinStData-based	Inflation
Waller, Thomas C.	BUDGETARY CONTROL OF THE DEVELOPMENT OF MANAGEMENT INFORMATION SYSTEMS	Houston	77	323	Field Study	Systems/ Computers
Walther, Larry M.	AN EMPIRICAL INVESTIGATION OF THE VALIDITY OF HISTORICAL COST/CONSTANT DOLLAR DATA ESTIMATION MODELS	Okl St	80	235	FinStData-based	Inflation
Ward, Dalton Dewey	A DELPHI SURVEY OF RELIANCE UPON INTERNAL AUDITORS AND THEIR WORK BY EXTERNAL AUDITORS DURING FINANCIAL AUDITS.	Texas	79	382	Field Study	Auditing
Ward, Danny Ray	AN EMPIRICAL INVESTIGATION INTO THE ACQUISITION AND MERGER OF PROFESSIONAL ACCOUNTING PRACTICES IN THE STATE OF LOUISIANA.	La Tech	79	235	Field Study	Profession
Warner, Paul D.	THE COST AND BENEFITS OF ASR- 177 REVIEWS: AN EMPIRICAL STUDY	NYU	81	84	Field Study	Financial
Waters, Gary Lynn	CRITERIA FOR DETERMINING THE APPROPRIATE TAX TREATMENT OF EXPENDITURES AS REPAIRS VERSUS IMPROVEMENTS: AN EMPIRICAL INVESTIGATION OF JUDICIAL DECISIONS.	Tenn	81	114	Archival	Tax
Watkins, Larry Edward	THE INFORMATION CONTENT OF SELECTED DISCLOSURES FOR MINING FIRMS: AN EXPERIMENTAL STUDY	Okl St	84	78	Experimental	Financial
Watkins, Paul Roger	PERCEIVED INFORMATION COMPLEXITY AND COGNITIVE STYLES: IMPLICATIONS FOR DECISION SUPPORT SYSTEMS DESIGN.	Arizona	80	396	Experimental	Managerial
Waymire, Gregory Brooks	AN EMPIRICAL ANALYSIS OF VOLUNTARY MANAGEMENT EARNINGS FORECASTS	Chicago	84		Field Study	Forecasts

Author	Title	School	Date	pp	Methodology	Topic
Weatherwax, Roy C.	AN EMPIRICAL INVESTIGATION OF THE EXISTENCE OF AN ACCOUNTING CONSTRAINT ON CAPITAL BUDGETING DECISION-MAKING	Wiscon	74	198	Field Study	Managerial
Weber, Richard P.	THE ALLOCATION OF CONSOLIDATED FEDERAL INCOME TAX LIABILITIES WITH SOME RELATED ACCOUNTING AND LEGAL IMPLICATIONS	Michigan	75	233	Archival	Tax
Weber, Ronald A.	AUDITOR DEC. MAKING: A STUDY OF SOME ASPECTS OF ACCURACY AND CONSENSUS, AND USEF OF A SIMUL. DEC. AID FOR ASSESS. OVERALL SYS. REL.	Minnesota	77	341	Experimental	Auditing
Webster, Stuart K.	AN EMPIRICAL EXAMINATION OF THE ASSOCIATION BETWEEN ACCOUNTING AND SHARE PRICE DATA AMONG STOCK LIFE INSURANCE COMPANIES	Iowa	75	133	Market- based	Financial
Wee, Warren	SELECTED INTERNAL ACCOUNTING CONTROL CHANGES IN U.S. BUSINESS FIRMS	U Wash	82	142	Field Study	Auditing
Weintrop, Joseph	AN EMPIRICAL INVESTIGATION INTO THE ECONOMIC IMPACT OF MANDATED LEASE DISCLOSURE REQUIREMENTS	Oregon	84	117	Experimental	Leases
Weirich, Thomas R.	A DETERMINATION OF THE ACCEPTABILITY OF USING ACCOUNTING DATA IN THE EXPLANATION AND PREDICTION OF RISK	Missouri	76	241	Market- based	Financial
Weis, William L.	AN EXPERIMENTAL INVESTIGATION OF SOME EFFECTS OF CONSOLIDATING COLLEGIATE FINANCIAL REPORTS	Wash	79	177	Experimental	Financial
Weiss, Dieter H.	AN EMPIRICAL STUDY ON THE FEASIBILITY OF RATIOS IN TRANSNATIONAL FINANCIAL ANALYSIS WITH REFERENCE TO GERMAN CORPORATIONS.	American	76	224	FinStData-based	International
Welch, Paul R.	PROBABILISTIC NATURE OF ACCOUNTING EARNINGS: MACROECONOMIC INFLUENCE AND EX ANTE PREDICTION	Florida	81	254	Model- based	Financial

Author	Title	School	Date	pp	Methodology	Topic
Welker, Donna Lynn	BACKGROUND FACTORS AND THE ANCHORING AND ADJUSTMENT HEURISTIC: AN EMPIRICAL INVESTIGATION (JUDGMENTAL BIASES)	Texas A&M	85	174	Experimental	Auditing
Welker, Robert B.	A DESCRIPTIVE COMPARISION OF THE JUDGEMENT FORMING PROCESS IN PERSONNEL SELECTION	Ariz St	77	253	Experimental	Profession
Wescott, Shari H.	AN ASSESSMENT OF THE ABILITY OF ACCOUNTING NUMBERS TO PREDICT MUNICIPAL GENERAL OBLIGATION BOND RATINGS	S Carol	82	191	Market- based	Not-for-profit
Westmoreland Geraldine	ELECTRIC UTILITIES' ACCT. FOR CONSTRUC. WORK IN PROGRESS: THE EFFECTS OF ALT. METH. ON THE FIN. STATEM., UTIL. RATES, AND MARKET TO BOOK RATIO	Florida	79	241	FinStData-based	Financial
Wetzel, Thomas Sterling	GAME THEORETIC SOLUTIONS APPLIED TO ACCOUNTING COST ALLOCATION: A LABORATORY EXPERIMENT.	Okl St	80	98	Experimental	Managerial
Whisnant, Susan R.	THE ATTITUDE OF ACCOUNTANTS AND OTHER SPECIALISTS EMPLOYED BY CPA FIRMS TO THE ETHICAL ISSUES OF MARKETING PROFESSIONAL SERVICES	Texas	76	328	Field Study	Ethics
White, Clinton Elwin, Jr.	AN EVALUATION OF THE DECISION MAKING EFFECTS OF THE AGGREGATION OF ACCOUNTING NUMBERS IN MANAGEMENT ACCOUNTING REPORTS: A FIELD EXPERIMENT.	Indiana	81	214	Experimental	Managerial
White, Debra M.	AN EMPIRICAL INQUIRY INTO THE EFFECT OF DIRECT & INDIRECT VOTING STRUCTURES ON THE EFFICIENT PROVISION OF PUBLIC GOODS	Okl St	80	203	Field Study	Tax
White, Godwin Thomas	AN EMPIRICAL INVESTIGATION OF THE CASH FLOW PREDICTABILITY OF HISTORICAL COST, GENERAL PRICE LEVEL, AND REPLACEMENT COST INCOME MODELS	VPI	83	223	Model- based	Inflation
White, Richard Alan	EMPLOYEE PREFERENCES FOR NONTAXABLE COMPENSATION: AN EMPIRICAL STUDY.	Ariz St	81	167	Experimental	Tax

Author	Title	School	Date	pp	Methodology	Topic
Whitt, Sue Y.	NEUTRALITY OF A TAX POLICY DEVICE: AN INQUIRY INTO THE EFFECTS OF THE ASSET DEPRECIATION RANGE SYSTEM	Arkansas	75	195	Archival	Tax
Whittenburg, Gerald Eugene	TAX REFORM IN BUSINESS COMBINATIONS: ANALYSIS OF TAX TREATMENT IN THE UNITES STATES AND SELECTED FOREIGN COUNTRIES.	Houston	76	205	Experimental	Tax
Whittington, Oliver R.	AN EXAMINATION OF THE EFFECTS OF ANALYTICAL EVIDENCE AND TIME BUDGETS ON AUDIT JUDGEMENTS	Houston	78	151	Experimental	Auditing
Wiehrs, Paula E.	AN EMPIRICAL STUDY OF CAPITAL INVESTMENT INCENTIVES IN AN INFLATIONARY ENVIRONMENT	S Carol	83	104	FinStData-based	Tax
Wiggins, Casper E.	EVALUATING INTERNAL CONTROL AND ALTERNATIVE COMPLIANCE TESTING PROCEDURES: A SIMULATION APPROACH	Tenn	82	104	Experimental	Auditing
Wiggins, Charles Donald	A DUAL BETA APPROACH TO PORTFOLIO ANALYSIS.	La Tech	76	133	Market- based	Financial
Wild, John Joseph	A MICROECONOMETRIC MODEL OF THE DETERMINANTS OF ACCOUNTING NUMBERS' SYSTEMATIC PROPERTIES	Wiscon	83	321	Model- based	Financial
Wilde, Harold Heye	A SURVEY OF THE ATTITUDES OF SOUTH DAKOTA SMALL BUSINESS OWNERS AND/OR MANAGERS TOWARDS SOCIAL RESPONSIBILITY ACCOUNTING.	Nebraska	81	185	Field Study	Social
Wilguess, John Harry	THE EXPERIENCE OF TAX PRACTITIONERS WITH THE TAX RETURN PREPARER RULES.	Arkansas	79	193	Field Study	Tax
Wilkerson, Jack Edward Jr.	AN ANALYTICAL AND EMPIRICAL EXAMINATION OF ECONOMIC DETERMINANTS OF THE AUDITOR REPORTING DECISION (CONTINGENCIES, UNCERTAINTIES)	Texas	84	280	Experimental	Auditing

Author	Title	School	Date	pp	Methodology	Topic
Williams, Hubert J.	CUE UTILIZATION IN AUDITOR'S GOING-CONCERN QUALIFICATION JUDGEMENTS: AN EMPIRICAL ANALYSIS	Georgia	82	191	Field Study	Auditing
Williams, John Joseph	CAPITAL MARKET REACTION TO FINANCIAL ACCOUNTING STANDARDS BOARD STATEMENT NO. 8	Penn St	78	213	Market- based	Foreign Currency
Williams, Paul F.	THE EVALUATIVE RELEVANCE OF SOCIAL INFORMATION	N Carol	77	288	Experimental	Social
Williams, Ralph Batchelder	REPORT ON INTERNAL CONTROL: IMPACT ON FINANCIAL ANALYSTS' EVALUATION OF A COMPANY.	S Calif	81		Experimental	Auditing
Willinger, Geoffrey L.	A CONTINGENT CLAIMS MODEL FOR PENSION COSTS	Fla St	82	140	Model- based	Pensions
Willis, Eugene	JOB SATISFACTION AND PERSONALITY TRAITS OF CPA'S	Cincinnati	75	108	Field Study	Profession
Willis, G. W.	A STUDY OF INVESTOR REACTION TO ACCOUNTING CHANGES REQUIRED BY FASB STATEMENT NO. 2 AND STATEMENT NO. 8	Txs A&M	77	229	Market- based	Accounting Changes
Wilner, Neil Alan	INFORMATION INDUCTANCE AND SFAS 8: A BEHAVIORAL EXPERIMENT.	Ohio St	80	259	Experimental	Foreign Currency
Wilson, Beverly	MODELING FOR OPTIMAL PRODUCTION DECISIONS AND PERFORMANCE CONTROL IN AGRICULTURE	Arizona	83	134	Model- based	Managerial
Wilson, Earl R.	AN EMPIRICAL ANALYSIS OF THE EFFECTS OF ACCOUNTING AND REPORTING PRACTICES ON MUNICIPAL BOND RATINGS AND BORROWING COSTS	Missouri	82	274	FinStData-based	Financial

Author	Title	School	Date	pp	Methodology	Topic
Wilson, James E.	DEVELOPMENT AND TESTING OF A CREDIT SCREENING METHOD	Miss St	81	163	Model- based	Managerial
Wilson, Michael D.	AN INVESTIGATION INTO THE USEFULNESS OF THE INFORMATION CONTAINED IN THE ACCOUNTING SYSTEM OF A MUNICIPALITY	Missouri	83	232	Field Study	Not-for-profit
Wilson, Peter Randall	AN ANALYSIS OF AUDITORS' PERCEPTION OF THE VALUE OF INFORMATION (DECISION-MAKING)	N Car	84	118	Field Study	Auditing
Wilson, Wayne R	THE USE OF PERMANENT LEARNING GROUPS IN TEACHING INTRODUCTORY ACCOUNTING	Oklahoma	82	184	Field Study	Education
Winters, Alan Joseph	UNAUDITED FINANCIAL STATEMENTS: A DELINEATION OF ISSUES, SURVEY OF PRACTICE, AND STATEMENT OF RESPONSIBILITY.	Txs Tech	74	357	Field Study	Auditing
Wiseman, Joanne W.	AN EMPIRICAL EXAMINATION OF THE CONTENTS AND ACCURACY OF VOLUNTARY CORPORATE POLLUTION CONTROL DISCLOSURES	N Carol	80	185	Field Study	Social
Woehrle, Stephen Luer	RESOURCE ALLOCATIONS IN A PERFORMANCE AUDITING SYSTEM: A GOAL PROGRAMMING-BASED REVIEW PROCEDURE.	Nebraska	78	147	Field Study	Not-for-profit
Wolf, Allen Edwin	MANAGERIAL ATTITUDES AND PERFORMANCE IN A HIGH PERFORMING AND LOW PERFORMING ENVIRONMENT: A COMPARATIVE TEST OF AN EXPECTANCY THEORY MODEL.	Harvard	74	327	Model- based	Managerial
Wolff, Bernard Christopher	A HIERARCHY OF ORGANIZATIONAL NEEDS AND ITS ACCEPTANCE BY TOP-LEVEL BUSINESS EXECUTIVES AND ACCOUNTANTS.	Arkansas	76	193	Field Study	Managerial
Wolfson, Mark A.	TOWARD AN UNDERSTANDING OF THE COMPLEMENTARY NATURE OF SECURITY PRICE AND NONSECURITY PRICE INFORMATION IN RELATIVE RISK PARAMETER EST.	Texas	77	132	Model- based	Financial

Author	Title	School	Date	pp	Methodology	Topic
Wood, Edwin A.	QUANTITATIVE FACTORS FOR INSTRUCTIONAL RESOURCES IN THE STATE UNIVERSITY SYSTEM OF FLORIDA	Florida	76	167	Field Study	Not-for-profit
Wooding, Giles Clement	THE AUDIT AND CONTROL OF REAL TIME DISTRIBUTED DATA BASE SYSTEMS	Geo Wash	84	186	Field Study	Auditing
Wooton, Charles W.	AN ANALYSIS OF THE POSSIBLE DOMINENCE BY THE BIG EIGHT ACCOUNTING FIRMS OF LARGE AUDIT CLIENTS	Miss St	82	302	FinStData-based	Auditing
Worrels, Cecil Eugene	AN ANALYSIS OF THE PUBLISHED WRITINGS OF ROBERT H. MONTGOMERY IN RELATION TO SELECTED DEVELOPMENTS IN AMERICAN PUBLIC ACCOUNTING.	Illinois	74	260	Archival	History
Worthington, James	AN ANALYSIS OF THE READIBILITY OF FOOTNOTES TO FINANCIAL STATEMENTS AND RECOMMENDATIONS FOR THEIR IMPROVEMENT	Missouri	76	224	FinStData-based	Statement Presentation
Wragge, John H.	COMPREHENSIVE SIMULATION MODELING IN HIGHER EDUCATION: THE STATE OF THE ART AND THE STABILITY OF THE ICCM	Houston	75	212	Field Study	Education
Wrege, William Thomas	ACCOUNTING INFORMATION NEEDED BY SELECTED STATE LEGISLATORS AND FISCAL OFFICERS	Kentucky	84	213	Field Study	Not-for-Profit
Wright, Arnold M.	AN EXAMINATION OF THE EFFECT OF ENVIRONMENTAL CUES ON AUDIT JUDGMENTS.	S Calif	79		Experimental	Auditing
Wright, Charlotte J.	AN ASSESSMENT OF THE EFFECTS OF NEWS ANNOUNCEMENTS OF STOCK PRICES OF OIL AND GAS PRODUCING COMPANIES	N Txs St	82	164	Market- based	Oil & Gas
Wright, William Frank	COGNITIVE INFORMATION PROCESSING AND INVESTMENT ANALYSIS.	Berkeley	75		Experimental	Financial

Author	Title	School	Date	pp	Methodology	Topic
Wu, Hsiang-fa	A STUDY OF FINANCIAL DECISION MAKING FOR PLANING AND CONTROLLING CENTRAL UTILITY PLANTS IN COLLEGES AND UNIVERSITIES	Txs Tech	75	294	Field Study	Not-for-profit
Wunder, Haroldene Fowler	CAPITAL FORMATION AND THE INVESTMENT CREDIT: AN EMPIRICAL STUDY.	S Carol	78	203	FinStData-based	Tax
Wygal, Donald Evans	AN EXPLORATORY STUDY OF PERFORMANCE AND PROCESS IN AN INDUSTRIAL SAFETY PROGRAM.	Pitt	77	181	Field Study	Managerial
Wyler, Wayne E.	THE USE OF ACCOUNTING IN THE ECOLOGICAL EVALUATION OF SEWAGE TREATMENT PLANTS	N Colo	75	193	Field Study	Social
Wyndelts, Robert Ward	TAX PLANNING AND AN ANALYSIS OF FEDERAL INCOME TAX LAWS: INVESTMENT DECISIONS IN REAL ESTATE.	Georgia	74	154	Experimental	Tax
Yahr, Robert B.	ARE THERE GA(A)PS IN FINANCIAL REPORTING FOR THE LIFE INSURANCE INDUSTRY	Nebraska	79	256	Model- based	Financial
Yang, David Chie Hwa	THE ASSOCIATION BETWEEN SFAS 33 INFORMATION AND BOND RATINGS	Columbia	85	145	FinStData-based	Inflation
Yeary, James D.	AN EMPIRICAL STUDY OF NON-SAMPLING ERRORS IN THE CONFIRMATION OF ACCOUNTS RECEIVABLE	Okl St	75	100	Experimental	Auditing
Yeater, David A.	THE IMPACT OF STATEMENT OF FAS NO. 8 ON CORPORATE VALUE	Cornell	78	172	FinStData-based	Foreign Currency
Yerkes, Russell E.	VARIATION IN ADHERENCE TO EXPRESSED RULES OF ETHICS BY THE ACCOUNTING PROFESSION AND SOME FACTORS ASSOCIATED WITH SUCH VARIATION	SUNY-Buf	75	366	Field Study	Ethics

Author	Title	School	Date	pp	Methodology	Topic
Young, Ralph L.	ACCOUNTING INSTRUCTION IN PUBLIC JR. (COMMUNITY) COLLEGES IN THE U.S.	N Txs St	74	179	Field Study	Education
Young, Richard Anthony	AGENCY MODELS OF COST VARIANCE INVESTIGATION DECISIONS: A NUMERICAL ANALYSIS	Ohio St	84	161	Field Study	Managerial
Young, S. Mark	THE EFFECTS OF SUBORDINATE'S PRIVATE INFORMATION AND PARTICIPATION ON BUDGETARY SLACK AND WORKER SATISFACTION IN A SIMULATED PRODUCTION SETTING	Pitt	83	175	Field Study	Managerial
Younkins, Edward Wayne	AN EXAMINATION OF PERCEPTIONS AND ACCEPTANCE OF ACCOUNTING INNOVATIONS AND CHANGES BY ACCOUNTING INTEREST GROUPS: IMPLICATIONS FOR THE FINANCIAL ACCOUNTING STANDARDS-SETTING PROCESS	Miss	84	320	Field Study	Standard-setting
Yunker, Penelope Jane	TRANSFER PRICING AND PERFORMANCE EVALUATIONS IN MULTINATIONAL CORPORATIONS: A SURVEY STUDY.	Saint Louis	81	225	Field Study	Managerial
Zaunbrecher, Hilary C.	THE IMPACT OF HUMAN RESOURCE ACCOUNTING ON THE PERSONNEL SELECTION PROCESS: AN EMPIRICAL STUDY	LSU	74	267	Experimental	Hum.Resource Acct.
Zavgren, Christine Virginia	A PROBABILISTIC MODEL OF FINANCIAL DISTRESS.	Nebraska	80	213	FinStData-based	Financial Ratios
Zawati, A. K.	THE RELIABILITY OF APPRAISAL METHODS IN DETERMING CURRENT ASSET VALUES: AN EMPIRICAL STUDY	LSU	77	178	Field Study	Inflation
Zebda, Awni M.	A MODEL FOR THE INVESTIGATION OF COST VARIANCES: THE FUZZY SET THEORY APPROACH	VPI	82	211	Model- based	Managerial
Ziebart, David A.	MODELING THE UTILIZATION OF ACCOUNTING DATA: AN EMPIRICAL STUDY	Mich St	83	156	Market- based	Financial

Author	Title	School	Date	pp	Methodology	Topic
Zimmerman, Jerold Lee	**INDIVIDUAL FINANCIAL DECISION-MAKING IN BASIC SCIENCE: A NORMATIVE AND DESCRIPTIVE STUDY.**	Berkeley	74		Field Study	Financial
Zuaiter, Farquoq Ahmad	**CASH MOVEMENT AS A BASIS FOR INCOME MEASUREMENT**	Txs Tech	74	197	FinStData-based	Financial

AUTHORS LISTED ALPHABETICALLY BY TOPIC

AUTHORS CATEGORIZED BY TOPIC

Bank Accounting

Bonds

Business Combinations

Business Segments

Cash Flows

Communication

Deferred Taxes

Depreciation

Earnings Per Share

Education

Ethics

Extraordinary Items

Financial (Misc. Topics)

Deines, Dan Stuart
Demotses, Andrew J.
Dhaliwal, Dan Singh
Dirsmith, Mark W.
Dodd, Peter Raymond
Dontoh, Alex Kwesi
Downes, David Howard
Duke, Donald E.
El-Arabi, Abdussalan
El-Badadawi, Mohammed H.
Elgers, Pieter Thomas
Elhassy, Juma'a
Etherington, Lois Deane
Ewing-Chow, Frank D.
Farmer, Martha K.
Farrelly, Gail E.
Fellingham, John C.
Fortin, Karen A.
Foster, George J.
Foster, Taylor William, III
Frecka, Thomas Jean
Fried, Haim D.
Gamble, George O.
Garsombke, Henry P.
Gaumnitz, Bruce
Godwin, Larry B.
Gray, O. Ronald
Grief, Louis Adrian
Grove, Hugh D.
Guttikonda, Ramamohana R.
Hadley, Galen D.
Hall, Thomas W.
Hamamad, Ahmed-Hany B.
Hamer, John Gwenffrud
Hammer, Lawrence H.
Hansen, Don R.
Harbecke, Paula A.
Harkins, Jeffrey Lynn
Harmon, William K.
Harrell, Horace W.
Hawkins, Ennis Milton
Helmi, Medhat A.
Hennessee, Patrick Arnold
Herrera, Fernando B.
Herring, Hartwell C.
Hinds, John E.
Hines, Charles Edmund, Jr.
Holzmann, Oscar Jorge
Hong, Sungbin Chun
Hopwood, William S.
Horwood, Joanne Lynn
Hoth, Gerald Blaine
Huber, Charles Courtland, Jr.
Huffman, Wilmer E.
Hull, Rita P.
Hussein, Mohammed E.
Ismail, Hamzah B.
Jenkins, David Randall
Johnson, Johnny R.
Johnson, Steven B.
Johnson, William B.
Jones, Richard W.
Jopling, Samuel Haigh, Jr.
Kahn, Nathan
Kamnikar, Judith A.
Kanodia, Chandra S.
Karmon, David James
Keck, John T.
Kellogg, Robert Leroy
Kelsy, Richard L.
Kemp, Robert S.
Kessler, Lawrence F.
Kettering, Ronald Clayton
Keys, David E.
Kirschman, Charles F.
Knutson, Dennis L.
Koogler, Paul R.
Kross, William J.
La Near, Richard E.
Lanen, William N.
Langefeld, Phillip A.
Lantz, Keith W.
Leftwich, Richard W.
Lemon, William Morley
Leong, Kenneth Kin On
Lew, Albert Yee-Hong
Libby, Robert
Livnat, Joshua
Lookabill, Larry L.
Lovins, W. Gene
Luthy, David H.
Lyn, Thomas
Mac Millan, Alistair R.
Magee, Robert Paul
Mapp, Johnnie A.
Marquis, Linda M.
Mayer- Sommer, Alan P.
McCabe, John C.
McCaslin, Thomas Eugene
McGillivray, Robert E.
McKeon, Joseph M.
McKinnon, Sharon M.
Meek, Gary Kenneth
Merei, Issam J.
Morse, Dale Clayton
Morton, James R.
Mulford, Charles W.
Munter, Paul H.
Murdock, Richard J.
Nair, Raghavan D.
Naloo, Man C.
Naser-Tavauolian, Mohsen
Newman, Donald Paul
Ng, David Siu Po
Nichols, David Lloyd
Ninsuvannakul, Prawit
Noreen, Eric W.
Nyadroh, Emmanuel
Mawuenyega Kwaku
O'Brien, Francis James
O'Doherty, Brian A.
Oliver, Janice B.
Oppong, Andrews
Orbach, Kenneth Ned
Ou, Jane Ai Jiuan
Owings, Guy W.
Oxner, Thomas H.
Palmon, Dan
Pan, Sheng-Der
Pannell, Richard L.
Paolasini, Arnold L.
Parsons, Gregory L.
Pastena, Victor S.
Patterson, Jeffrey L.
Paxton, William E.
Peyvandi, Ali Agha
Pincus, Morton P.
Potts, A. J.
Pratt, James H.
Preis, Nancy J.
Putnam, Donald F.
Ramakrishnan, Ram T. S.
Ramsey, Louis P.
Rao, Honnudike V.
Rao, Kailas J.
Reeder, David B.
Reeve, James M.
Ricchiute, David N.
Rich, Anne J.
Richardson, Frederick M.
Richardson, Gordon D.
Rivera Fernandez, Juan M.
Rodgers, Waymond
Rosanas, Josep M.
Rouse, Robert W.
Roy, Stephen P.
Rozanski, Eugene R.
Saghafi, Ali
Salimi, Anwar Yazdani
Samuelson, Bruce A.
Sandretto, Michael J.
Santos, Dante E.
Schepanski, Albert A.
Schmutte, James L.
Schroeder, Nicholas W.
Schugart, Gary L.
Sefcik, Stephen E.
Sharp, Durwin L.
Sharp, Robert F.
Sheteini, Idris A.
Siegel, Joel G.
Silhan, Peter A.
Simkins, Allen F.
Singh, Dan
Skantz, Tereance R.
Smith, David B.
Snowball, Douglas A. Thomas
Spero, Abba V.
Spero, Leslie Lawrence
Stanga, Keith G.
Steedle, Lamont F.
Stephens, Ray G.
Stolar, Robert W.

Stout, David E.
Sutton, Timothy G.
Swanson, Gale A.
Taylor, Barbara
Thakkar, Rashmi Bhanuchandra
Thompson, Carolyn L.
Thompson, Joel E.
Tillery, Jean Dupree
Tower, Ralph Burnett, Jr.
Traugh, Helen M.
Ugault, Michel
Van Breda, Michael F.
Veazey, Richard E.
Verrecchia, Robert Ernest
Vickery, Don W.
Vives, Antonio
Volkan, Ara G.
Volkert, James F.
Wagner, Robin M
Warner, Paul D.
Watkins, Larry Edward
Webster, Stuart K.
Weirich, Thomas R.
Weis, William L.
Welch, Paul R.
Westmoreland, Geraldine
Wiggins, Charles Donald
Wild, John Joseph
Wilson, Earl R.
Wolfson, Mark A.
Wright, William Frank
Yahr, Robert B.
Ziebart, David A.
Zimmerman, Jerold Lee
Zuaiter, Farquoq Ahmad

Financial Distress

Anyanwa, Casimar I.
Hamer, Michelle M
Lau, Amy Hing-Ling
Moores, Charles T.
Parker, Hugh J.
Tennyson, Barney Mack, III

Financial Ratios

Blann, Jack Ralph
Bristol, James Tadsen
Brown, Ronald D.
Courtis, John K.
Elkhorouf, Farouk W.
Espahbodi, Hassanali
Faisal, Abdullah M.
Kiddoo, Robert James
Legault, Michel
Marquette, Roberta Penny
O'Rourke, Vincent
Pare, Paul-Victor
Park, Joengdae
Selph, Carl J.
Shimerda, Thomas A.
Stephens, Lynn M.
Trapnell, Jerry E.
Zavgren, Christine Virginia

Forecasts

Ahern, John T.
Al-Rai, Ziad Khalil
Alford, Robert M.
Asebrook, Richard J.
Azzeh, Jawad Jawdat
Baldwin, Bruce A.
Berk, Joel Lee
Beshara, Robert Labib
Boynton, William C.
Brecha, Sonia A.
Campbell, David R.
Carter, Charles Edward
Cheever, John K.
Cianciolo, Salvatore T.A.
Cox, Clifford Theodore
Croll, David Bruce
Foote, Paul S.
Fries, Clarence E.
Gift, Michael J.
Gingras, Russell T.
Giroux, Gary Alan
Hassell, John M.
Hock, Clayton Allen
Holley, Charles L.
Hudson, Jean Marie Baldwin
Hyon, Yong-Ha
Janell, Paul Andrew
Keith, Richard Lyman
Kim, Kun Jang
Kim, Kung J.
Leese, Wallace R.
Lobo, Gerald Joseph
McMenimen, Leo Joseph
Min, Han Ki
Naoum, Christos
Neumann, Reuben
Olson, Stevan K.
Patell, James M.
Penman, Stephen H.
Philipich, Kirk Lynn
Porter, Gary A.
Reed, Barbara L.
Schreiner, Paul W.
Shelton, Fred A.
Snyder, Andrew G.
Taylor, William J.
Tosanguan, Prayoon
Waymire, Gregory Brooks

Foreign Currency

Bindon, Kathleen Jo Ranney
Cheng, Thomas Tong
Duangploy, Orapin
Glover, Robert I.
Graham, Lynford E.,Jr.
Gray, Dahli
Guithues, Denise Michele
Harris, Trevor S.
Haselkorn, Michael
Jain, Rohit
Kablan, Abdelsalam Ali
Kim, Hyuk
McMath, Herbert Kent
Nance, Jon Roland
Ndubizu, Gordian Anumudu
Rupp, Galen L.
Salatka, William Kenneth
Troberg, Pontus Henrik
Urbancic, Frank Robert
Williams, John Joseph
Wilner, Neil Alan
Yeater, David A.

History

Alvara, Martenelli
Andrews, Wesley T.
Bryson, Roscoe E.
Bulmash, Gary F.
Butler, Daniel L.
Coffey, William J.
Cooper, William David
Dillon, Gadis J.
Foroughi, Tahirih T.
Fox, James G.
Hilton, Joseph Norwood
Humma, Nancy K.
Hunthausen, John Matthew
Krebs, Joseph F.
Lubell, Myron Samuel
Merino, Barbara D.
Moseley, Owen B.
Potts, James H.
Worrels, Cecil Eugene

Human Resource Accounting

Bayes, Paul E.
Czarsty, Steven L.
Ehrenreich, Keith B.
Flowers, Vincent S.
Gillespie, Jackson Floyd
Granger, Courtenay L.
Hendricks, James A.
Lacey, John M.
Ogan, Pekin
Paperman, Jacob B.
Sangeladji, Mohamad
Tolouian, Pouran
Tomassini, Lawrence A.
Walker, John P.
Zaunbrecher, Hilary C.

Income Smoothing

Inflation Accounting

Interest Capitalization

Interim Statements

International

Inventories

Investments

Leases

Cho, Paek Je
Emore, James Robert
Geller, Arthur Neal
Kuo, Horng-Ching
Oliver, Thomas W.
Parry, Robert W.
Pfeiffer, Glenn M.
Ro, Byung-Tak
Sager, Clayton R.
Slaymaker, Adrianne Lee Einfeldt
Suadi, Arief
Thompson, Robert B.
Weintrop, Joseph

Managerial

Abdel-fattah, Zakaria F.
Abdullah, W. Moustafa
Aboul-Ezz, Mohamed El-Said
Abu-Romman, Mohammed A.
Adelsman, Rony Mark
Aiyama, Toshikazu
Alhumaid, Abdulrhman I.
Alworth, Charles Houston
Anyane-Ntow, Kwabena
Armitage, Howard M.
Arvey, Richard E.
Ashorn, Leroy W.
Atkinson, Anthony A.
Badi, Mahmoud Muhyadin
Baiman, Stanley
Baker, Charles Richard
Banker, Rajiv Dushyant
Bao, Da-Hsien
Bartenstein, Edwin
Bartkowski, Richard J.
Bartlett, Roger Wallace
Bavish, Vinod Bapalal
Beam, Thomas J.
Bean, Russell D.
Becker, Edward A.
Benbasat, Izak
Biddle, Gary Clark
Biggs, Stanley F.
Bodnar, George H.
Bourne, Frances Yvonne
Bourne, Lowell D.
Braide, January Miller
Brown, Barbara
Brown, Clifton E.
Brown, James France, Jr.
Brownell, Peter
Bullock, James H.
Bush, James L.
Campbell, Penolope S.
Capettini, Robert Joseph
Carruth, Paul Joseph
Carter, Donald G.
Caspari, John A.
Cassell, Michael N.
Chalos, Jean-Pierre
Chaney, Paul K.
Chang, Davis L.
Chatham, Thomas West
Chee, Yong Hee
Cheng, Cheng-shing
Chiang, Hung-Fu
Christensen, John Asmus
Collins, Everett F.
Colson, Robert Henry
Cottell, Philip G.
Cress, William Peter
Crichfield, Timothy Ryan
Cummings, Robert R.
Damtew, Desta
Daroca, Frank Peter, Jr.
Dillon, Ray D.
Dittman, David Arthur
Dougherty, Frank P.
Dozier, Donald D.
Dudley, Lola W.
Earnest, Kenneth Roger
Eggleton, Ian Richard Carfrae
Eliraqi, Iraqi A.
Elmallah, Amin A.
Euske, Kenneth J.
Ferris, Kenneth R.
Friedlob, George Thomas
Gangolly, Jagdish Shivshanker
Geiser, Eugene G.
Giacomino, Don Edward
Glick, John R.
Gomaa, Ismail I.
Graul, Paul R.
Gunn, Sanford Charles
Haka, Susan F.
Hanks, George F.
Harmon, Kay Poston
Harr, David James
Harrell, Adrian M.
Harris, William T.
Harrison, Paul D.
Harvey, Barron Henry
Hassanin, Badr E.
Hayes, David C.
Healy, Paul M.
Hegstad, Larry Paul
Henaidy, Hamid Mohamad
Hilton, Ronald W.
Hinton, Walter V.
Hirsch, Maurice L.
Hopkins, W. Clyde
Hoskin, Robert Ellsworth
Hosseini, Ahmad
Hunt, Herbert G.
Hyman, Ladelle M.
Irvine, Vernon B.
Ismail, Badr El-Din Hassanin
Izumi, Marleen M
Jacobs, Frederic H.
Jaikumar, Vaiyapuri
Joy, Arthur C Jr.
Kaufman, Jerry M.
Kiani-Aslani, Rajabaldi
Kim, Song Ki
Kim, Soon-Kee
Kin, Joon S.
King, Jerry G.
Klein, Hans Emil
Lambert, Richard A.
Lamm, David Vincent
Lander, Gerald Harold
Lawler, William C.
Lee, Chan M.
Lee, Orland Sherer
Lere, John C.
Liao, Mawsen
Lin, W. Thomas
Luzi, Andrew D
Mackey, James Thomas
Maher, Michael William
Mansour, Fathi A.
Martin, Dale R.
Mays, Robert Leland, Jr
McAlum, Harry G.
McClendon, Thurrell O.
Meddaugh, Edsil James
Merchant, Kenneth Allen
Merrill, Gregory Bruce
Middaugh, Jack Kendall II
Miller, James Jerome
Mirghani, Mohamed Ali
Namazi, Mohammed
Newhouse, Benjamin
Nitterhouse, Denise
Okpechi, Simeon O.
Ormsby, Susan Y.
Owens, Robert Willis
Park, Hai G.
Penno, Mark C.
Peters, Richard M.
Petro, Louis W.
Phillips, Thomas E.
Pitre, Richard
Pitt, Harold R.
Rasch, Ronald H.
Raslan, Maher Mahmoud
Raval, Vasant H.
Redding, Rodney J.
Reveley, Thomas R.
Richards, Evan W.
Riise, Arne J.
Rivers, Richard A.
Robinson, Michael A.
Roemmich, Roger A.
Rosenzweig, Kenneth Y.
Rwegasiru, Kami
Saldana, Cesar G.
Sap, Richard W.
Sardinha, Jose C.
Sarhan, Mostafa H.
Schweikart, James
Sellers, Fred Evans

Selto, Frank H.
Shields, Michael D.
Shin, Joon Y.
Simon, Daniel T.
Smith, Emmett D.
Smith, James F.
Smith, Janice A.
Soliman, Soliman Youssef
Starr, Douglas Alan
Stocks, Kevin Dayna
Sunby, Lawrence C.
Tawfik, Mohamed Sherif
Taylor, Robert Earl
Thomas, Michael Francis
Thomas, Phyllis L.
Tiessen, Peter
Tiller, Mikel Glen
Tishlias, Dennis P.
Tomczyk, Stephen H.
Toole, Howard R.
Turki, Hedi
Tyler, June Diane
Tzur, Joseph
Umapathy, Srinivasan
Vidulich, Barbara Bader
Visse, Richard H.
Wade, Daniel Eugene
Waegelein, James F.
Watkins, Paul Roger
Weatherwax, Roy C.
Wetzel, Thomas Sterling
White, Clinton Elwin, Jr.
Wilson, Beverly
Wilson, James E.
Wolf, Allen Edwin
Wolff, Bernard Christopher
Wygal, Donald Evans
Young, Richard Anthony
Young, S. Mark
Yunker, Penelope Jane
Zebda, Awni M.

Mutual Funds

Baker, Paul D.
Hoshower, Leon B.
Keating, John L.

Not-for-profit

Adibi-Adeyiga, Abidemi Janet
Al-Bassam, Sadik Mohammed
Amry, Mohammed A.
Atieh, Sulayman H.
Badawi, Ibrahim Mohamed
Baker, Jack D.
Berkshire, Stewart, Jr.
Berry, Maureen H.
Besser, Lance J.
Bokemeier, L. Charles
Bowlin, William Frank
Bozanich, Peter Kenneth
Bradley, Bryce T.
Brock, Barbara H.
Brooks, Eugene H.
Bryan, Edward L.
Carlson, Frederic J.
Charlton, Richard E., Jr.
Chung, Yu to
Conway, Lucian G.
Covaleski, Mark Anthony
Crain, Gilbert W.
Creech, Janie L.
Dittenhofer, Mortimer A.
Dodson, Nita Jean Jones
Dunn, William M.
Ebey, Carl Finley
El-Gehawe, Abdelsalam Ali
Engstrom, John G.
Fane, Gary R.
Gabhart, David L.
Gaffney, Mary Anne
Gallun, Rebecca A.
Gavin, Thomas A.
Goodhart, Edward S.
Griffin, Richard Bradley
Hall, Steven D.
Haugland, Jerry Lee
Hays, Larry Lynn
Herrera, Olga B.
Hodges, Richard L.
Holder, William W.
Howard, Thomas P.
Hughes, Jesse W.
Jablonsky, Stephen F.
Jadallah, Salih Mahmoud
Johnson, Walter L.
Kennett, Danny L.
Knight, Lee Goodpaster
Krueger, James M.
Lewis Tom Dean
Lomax, Victor William Jr.
Magann, Julia H.
Menon, Krishnagopal
Messmer, Victor C.
Miller, Roger O
Mills, John Robert
Minmier, George S.
Mykelburst, Harold N.
Neumann, Bruce Richard
Newman, Bruce R.
Nichols, Richard L.
Nunamaker, Thomas R.
Parmley, William K.
Parrish, Lillian C.
Patton, James M.
Peacock, Kenneth E.
Plewa, Franklin J.
Posey, Roderick B.
Pumhrey, Lela Dale
Raman, Krishnamurthy K.
Reed, Sarah Auman
Rees, David A.
Reid, George R.
Rexroad, William M.
Reynolds, Ruthie
Robbins, Walter A.
Rowe, Thomas Milton
Ruffner, Roy A.
Sage, Lloyd George
Schipper, Katherine
Schueller, Robert H.
Selin, John R.
Seville, Mary Alice
Sharp, Florence C.
Sherman, H. David
Shoulders, Craig D.
Smith, Roy
Suleiman, Nader A.
Tai, Benjamin Yuk-Kwong
Talbott, John Cotton
Talib, Moechtar
Traub, Jack
Wade, Charles Murray
Wallace, Wanda A.
Wescott, Shari H.
Wilson, Michael D.
Woehrle, Stephen Luer
Wood, Edwin A.
Wrege, William Thomas
Wu, Hsiang-fa

Oil & Gas

Avard, Stephen L.
Bell, Timothy Barnes
Buchanan, Phillip G.
Burnaby, Priscilla A.
Chope, Roger Allen
Conn, Carolyn Terrell
Doran, Benjamin Michael
DuBois, Donoly A.
Elmadfai, Abdulfattah O.
Etebari-Khorasgani, Ahmad
Feller, Robert E.
Haskin, Daniel L.
Huang, Jiunn-Chang
Hussain, Inam
Kennedy, Dennis T.
Mannino, Ronald C.
Moser, Duane
Naggar, Ali K
Novin, Adele M.
Oien, M. Burton
Simiar, Farhad
Smith, Abbie Jean
Tarabzune, Muhiadin Rashad
Vent, Glenn A.
Wright, Charlotte J.

Pensions

Bayer, Frieda Anna Forcht

Cavanagh, Walter Forbes
Godfrey, L. Howard
Gordon, Irene Malinda
Green, Mitzi Chandler
Hamdallah, Ahmed El Sayed
Holland, Roger G.
Landsman, Wayne Robert
Maher, John Joseph
Mielke, David E.
Parker, Mary V.
Sil, Amar Nath
Stone, Mary Sheetz
Sullens, Robert T.
Swindle, Charles B.
Tosh, David Edward
Willinger, Geoffrey L.

Profession

Abraham, Stanley C.
Alvis, John M.
Anderson, Thomas N., Jr.
Ballew, Van B.
Barker, Robert L.
Barton, M. Frank, Jr.
Beed, Teresa Kathryn
Benke, Ralph L.
Bottin, Ronald R.
Bracken, Robert M.
Buckley, Charles E.
Buehlmann, David M.
Bullen, Maria L.
Campbell, Terry Lee
Clowery, Grant M.
Crowley, Robert M.
Cunningham, Billie Marie
Davies, Jonathan J.
Davis, Stanley Ward
Dennis, David K.
Dickinson, Harry Dawideit
Dillard, Jesse F.
Douglas, Sharon M.
Douma, Irene K.
Fay, Jack R.
Feibelkorn, George A.
Goodman, Leonard
Grabski, Severin V.
Groner, Michael I.
Guttmann, Paul Eston
Harper, James C.
Heaston, Patrick H.
Henderson, James Randal
Hicks, James O., Jr.
Hill, Robert W.
Hooks, Karen Leah
Hooper, Herbert P.
Jacobs, Frederick R.
Jacoby, Philip F.
Jiambolvo, James J.
Johnson, Douglas A
Johnson, Sidney Bruce
Karbens, John P.
Kilgore, Ronald W.
Klein, Kyle H.
Lammers, Lucille E.
Lasater, David B.
Lea, Kenneth R.
Levine, Marc
Lynn, Susan A.
Maloo, Man Chand
Marks, Marcus Francis
Marshall, Clifford L.
Martin, Jimmy W.
Maupin, Rebekah J.
Moore, John Oliver
Newton, Grant W.
Olds, Philip R.
Olsen, Ronnie Gary
Ratliff, Richard L.
Rosen, Louis I.
Rymer, Victoria Sharp
Sanderson, George Norman
Saunders, Gary J.
Scheiner, James H.
Schroeder, Richard G.
Senatra, Phillip T.
Shields, Paul D.
Siegel, Gary H.
Skousen, Clifford R.
Smith, Alvin G.
Smith, George S.
Smith, James D.
Smith, Lawrence M.
Tantral, Panadda
Tassin, Maurice F.
Ward, Danny Ray
Welker, Robert B.
Willis, Eugene

Quarterly Data

Bengharbia, Salem M.
Givoly, Dan
Griffin, Paul A.
Hutchins, Ronald Earl
Pelz, Ulrich
Phillips, Mary
Putnam, Karl B.

Real Estate

Hamilton, Marshall Lee
Powell, Norma C.

Research & Development

Adams, Steven J.
Bazaz, Mohammad Sadegh
Brugger, Karl A.
Dukes, Roland Edward
Hein, Cheryl Donnithorne
Joseph, Harold W.
Nix, Paul E.
Sinning, Kathleen E.
Tranter, Terry L.
Vigeland, Robert L.

Social

Blank, Mark M.
Burton, Eric J.
Cargile, Barney Ray
Cherry, Alan Abraham
Corbett, Barker D.
Corriher, Jacob D.
Dilley, Steven Charles
El-Gawhary, Ali Mohamed
Fletcher, John Cameron
Freedman, Martin
Granger, Mitchell Parker, II
Hurley, James F.
Ingram, Robert W.
Kunkel, James Gregory
Kwon, Young K.
Langeuin, Marcel
Lewis, Stanley X.
Lindblom, Christi K.
McFerrin, William D.
McKay, Frances Ellen
Neimark, Marilyn
Ratcliffe, Thomas H.
Roser, Sherman R.
Roth, Harold P.
Rueschhoff, Donald S.
Shane, Philip B.
Spicer, Barry H.
Stern, Myles S.
Stevens, William Patrick
Stiner, Frederic M.
Tipgos, Manuel A.
Wilde, Harold Heye
Williams, Paul F.
Wiseman, Joanne W.
Wyler, Wayne E.

Standard-setting

Chewning, Eugene G. Jr.
Dereshiwsky, Mary Irene
Devine, Wilfred Francis
Hendricks, Arthur George
Hiltebeitel, Kenneth Merrill
McKee, Arnold J.
Porter, Mattie C.
Puro, Marsha B.
Younkins, Edward Wayne

Statement of Chgs In Fin.Position

Allen, George Louis
Brownlee, Earl R.
Cherny, Julius

Nagoda, Robert John, II
Nissing, Burton J.
Nordhauser, Susan Litt
O'Connor, Walter Francis
O'Dell, Michael Arthur
O'Neil, Cherie Jeanne
Oatsvall, Rebecca Johnson
Oestreich, Nathan Alan
Olivera, Herbert Ernest
Osborn, John Paul
Ostrowski, Barbara A.
Outslay, Edmund
Panich, Richard Louis
Parker, Seth K.
Pearson, Della A.
Pollard, William B.
Pope, Thomas R.
Posey, Clyde L.
Pulliam, Dale R.
Raabe, William A.
Rans, Donald L.
Reeder, Janis R.
Reese, Craig E.
Renfer, Karin
Rhee, Thomas A.
Richardson, Willie
Robinson, John R.
Robison, John C.
Rogow, Robert B.
Rolfe, Robert J.
Ross, Ronald S.
Samson, William D.
Sayre, Julian R.
Schell, Wayne Morris
Schroeder, Jack D.
Schwartz, Bill N.
Seamans, Dana Gerald
Seat, Donald L.
Singleton, William R.
Spede, Edward C.
Stagliano, Anthony J.
Stewart, Dave Nelson
Stillabower, Linda May
Stout, Gary Raymond
Streer, Paul J.
Streffeler, John M.
Strobel, Caroline D.
Sullivan, Mark James
Swad, Randy Gene
Swanson, Robert Dean
Swenson, Charles William
Swingen, Judyth
Syck, Lawrence J.
Taylor, Ronald Leslie
Thompson, Steven Craig
Tripp, John Cassius
Tucker, Michael James
Vawter, Charles L.
Waters, Gary Lynn
Weber, Richard P.
White, Debra M.
White, Richard Alan
Whitt, Sue Y.
Whittenburg, Gerald Eugene
Wiehrs, Paula E.
Wilguess, John Harry
Wunder, Haroldene Fowler
Wyndelts, Robert Ward

AUTHORS LISTED ALPHABETICALLY BY METHODOLOGY

AUTHORS CATEGORIZED BY METHODOLOGY

Archival

Alidina, Mohamed
Alvara, Martenelli
Anderson, Kenneth E.
Anderson, Philip Neil
Andrews, Wesley T.
Aukerman, Richard A.
Azzeh, Jawad Jawdat
Bartenstein, Edwin
Bartlett, Henry C.
Beirne, Thomas Joseph, Jr.
Bond, James G.
Boyd, Joseph L.
Brock, Barbara H.
Bryson, Roscoe E.
Bulmash, Gary F.
Butler, Daniel L.
Cain, James E.
Cairns, Scott N.
Capps, Robert S.
Carr, Janice Lynn
Coffey, William J.
Collins, Julie Haney
Colvard, Robert Gene
Committe, Bruce E.
Cooper, William David
Crowley, Robert M.
Cunningham, Billie Marie
Davies, Jonathan J.
Davis, Lee Edward
DeCelles, Michael D.
Degnan, Theodore
DeVries, Joann S.
Donelly, David P.
Englebrecht, Ted Dewin
Ensly, Chula G.
Fantl, Irving L.
Fesmire, Walker E.
Fitzgerald, Michael N.
Flesher, Tonya Kay
Flowers, Vincent S.
Frantz, Irving L.
Gardner, Robert L.
Gatley, Mary Sue
Goetz, Joseph F.
Green John L.
Groner, Michael I.
Halperin, Robert M.
Hardman, Oswald C.
Harline, Norman L.
Hilton, Joseph Norwood
Holland, Michael L.
Hooper, Herbert P.
Humma, Nancy K.
Hunthausen, John Matthew
Hunthausen, S. J.
Izumi, Marleen M
Jacobs, Frederick R.
Jones, Sally Morrow
Jordan, William F.
Joy, David Walter
Karlinsky, Stewart Sheldon
Kimbrell, James A.
Kneer, Daniel Charles
Kozub, Robert M.
Kramer, John L.
Krebs, Joseph F.
Krueger, Lavern Eldon
Lacy, Melvin E.
Larkins, Ernst R.
LaRue, David Wayne
Lassila, Dennis Ray
Lathen, William Clifford
Lett, Samuel Lafayette
Lubell, Myron Samuel
Madeo, Silvia A.
Maloney, David Mitchell
Marquardt, John D.
McCarty, Naomi J.
McClure, Malcolm M.
Merino, Barbara D.
Misiewicz, Kevin
Moseley, Owen B.
Nagoda, Robert John, II
Nissing, Burton J.
O'Connor, Walter Francis
Oatsvall, Rebecca Johnson
Oestreich, Nathan Alan
Olivera, Herbert Ernest
Osborn, John Paul
Outslay, Edmund
Panich, Richard Louis
Pannell, Richard L.
Pollard, William B.
Pope, Thomas R.
Posey, Clyde L.
Potts, James H.
Reeder, Janis R.
Reese, Craig E.
Rezac, Reginald N.
Riise, Arne J.
Roberts, Ray
Robison, John C.
Rolfe, Robert J.
Ross, Ronald S.
Ruland, Robert G.
Samson, William D.
Schell, Wayne Morris
Schroeder, Jack D.
Seamans, Dana Gerald
Seat, Donald L.
Silvester, Wilfred H.
Smith, George S.
St. Pierre, Kent Edgar
Steinbart, Paul John
Stewart, Dave Nelson
Stillabower, Linda May
Strecker, Mary F.
Streer, Paul J.
Swanson, Robert Dean
Swenson, Charles William
Swingen, Judyth
Syck, Lawrence J.
Tantral, Panadda
Teichman, Ronald J.
Thompson, Steven Craig
Tripp, John Cassius
Tucker, James Joseph III
Verreault, Kathryn M.
Wagner, Charles R.
Waters, Gary Lynn
Weber, Richard P.
Whitt, Sue Y.
Worrels, Cecil Eugene

Experimental

Abdolmohammadi, Mohammed J.
Adelsman, Rony Mark
Aiyama, Toshikazu
Ajinkaya, Bipin B.
Alexander, Robin A.
Anderson, Donald Terry
Anderson, Matthew J.
Anderson, Thomas N., Jr.
Arnett, Stephen J.
Arvey, Richard E.
Ashton, Alison Marie Hubbard
Attaway, Alan N.
Atwood, K. Edward
Austin, Kenneth R.
Bailey, Charles Daniels
Bailey, Kieffer Edwin, III
Bailey, William Tansley
Bamber, Edward Michael
Bao, Da-Hsien
Barnett, Andrew H.
Barron, Rhelda W.
Bartkowski, Richard J.
Barton, Thomas L.
Baxter, Clifton A.
Bayes, Paul E.
Beam, Thomas J.
Beck, Paul J.
Benbasat, Izak
Bennett, Shelby Dill
Benson, Vaughn Leon
Bentsen, Elesa J.W.
Black, Robert L.
Boland, Richard James, Jr.
Boley, Richard Dale
Booker, Quinton
Boritz, Jefim E.
Bourne, Lowell D.
Bowman, Betty R.
Boyd, James H.
Boyett, Arthur S., III
Broden, Berry C.
Brook, Edna Mae

Brown, Clifton E.
Brown, Surdo
Brownell, Peter
Bryant, Murray J.
Burke, Richard Collingwood
Butler, David H.
Byars, Richard B.
Campbell, Penelope S.
Capettini, Robert Joseph
Cargile, Barney Ray
Carruth, Paul Joseph
Carter, Charles Edward
Casey, Cornelius John, Jr.
Chalos, Jean-Pierre
Chang, Davis L.
Chen, Kung-Hong
Cherry, Alan Abraham
Chevalier, Gilles
Chewning, Eugene G. Jr.
Christmore, Patricia C.
Cianciolo, Salvatore T.A.
Clark, Corolyn Elizabeth
Collins, Dennis John
Compton, Ted R.
Croll, David Bruce
Crosby, Michael Alan
Crum, Robert P.
Daroca, Frank Peter, Jr.
Dau, Khalifa A.
Davidson, David
Davidson, Lewis Franklin
Dickens, Thomas L.
Dillard, Jesse F.
Dillaway, Manson Peter
Dombrowski, Robert F.
Dorr, Patrick B.
Doty, Edwin A.
Dougherty, Frank P.
Doupnik, Timothy S.
Drummings, Sandra T.
Duangploy, Orapin
Duke, Gordon Leon
Duncan, William A.
Dungan, Christopher W.
Dworin, Lowell
Dykxhoorn, Hans J.
Earnest, Kenneth Roger
Eggleton, Ian Richard Carfrae
El-Arabi, Abdussalan
El-Badadawi, Mohammed H.
El-Maksy, Mostafa M.
Elhassy, Juma'a
Emore, James Robert
Enis, Charles Richard
Etherington, Lois Deane
Ewing-Chow, Frank D.
Farmer, Larry E.
Fazzi, Charles
File, Richard Garrison
Fisher, Ted Lance
Flaherty, Daniel J.
Fletcher, John Cameron
Ford, Donald H.
Frakes, Albert H.
Friedman, Mark Edward
Fulks, Daniel Lee
Gaber, Brian G.
Gaertner, James F.
Gangolly, Jagdish Shivshanker
Geary, Kent M.
Geary, William Thomas
Gibbins, Michael
Glazer, Alan S.
Glezen, G. William, Jr.
Godfrey, Robert F.
Golden, Mary Rolwing
Gomaa, Ismail I.
Gramling, Lawrence J.
Gray, Dahli
Greenberg, Robert R.
Groft, William L.
Grove, Hugh D.
Grudnitski, Gary Martin
Guber, Quentin N.
Hamdallah, Ahmed El Sayed
Hamer, John Gwenffrud
Hammer, Lawrence H.
Hanks, George F.
Harper,Robert W.,Jr.
Harper, Thomas Robert
Harr, David James
Harrell, Adrian M.
Harris, William T.
Harsha, Phillip D.
Haskin, Daniel L.
Hassell, John M.
Hawkins, Ennis Milton
Helleloid, Richard Trygve
Heller, Kenneth H.
Henaidy, Hamid Mohamad
Hicks, Margaret
Hicks, Samuel A.
Hiltebeitel, Kenneth Merrill
Hinds, John E.
Hirsch, Maurice L.
Hitzig, Neal B
Hoffman, David E.
Hoffman, Michael J.
Holmen, Jay Scott
Holmes, James R.
Honea, James Harold
Hopewell, Rita Jean
Hoskin, Robert Ellsworth
Howard, Thomas P.
Howe, Keith R.
Hreha, Karen Sue
Hull, Rita P.
Ibrahim, Mohamed El Hady
Ismail, Hamzah B.
Jackson, Anthony Wayne
Jamison, Robert Watt, Jr.
Jenne, Stanley E.
Johnson, William B.
Joyce, Edward J.
Kaplan, Steven E.
Karan, Vijay
Karvel, George Raymond
Kelsy, Richard L.
Kennedy, Helen Augusta Davis
Kennelley, Michael Dean
Kermis, George F.
Kessler, Lawrence F.
Keys, David E.
Kida, Thomas Edward
Kim, Joon Seuk
Kin, Joon S.
Kiringoda, Dayal
Knechel, Warren Robert
Koch, Bruce S.
Koeppen, David R.
Kreuze, Jerry Glenn
Kulsrud, William Norman
Kushel, Paul Steven
Landsman, Wayne Robert
Larcker, David F.
Lathan, Malcolm H.
Lee, Johng Yul
Lee, Patsy L.
Leese, Wallace R.
Leichti, Janet Lynn Colbert
Lemon, William Morley
Lilly, Martha S.
Limberg, Stephen T.
Lin, W. Thomas
Liu, Chao M.
Luthy, David H.
Luzi, Andrew D
Mackey, James Thomas
Maher, John Joseph
Maher, Michael William
Mangold, Nancy Rueyhwa
Marquis, Linda M.
Maydew, Gary L.
Mayper, Alan G.
Mays, Robert Leland, Jr
McCabe, John C.
McEldowney, John Eugene
McKay, Frances Ellen
McKinley, Sue H.
Meddaugh, Edsil James
Meixner, Wilda Furr
Melcher, Trini U.
Messier, William Francis Jr.
Meyer, Kent Wyatt
Michaelson, Robert H.
Middaugh, Jack Kendall II
Mills, John Robert
Moffie, Robert Paul
Monger, Rodney Frank
Moran, Ceil Marie
Murphy, Kevin E.
Nair, Raghavan D.
Nanni, Alfred John Jr.

Nathan, Kevin Stuart
Neidermeyer, Adolph A.
Neilson, Denis Peter
Nitterhouse, Denise
Norris, Daniel M.
O'Dell, Michael Arthur
Oliver, Janice B.
Ostrowski, Barbara A.
Pan, Sheng-Der
Pany, Kurt J.
Park, Hai G.
Parker, Larry M.
Paul, John W.
Pawliczek, Ronald B.
Phillips, Thomas James Jr.
Plumlee, Roy D.
Pocano, Thomas M.
Porcano, Thomas M.
Porter, Leslie R.
Pratt, James H.
Pulliam, Dale R.
Pushkin, Ann B.
Raabe, William A.
Raiborn, Cecily A.
Raslan, Maher Mahmoud
Ratcliffe, Thomas H.
Rebele, James Edward
Reckers, Philip M.
Redding, Rodney J.
Reeve, James M.
Reveley, Thomas R.
Rich, Anne J.
Richardson, Frederick M.
Robinson, Christopher Michael
Robinson, Michael A.
Rogow, Robert B.
Rohrbach, Kermit J.
Romney, Marshall B.
Rupp, Galen L.
Rymer, Victoria Sharp
Sardinha, Jose C.
Saul, William E.
Sayre, Julian R.
Schepanski, Albert A.
Schmutte, James L.
Schneider, Arnold
Schwartz, Bill N.
Selling, Thomas I.
Selto, Frank H.
Shields, Michael D.
Shook, Charles H.
Sil, Amar Nath
Silhan, Peter A.
Simkins, Allen F.
Skeith, Arlette W.
Slavin, Nathan S.
Smieliauskas, Waldemar J.
Smith, James F.
Smith, Wilbur Irvin
Sneed, Florence Richwood
Snowball, Douglas Alexander Thomas
Solomon, Ira
Sorkin, Horton L.
Stambaugh, Clyde T.
Starr, Douglas Alan
Steedle, Lamont F.
Stephens, Ray G.
Stewart, John Ray
Stivers, Bonnie La Von Philbrook
Stocks, Kevin Dayna
Stone, Ronald Summer
Strobel, Caroline D.
Stryker, Judson P.
Tabor, Richard Herbert
Taylor, Barbara
Taylor, Robert Earl
Thomas, Phyllis L.
Thompson, James H.
Tiessen, Peter
Tiller, Mikel Glen
Tishlias, Dennis P.
Tolouian, Pouran
Tomassini, Lawrence A.
Tosh, David Edward
Troxel, Terri E.
Truitt, Jack F.
Tyler, June Diane
Vent, Glenn A.
Vidulich, Barbara Bader
Visse, Richard H.
Volkert, James F.
Watkins, Larry Edward
Watkins, Paul Roger
Weber, Ronald A.
Weintrop, Joseph
Weis, William L.
Welker, Donna Lynn
Welker, Robert B.
Wetzel, Thomas Sterling
White, Clinton Elwin, Jr.
White, Richard Alan
Whittenburg, Gerald Eugene
Whittington, Oliver R.
Wiggins, Casper E.
Wilkerson, Jack Edward Jr.
Williams, Paul F.
Williams, Ralph Batchelder
Wilner, Neil Alan
Wright, Arnold M.
Wright, William Frank
Wyndelts, Robert Ward
Yeary, James D.
Zaunbrecher, Hilary C.

Field Study

Abdeen, Adan Muhammed
Abdel-fattah, Zakaria F.
Abdoelkadir, Katjep K.
Abdullah, W. Moustafa
Aboul-Ezz, Mohamed El-Said
Abraham, Stanley C.
Adams, Barbara Louise
Adelberg, Arthur H.
Adibi-Adeyiga, Abidemi Janet
Al-Bassam, Sadik Mohammed
Al-Shuaib, Shaib A.
Albrecht, William S.
Alford, Robert M.
Alhumaid, Abdulrhman I.
Alkafaji, Yass A.
Allen, George Louis
Alsultan, Sultan M.
Alsup, Rodney Glen
Alvis, John M.
Alworth, Charles Houston
Amenkhienam, Felix Ehichoya
Amry, Mohammed A.
Anderman, Steven G.
Anderson, Earl H.
Anyane-Ntow, Kwabena
Armitage, Howard M.
Armstrong, Mary Beth
Arrington, Cecil E.
Asebrook, Richard J.
Ashorn, Leroy W.
Atieh, Sulayman H.
Badawi, Ibrahim Mohamed
Badi, Mahmoud Muhyadin
Badran, Sanaa M.
Baingridge, Dunham R.
Baker, Jack D.
Baldwin, Duane E.
Ballew, Van B.
Banatte, Jean-Marie
Banker, Rajiv Dushyant
Barker, Robert L.
Barkman, Arnold I.
Bartlett, Roger Wallace
Barton, M. Frank, Jr.
Baudin, Jerry J.
Bavish, Vinod Bapalal
Bayless, Mark E.
Bayou, Mohammed E.
Bazaz, Mohammad Sadegh
Bean, Russell D.
Becker, Edward A.
Beed, Teresa Kathryn
Benke, Ralph L.
Bennett, Jerome Vincent
Berkshire, Stewart, Jr.
Bermudez, Andres
Berry, Leonard E.
Besser, Lance J.
Bettinger, Cynthia Ann Rabby
Biggs, Stanley F.
Bindon, Kathleen Jo Ranney
Birkett, Brenda S.
Birrer, George Eddy
Blank, Mark M.
Bodnar, George H.

Bokemeier, L. Charles
Boockholdt, James Lee
Boodai, Khalid M.
Bostwick, William Jackson
Bottin, Ronald R.
Bowlin, William Frank
Bozanich, Peter Kenneth
Bracken, Robert M.
Brackner, James Walter
Bradley, Bryce T.
Braun, Robert M.
Brewer, Carl Wm.
Brooks, Eugene H.
Brown, Barbara
Brown, Howard J.
Brown, Paul R.
Brownlee, Earl R.
Buckley, Charles E.
Buehlmann, David M.
Bullen, Maria L.
Burke, Mimi
Burns, Jane Offutt
Burton, Eric J.
Bush, James L.
Byrd, David Blackwell
Byrd, Sandra Darlene
Campbell, Jane E.
Campbell, Terry Lee
Campbell, Walter M.
Carlson, Frederic J.
Carney, Keith T.
Carpenter, Vivian Laverne
Carter, Donald G.
Carter, Jack L.
Cashell, James Douglass
Caspari, John A.
Cassell, Michael N.
Chapman, William C.
Charlton, Richard E., Jr.
Chatham, Thomas West
Cheng, Ting-Wong
Cherny, Julius
Chiang, Hung-Fu
Clark, Wilbur R.
Clay, Raymond J.
Clowery, Grant M.
Coakley, James R.
Coffee, Carl D.
Colgan, Joseph C.
Collins, Everett F.
Colson, Robert Henry
Conn, Carolyn Terrell
Conway, Lucian G.
Corbett, Barker D.
Cornick, Michael F.
Correia, Ernest V.
Corriher, Jacob D.
Covaleski, Mark Anthony
Cox, James S.
Crain, Gilbert W.
Creech, Janie L.
Cress, William Peter
Crockett, James R.
Dalton, Michael A.
Damtew, Desta
Danos, Paul P.
Davis, Dale Allen
Davis, Henry Holbrook
Davis, James R.
Davis, Stanley Ward
Dawkins, Louis E.
Dawkins, Sarah E.
Dawley, Donald L.
Deck, Alan Bruce
Deitrick, James W.
Dennis, David K.
Dennis- Escoffier, Shirley
Dereshiwsky, Mary Irene
Devine, Wilfred Francis
Diamond, Michael A.
Dickinson, Harry Dawideit
Dilley, Steven Charles
Dillon, Ray D.
Dinius, Sara Holton
Dirsmith, Mark W.
Dittenhofer, Mortimer A.
Dittman, David Arthur
Dodson, Nita Jean Jones
Donahue, Marlene S.
Douglas, Sharon M.
Douma, Irene K.
Dozier, Donald D.
Driscoll, Donna Ann
Dudley, Lola W.
Dunn, William M.
Dykes, Linda Muckenfuss
Ebey, Carl Finley
Edmonds, Thomas Paul
Egenold, Robert V.
Ehrenreich, Keith B.
Eisenman, Seymour L.
El-Gehawe, Abdelsalam Ali
Ellison, David J.
Elsea, John Edward
Engle, Terry J.
Engstrom, John G.
Euske, Kenneth J.
Fairchild, Joseph V.
Fane, Gary R.
Farrar, Robert H.
Fasci, Martha Alicia
Fay, Jack R.
Feibelkorn, George A.
Ferris, Kenneth R.
Fields, Kent T.
Fleming, Mary Madonna Katzer
Flesher, Dale L.
Flory, Steven M.
Foroughi, Tahirih T.
Fowler, Anna Cook
Freedman, Martin
Friedberg, Alan H.
Gaffney, Mary Anne
Gangouli, Gourganga
Gavin, Thomas A.
Gean, Gilbert Farrell
Giacoletti, Robert R.
Giacomino, Don Edward
Gillett, John W.
Giroux, Gary Alan
Glick, John R.
Godwin, Larry B.
Gokarn, Rajul Yoganand
Goodhart, Edward S.
Goodman, Leonard
Govindarajan, V.
Grabski, Severin V.
Graci, Samuel P.
Graham, Lynford E.,Jr.
Granger, Courtenay L.
Granger, Mitchell Parker, II
Gray, O. Ronald
Green, Mitzi Chandler
Grierson, Peter Robert
Griffin, Richard Bradley
Gunn, Sanford Charles
Guttikonda, Ramamohana R.
Guttmann, Paul Eston
Hadley, Galen D.
Haka, Susan F.
Hall, James Arthur
Hall, Steven D.
Hall, Thomas W.
Hamilton, Marshall Lee
Harkins, Jeffrey Lynn
Harmon, Kay Poston
Harper, James C.
Harris, Robert W.
Harrison, Kenneth Eugene
Harrison, Paul D.
Hartgraves, Al L.
Harvey, Barron Henry
Haskins, Mark Eugene
Hatami, Roben
Haugland, Jerry Lee
Hawkins, Charles E.
Hayes, David C.
Hays, Larry Lynn
Heaston, Patrick H.
Hegstad, Larry Paul
Heian, James Bernard
Hein, Cheryl Donnithorne
Helms, Flenn Lindley
Hemmingway, James R.
Henderson, James Randal
Herrera, Olga B.
Hicks, James O., Jr.
Hill, Robert W.
Hiltner, Arthur H.
Hines, Charles Edmund, Jr.
Hinton, Walter V.
Hodges, Richard L.
Holder, William W.

Holt, Doris L.
Holtfreter, Robert Eugene
Hooks, Karen Leah
Hopkins, Bobbie H.
Hopkins, W. Clyde
Horlick, Geoffrey Richard
Hughes, Jesse W.
Hurley, James F.
Hussain, Inam
Hussein, Mohammed E.
Hyman, Ladelle M.
Irvine, Vernon B.
Jablonsky, Stephen F.
Jackson, Betty R.
Jacoby, Philip F.
Jadallah, Salih Mahmoud
Jagolinzer, Philip
Jiambolvo, James J.
Johnson, Douglas A
Johnson, Kenneth L.
Johnson, Raymond N.
Johnson, Sidney Bruce
Johnson, Walter L.
Johnston, James G.
Jones, Richard W.
Joy, Arthur C Jr.
Kagle, Arthur Renn
Kaliska, Burton S.
Kamnikar, Judith A.
Kandiel, El Sayed H. A.
Kanter, Howard Allen
Karbens, John P.
Kauder, William F.
Keck, John T.
Kelley, Timothy Patrick
Kennett, Danny L.
Kiani-Aslani, Rajabaldi
Kilgore, Ronald W.
Kilpatrick, Joyce
Kim, Hyo Seuk
Kimura, Joseph H.
King, Jerry G.
Kirkpatrick, Donald Clay
Kissinger, John N.
Klein, Hans Emil
Klein, Kyle H.
Klien, Lawrence A.
Knapp, Michael C.
Knight, Barry Allan
Knight, Lee Goodpaster
Knight, Royal E.
Knutson, Dennis L.
Koester, Robert J.
Kordi, Khalil A. Khalil
Kreiser, Lawrence A.
Krueger, James M.
Kucic, Anthony R.
Kunitake, Walter Kunio
Kuo, Horng-Ching
Lacey, John M.
Lake, Robert C.
Lam, Wai Ping
Lambert, Kenneth R.
Lamm, David Vincent
Lammers, Lucille E.
Lander, Gerald Harold
Langer, Russell D.
Langeuin, Marcel
Lasater, David B.
Lavin, David
Lea, Kenneth R.
Lee, Orland Sherer
Leong, Kenneth Kin On
Lere, John C.
Levine, Marc
Lewis Tom Dean
Lewis, Barry Leroy
Lewis, Lawrence D.
Lewis, Stanley X.
Libby, Robert
Lieberman, Arthur Z.
Lindblom, Christi K.
Listro, John P.
Lovdal, Michael Lawrence
Lynn, Susan A.
Mandell, Steven Leslie
Margheim, Loren L.
Marks, Marcus Francis
Markwalder, Alice M.
Marshall, Clifford L.
Martin, Charles L.
Martin, Dale R.
Martin, Jimmy W.
Mattson, Lucretia W.
Maupin, Rebekah J.
Mayer- Sommer, Alan P.
McAlum, Harry G.
McCaslin, Thomas Eugene
McClendon, Thurrell O.
McCormack, Vincent Francis
McEnroe, John Edward
McGillivray, Robert E.
McKean, Gerald William
McKinnon, Sharon M.
McMath, Herbert Kent
Merei, Issam J.
Messmer, Victor C.
Michalka, William J.
Milano, Duane R.
Milburn, John A.
Miller, James Jerome
Miller, Roger O
Min, Han Ki
Minmier, George S.
Mirghani, Mohamed Ali
Moneef, Abdullah Ali
Monroe, Gary S.
Monroe, John E.
Moore, John Oliver
Moore, Phillip M.
Mutchler, Jane F.
Mykelburst, Harold N.
Nagarajan, Nandu Jaishankar
Naggar, Ali K
Nathan, Edward C.
Neimark, Marilyn
Neumann, Reuben
Newman, Bruce R.
Newton, Grant W.
Newton, Lauren K.
Nichols, Richard L.
Niemeyer, Ronald Duane
Noel, James Carl
Nosari, John Stanley
Nunamaker, Thomas R.
Nunley, Terry J.
Nutter, David E.
O'Neil, Cherie Jeanne
Ogan, Pekin
Oion, M. Burton
Okpechi, Simeon O.
Olds, Philip R.
Oliver, Joseph Robert
Olsen, Ronnie Gary
Olson, Stevan K.
Ormsby, Susan Y.
Ovadia, Arie
Overbey, John T.
Owens, Robert Willis
Owings, Guy W.
Palmon, Dan
Palmrose, Zoe-Vonna
Paperman, Jacob B.
Parker, Seth K.
Parmley, William K.
Parrish, Lillian C.
Pattison, Diane D.
Patton, James M.
Paxton, William E.
Pearson, Della A.
Pearson, Michael A.
Peters, Richard M.
Philipich, Kirk Lynn
Phillips, Thomas E.
Pincus, Karen Vandermause
Pitre, Richard
Plewa, Franklin J.
Porter, Mattie C.
Potts, A. J.
Pumhrey, Lela Dale
Purvis, S.E.C.
Raiborn, Debra D.
Raman, Krishnamurthy K.
Rankin, Larry J.
Rans, Donald L.
Rao, Honnudike V.
Rao, Kailas J.
Ratliff, Richard L.
Raval, Vasant H.
Reber, Dennis L.
Reed, Ronald O.
Reed, Sarah Auman
Rees, David A.

Reinstein, Alan
Remmele, David Alan
Renfer, Karin
Reynolds, Ruthie
Rhee, Thomas A.
Ricchiute, David N.
Richards, Evan W.
Richardson, Willie
Rittenberg, Larry E.
Rivera Fernandez, Juan Manuel
Robbins, Walter A.
Roberts, Martin B.
Rodgers, Fay H.
Roemmich, Roger A.
Rogers, Richard L.
Rosen, Louis I.
Rosenzweig, Kenneth Y.
Roser, Sherman R.
Rouse, Robert W.
Rowe, Thomas Milton
Rueschhoff, Donald S.
Ruffner, Roy A.
Russell, Keith A.
Rwegasiru, Kami
Salatka, William Kenneth
Saldana, Cesar G.
Samuelson, Bruce A.
Sanderson, George Norman
Sangeladji, Mohamad
Sannella, Alexander
Sap, Richard W.
Sardians, Joseph L.
Sarhan, Mostafa H.
Saubert, Lynn K.
Saunders, Gary J.
Sbrocchi, Frank L.
Schilit, Howard M.
Schipper, Katherine
Schmidgall, Raymond S.
Schroeder, Mary S.
Schroeder, Nicholas Waldo
Schroeder, Richard G.
Schueller, Robert H.
Schultq, Joseph J.
Schultz, Norman O.
Schwarzbach, Henry R.
Schweikart, James
Selin, John R.
Sellers, Fred Evans
Senatra, Phillip T.
Seville, Mary Alice
Shaltout, Mohanned K.
Shane, Philip B.
Sharp, Durwin L.
Sharp, Florence C.
Sheldahl, Terry K.
Sheriff, Jimmy D.
Sherman, H. David
Shields, Paul D.
Shoulders, Craig D.
Shriver, Keith Alva
Siegel, Gary H.
Siegel, Joel G.
Simon, John R.
Skousen, Clifford R.
Slaymaker, Adrianne Lee Einfeldt
Smith, Alvin G.
Smith, James D.
Smith, Janice A.
Smith, Lawrence M.
Smith, Maureen H.
Smith, Roy
Soloman, Lanny M.
Spede, Edward C.
Stanga, Keith G.
Steed, Steve Alan
Stern, Myles S.
Stiner, Frederic M.
Stout, Gary Raymond
Stratton, William O.
Streffeler, John M.
Stumbaugh, Charles C.
Suleiman, Nader A.
Sumners, Glenn Earl
Sunby, Lawrence C.
Sutton, Timothy G.
Swad, Randy Gene
Swearingen, James G.
Tai, Benjamin Yuk-Kwong
Talbott, John Cotton
Talib, Moechtar
Tang, Roger Y.
Tassin, Maurice F.
Taylor, Robert D.
Taylor, Ronald Leslie
Thomas, Michael Francis
Thompson, Billy D.
Thompson, Carolyn L.
Thompson, John A.
Thompson, Robert B.
Tillery, Jean Dupree
Tondkar, Rasoul H.
Traub, Jack
Trigg, Rodger R.
Tucker, Michael James
Tull, Guy L.
Tully, Gregory John
Turki, Hedi
Uddin, M. Jamir
Umapathy, Srinivasan
Van Dongen, William Orson
Van Zante, Neal R.
Vawter, Charles L.
Verreault, Daniel Arthur
Verschoor, Curtis C.
Vicknair, David B.
Wade, Charles Murray
Wade, Daniel Eugene
Wallace, Wanda A.
Waller, Thomas C.
Ward, Dalton Dewey
Ward, Danny Ray
Warner, Paul D.
Waymire, Gregory Brooks
Weatherwax, Roy C.
Wee, Warren
Whisnant, Susan R.
White, Debra M.
Wilde, Harold Heye
Wilguess, John Harry
Williams, Hubert J.
Willis, Eugene
Wilson, Michael D.
Wilson, Peter Randall
Wilson, Wayne R.
Winters, Alan Joseph
Wiseman, Joanne W.
Woehrle, Stephen Luer
Wolff, Bernard Christopher
Wood, Edwin A.
Wooding, Giles Clement
Wragge, John H.
Wrege, William Thomas
Wu, Hsiang-fa
Wygal, Donald Evans
Wyler, Wayne E.
Yerkes, Russell E.
Young, Ralph L.
Young, Richard Anthony
Young, S. Mark
Younkins, Edward Wayne
Yunker, Penelope Jane
Zawati, A. K.
Zimmerman, Jerold Lee

Financial Statement Data-Based

Abdulkade, Abdullah
Adams, Steven J.
Agudelo, Jaime
Akpa, Abimaje
Al-Ghamdi, Saad Attieah
Al-Tassan, Mohammad Saleh
Al-Yamani, Abdullah G.
Aono, June Yoshiko
Arnold, Jerry L.
Atamna, Said
Avard, Stephen L.
Bailey, Larry P.
Bait-Elmel, Mohammed A.
Baldwin, Bruce A.
Barrack, John B.
Bartley, Jon W.
Basohlu, Basalet
Bayer, Frieda Anna Forcht
Beard, Larry H.
Berk, Joel Lee
Bhamornsiri, Surasakdi
Biddle, Gary Clark
Bitner, Larry Newell
Blann, Jack Ralph
Bowman, Robert G.

Boynton, William C.
Bravo Herrera, Fernando
Brecha, Sonia A.
Bristol, James Tadsen
Brooks, John E.
Broom, Lowell S.
Brown, James France, Jr.
Brugger, Karl A.
Buchanan, Phillip G.
Burrows, Ronnie J.
Caldwell, Charles William
Carpenter, Jon Robert
Carter, William K.
Chaloupecky, KentE.
Chant, Peter D.
Chumley, Delbert W.
Chung, Yu to
Clark, Myrtle W.
Clark, Ronald L.
Collins, James F.
Collins, James R.
Cottell, Philip G.
Cox, Billie Don
Cress, James L.
Cummings, Robert R.
Danese, Stephen
Davis, Harry
Dawson, Ted
De Moville, Wiggens B.
Debessay, Araya
Demotses, Andrew J.
Dennis, Hubert L.
DeRidder, Jerome J.
Dhaliwal, Dan Singh
Dharan, Bala Ganga
Dillon, Gadis J.
Drury, Donald H.
Eichenseher, John Walter
Elkhorouf, Farouk W.
Engler, Calvin
Espahbodi, Hassanali
Espahbodi, Reza
Faircloth, Archie W.
Faisal, Abdullah M.
Farrelly, Gail E.
Feller, Robert E.
Fleming, Robert J.
Fonfeder, Robert
Foote, Paul S.
Fortin, Karen A.
Foster, Taylor William, III
Frazier, Katherine Beal
Fried, Haim D.
Friedlob, George Thomas
Fries, Clarence E.
Frigo, Mark Louis
Fry, Nichola E.
Gabhart, David L.
Gamble, George O.
Gibson, Robert W.
Glover, Robert I.
Godfrey, L. Howard
Goma, Ahmed Tawfik
Greenberg, Ralph Howard
Grief, Louis Adrian
Groomer, Stephen M.
Guithues, Denise Michele
Habib, Abo-el-yazeed
Hamer, Michelle M
Hartman, Bart P.
Haselkorn, Michael
Hasselback, James R.
Healy, Paul M.
Helmi, Medhat A.
Hendricks, Arthur George
Hennessee, Patrick Arnold
Herrera, Fernando B.
Hinrichs, Anella Sue Noel
Hock, Clayton Allen
Hohl, Katherine J.
Holley, Charles L.
Holt, Robert Nisbet, Jr.
Holzmann, Oscar Jorge
Hopkins, Albert W.
Hosseini, Ahmad
Hoth, Gerald Blaine
Huff, Thomas Edward
Hunt, Herbert G.
Huss, Harry F.
Icerman, Joe D.
Icerman, Rhoda C.
Ingram, Robert W.
Iqbal, Mohammed Z.
Izard, C. Douglass
Jain, Mahesh C.
Janell, Paul Andrew
Janson, Kenneth R.
Jarnagin, Bill D.
Jolly, Stephen Alton
Jopling, Samuel Haigh, Jr.
Joseph, Harold W.
Kang, Jai S.
Keating, John L.
Kee, Robert Carl
Keith, Richard Lyman
Ketz, John E.
Khumawala, Saleha B.
Kiddoo, Robert James
Kiel, Mark
Kimmell, Dennis L.
Knauf, Janine Bernice
Lanen, William N.
Lau, Amy Hing-Ling
Lau, Chor Tin
Laverdiere, Raymond G.
Lawler, William C.
Leftwich, Richard W.
Levitan, Alan S.
Lippitt, Jeffrey William
Lomax, Victor William Jr.
Lorek, Kenneth S.
Mac Millan, Alistair R.
Madison, Roland L.
Magann, Julia H.
Mano, Ronald M.
Maples, Lawrence D.
Marquette, Roberta Penny
Marting, Edward D.
Mayne, Frank Andrews
Mazhin, Reza
McConnell, Donald K. Jr.
McKee, Arnold J.
McKee, Thomas F.
McKeon, Joseph M.
McKnight, Reed Harrision
McMenimen, Leo Joseph
McNamara, James Bray
Means, Kathryn M.
Menon, Krishnagopal
Mensching, James Richard
Merrill, Gregory Bruce
Merz, Charles M.
Messere, Carl J.
Monahan, Thomas F.
Moore, John T.
Moores, Charles T.
Morgan, Robert George
Morton, James R.
Moses, Orrin D.
Murdoch, Brock Gordon
Nance, Jon Roland
Neumann, Bruce Richard
Newhouse, Benjamin
Nichols, David Lloyd
Nieminsky, Arthur C.
Nix, Paul E.
Noe, Joann M.
Norton, Curtis L.
O'Rourke, Vincent
Ogunjimi, Emmanuel O.
Ou, Jane Ai Jiuan
Oxner, Thomas H.
Paolasini, Arnold L.
Pare, Paul-Victor
Parker, Hugh J.
Parry, Robert W.
Pastena, Victor S.
Peacock, Kenneth E.
Peyvandi, Ali Agha
Posey, Roderick B.
Powell, Norma C.
Powers, Marian
Preis, Nancy J.
Prober, Larry M.
Puro, Marsha B.
Ramsey, Louis P.
Rayburn, Frank R.
Reed, Ira M.
Reeder, David B.
Reneau, James H.
Rexroad, William M.
Robinson, John R.
Rue, Joseph C.

Ruland, William J.
Sage, Lloyd George
Saghafi, Ali
Sami, Heibatollah
Sanborn, Robert H.
Santos, Dante E.
Savage, Linda J.
Schneider, Harold C.
Schoch, Hubert P.
Schroeder, Douglas A.
Schugart, Gary L.
Schwartz, Kenneth B.
Selph, Carl J.
Shalchi, Hossein
Sharp, Robert F.
Sheldon, Debra
Shimerda, Thomas A.
Simiar, Farhad
Simon, Daniel T.
Singh, Dan
Singleton, William R.
Skekel, Ted D.
Smith, Emmett D.
Smith, Howard Gromel
Smith, Julian D.
Snow, Charles J.
Snyder, Andrew G.
Spero, Leslie Lawrence
Stagliano, Anthony J.
Stephens, Lynn M.
Stevenson, Francis Liddell Jr.
Stout, David E.
Strickland, Sherre Geane
Sullens, Robert T.
Sullivan, Mark James
Swanson, Edward P.
Sweeney, Janet Ann Lawson
Swindle, Charles B.
Tackett, James A.
Tarabzune, Muhiadin Rashad
Taylor, Martin E.
Taylor, William J.
Tennyson, Barney Mack, III
Tomczyk, Stephen H.
Toole, Howard R.
Tosanguan, Prayoon
Tower, Ralph Burnett, Jr.
Tranter, Terry L.
Trapnell, Jerry E.
Trebby, James P.
Troberg, Pontus Henrik
Ugault, Michel
Urbancic, Frank Robert
Waegelein, James F.
Wallace, William Duane
Walther, Larry M.
Weiss, Dieter H.
Westmoreland, Geraldine
Wiehrs, Paula E.
Wilson, Earl R.
Wooton, Charles W.
Worthington, James
Wunder, Haroldene Fowler
Yang, David Chie Hwa
Yeater, David A.
Zavgren, Christine Virginia
Zuaiter, Farquoq Ahmad

Market-Based

Aharony, Joseph
Ahmed, Sania T.
Al-Rai, Ziad Khalil
Alderman, Charles W.
Allen, Steven A.
Anthony, Murray S.
Anyanwa, Casimar I.
Applewhite, George
Atiase, Rowland Kwame
Ayers, Frances Lynch
Bahjatt, Mohammed F.
Baker, Paul D.
Baker, Richard Edward
Balogun, Jacob Olakayode
Banks, Doyle Wesley
Bao, Ben Hsien
Baran, Arie
Bartczak, Norman Joseph
Basu, Sanjoy
Bates, Homer L
Bathke, Allen William, Jr.
Beatty, Randolph P.
Bell, Timothy Barnes
Bengharbia, Salem M.
Benjamin, Wahjudi Prakarsa
Beshara, Robert Labib
Bishop, Ashton Coles, Jr.
Black, Thomas Gilbert
Block, Linda Joyce
Boes, Richard Fred
Bomber, Linda S.
Boren, Adrian W.
Bremser, Wayne G.
Briner, Russell F.
Brown, Robert M.
Brown, Ronald D.
Bublitz, Bruce Orval
Buchman, Thomas A.
Burgstahler, David Curtis
Burnaby, Priscilla A.
Campbell, David R.
Cantz, Keith W.
Cheever, John K.
Cheng, Thomas Tong
Cheung, Joseph K.
Cho, Paek Je
Choi, Sung Kyu
Chope, Roger Allen
Chow, Chee Woo
Christie, Andrew Allan
Clancy, Donald Keith
Collins, William A.
Courtenay, Stephen M.
Courtis, John K.
Cox, Clifford Theodore
Cox, Ellen F.
Cox, Michael A.
Craig, Darryl L.
Cready, William Montgomery
Curatola, Anthony P.
D'Souza, Rudolph E.
Daley, Lane A.
Davis, Darrel Wilber
Davis, Robert R.
Defeo, John V.
Deines, Dan Stuart
Dietrich, James Richard
Dodd, Peter Raymond
Doran, Benjamin Michael
Dowell, Claud D.
Downes, David Howard
DuBois, Donoly A.
Dukes, Roland Edward
El-Gawhary, Ali Mohamed
El-Leithy, Fouad M.
Elgers, Pieter Thomas
Elliott, John A.
Ernst, John D.
Etebari-Khorasgani, Ahmad
Farmer, Martha K.
Fellingham, John C.
Fertuck, Leonard J.
Fleenor, William C.
Foster, George J.
Frecka, Thomas Jean
Freeman, Jack Louis
Freeman, Robert N.
Garsombke, Henry P.
Gaumnitz, Bruce
Geller, Arthur Neal
Gheyara, Kelly Framroze
Gift, Michael J.
Gingras, Russell T.
Givoly, Dan
Gordon, Irene Malinda
Grant, Edward B.
Griffin, Paul A.
Hale, Jack A.
Hamamad, Ahmed-Hany B.
Hamilton, Robert E.
Hansen, Don R.
Harbecke, Paula A.
Harmon, William K.
Harrell, Horace W.
Harris, Trevor S.
Harrison, Walter T.
Haw, In-Mu
Hayes, Randall Bryant
Hendricks, James A.
Hillison, William A.
Holthausen, Robert Wood
Hopkins, Merle W.
Hopkins, Raymond F.

Hoshower, Leon B.
Huang, Jiunn-Chang
Huber, Charles Courtland, Jr.
Huffman, Wilmer E.
Hutchins, Ronald Earl
Hyon, Yong-Ha
Izan, Haji Y.
Jain, Rohit
Jenkins, David Randall
Johnson, Johnny R.
Kablan, Abdelsalam Ali
Kahn, Nathan
Kamin, Jacob Y.
Kanaan, Georges Kaissar
Kanodia, Chandra S.
Karmon, David James
Keller, Stuart B.
Kellogg, Robert Leroy
Kennedy, Dennis T.
Kettering, Ronald Clayton
Kim, Hyuk
Kim, Kun Jang
Kim, Kung J.
King, Raymond Dean
Klemme, Dana K.
Koogler, Paul R.
Kramer, Sandra Smith
Kross, William J.
La Near, Richard E.
Lakonishok, Josef
Lane, Michael R.
Langefeld, Phillip A.
Lantz, Keith W.
Legault, Michel
Lew, Albert Yee-Hong
Lish, G. Rex
Livnat, Joshua
Lobo, Gerald Joseph
Lookabill, Larry L.
Lovins, W. Gene
Lyn, Thomas
Magee, Robert Paul
Manegold James G.
Mannino, Ronald C.
McAllister, John Peter
Meek, Gary Kenneth
Mohr, Rosanne Marie
Morris, Michael Henry
Morse, Dale Clayton
Moser, Duane
Moustafa, Salah
Mulford, Charles W.
Munter, Paul H.
Murdock, Richard J.
Murray, Dennis Francis
Naoum, Christos
Naser-Tavauolian, Mohsen
Ndubizu, Gordian Anumudu
Ng, David Siu Po
Nichols, William Donald
Novin, Adele M.
Nyadroh, Emmanuel M. Kwaku
O'Brien, Francis James
O'Keefe, William T.
Oliver, Thomas W.
Oppong, Andrews
Parikh, Rajeev N.
Patell, James M.
Patterson, Jeffrey L.
Pelz, Ulrich
Penman, Stephen H.
Pfeiffer, Glenn M.
Phillips, Mary
Pincus, Morton P.
Pitman, Marshall K.
Pitt, Harold R.
Porter, Gary A.
Powers, Marian
Putnam, Karl B.
Reed, Barbara L.
Rice, Steven J.
Richardson, Gordon D.
Ricks, William E.
Ro, Byung-Tak
Roth, Harold P.
Roy, Stephen P.
Rozanski, Eugene R.
Ryerson, Frank E.
Saftner, Donald V.
Sager, Clayton R.
Sandretto, Michael J.
Schaefer, Thomas F.
Schreiner, Paul W.
Scott, Edward R.
Sefcik, Stephen E.
Selama, Yehia A.
Sepe, James F.
Shelton, Fred A.
Short, Daniel G.
Sinning, Kathleen E.
Smith, Abbie Jean
Smith, David B.
Soroosh Joo, Jalaleddin
Spero, Abba V.
Spiceland, J. David
Spicer, Barry H.
Sterner, Julia Ann
Stevens, William Patrick
Stone, Kenneth E.
Stone, Mary Sheetz
Suadi, Arief
Sunder, Shyam
Tanju, Murat N.
Thakkar, Rashmi Bhanuchandra
Thomas, Charles William
Thomas, Lynn R.
Thompson, Forrest
Thompson, Joel E.
Twombly, John Roger
Uruwink, David R.
Ushman, Neal L.
Vigeland, Robert L.
Vives, Antonio
Vruwink, David R.
Webster, Stuart K.
Weirich, Thomas R.
Wescott, Shari H.
Wiggins, Charles Donald
Williams, John Joseph
Willis, G. W.
Wright, Charlotte J.
Ziebart, David A.

Model- Based

Abu-Romman, Mohammed A.
Adam, Shiraz Noor- mohamed
Ahern, John T.
Alberni, Carlos W.
Anthony, Joseph Harry
Antle, Ricky Lee
Ariyo, Ademola
Arlinghaus, Barry Paul
Atkinson, Anthony A.
Baber, William Russell
Baiman, Stanley
Baker, Charles Richard
Baker, Robert Louis
Berry, Maureen H.
Bizzell, Allen H.
Blocher, Edward J.
Bloom, Robert
Borthick, Alice F.
Bostrom, Donald E.
Bourne, Frances Yvonne
Bowen, Robert Michael
Boyles, Jesse V.
Brady, Thomas J.
Braide, January Miller
Brecht, Howard David
Bryan, Edward L.
Bullock, James H.
Bylinski, Joseph Henry
Callaghan, David Richard
Campbell, William Dennis
Cavanagh, Walter Forbes
Cerva,John A
Chan, James L.
Chan, Yee Ching Lilian
Chaney, Paul K.
Chee, Yong Hee
Cheng, Cheng-shing
Cheng, Peter
Christensen, John Asmus
Cirtin, Arnold Lee
Collins, Lane G.
Cowen, Scott S.
Craft, Clifford Justin, III
Crichfield, Timothy Ryan
Cunningham, Gary M.
Czarsty, Steven L.
De Jong, Douglas V.
DeAngelo, Linda Elizabeth

Dontoh, Alex Kwesi
Duke, Donald E.
Eliraqi, Iraqi A.
Elmadfai, Abdulfattah O.
Elmallah, Amin A.
Evens, John Henry
Everett, John O.
Farmer, Timothy Alan
Fedorowicz, Jane
Fox, James G.
Friedman, Laurence A.
Gallun, Rebecca A.
Geiser, Eugene G.
Gelinas, Ulric Joseph, Jr.
Gillespie, Jackson Floyd
Graul, Paul R.
Grimlund, Richard A.
Groff, James Edward
Hassanin, Badr E.
Helal, Samir
Herring, Hartwell C.
Hilton, Ronald W.
Hines, Danny R.
Holland, Roger G.
Hong, Sungbin Chun
Hopwood, William S.
Horwood, Joanne Lynn
Hudson, Jean Marie Baldwin
Hughes, John Silver, III
Hughes, Marilynn L.
Ismail, Badr El-Din Hassanin
Jacobs, Frederic H.
Jaikumar, Vaiyapuri
Johnson, Steven B.
Kaufman, Jerry M.
Kemp, Robert S.
Kim, Song Ki
Kim, Soon-Kee
Kirkpatrick, Thomas L.
Kirschman, Charles Frederick
Ko, Wansuk Matthew
Krogstad, Jack L.
Kunkel, James Gregory
Kwon, Young K.
Lambert, Richard A.
Laudeman, Max A.
Lee, Chan M.
Lewis, Eddie M.
Liao, Mawsen
Malone, Fannie Lee
Maloo, Man Chand
Mansour, Fathi A.
Mapp, Johnnie A.
Mboya, Fratern M.
McCarthy, William E.
McFerrin, William D.
McMickle, Peter L.
Mensah, Yaw Mireuk
Merchant, Kenneth Allen
Mielke, David E.
Mintz, Steven M.
Naloo, Man C.
Namazi, Mohammed
Newman, Donald Paul
Ninsuvannakul, Prawit
Nordhauser, Susan Litt
Noreen, Eric W.
O'Doherty, Brian A.
O'Keefe, Hubert A.
Orbach, Kenneth Ned
Park, Joengdae
Park, Soong H.
Parker, Mary V.
Parsons, Gregory L.
Patz, Dennis H.
Penno, Mark C.
Petro, Louis W.
Putnam, Donald F.
Ramakrishnan, Ram T. S.
Ransom, Charles R.
Rasch, Ronald H.
Read, William Joseph
Reid, George R.
Rivers, Richard A.
Rodgers, Waymond
Rosanas, Josep M.
Salimi, Anwar Yazdani
Salter, John H.
Scheiner, James H.
Schmidt, Richard J.
Shaaban, Hamed A.
Sharifi Fardi, Moshen
Sheteini, Idris A.
Shin, Joon Y.
Skantz, Tereance R.
Soliman, Soliman Youssef
Srinidhi, Bindiganavale Narayan
Srivasteva, Rajendre P.
Stolar, Robert W.
Swanson, Gale A.
Tabor, John George
Tawfik, Mohamed Sherif
Techavichit, Joseph Virachai
Thibadoux, Gregory Maurice
Tipgos, Manuel A.
Traugh, Helen M.
Tse, Senyo Yawo
Tzur, Joseph
Van Breda, Michael F.
Vanecek, Michael Thomas
Veazey, Richard E.
Verrecchia, Robert Ernest
Vickery, Don W.
Volkan, Ara G.
Vorherr, Phillip H.
Wagner, Robin M
Walker, John P.
Welch, Paul R.
White, Godwin Thomas
Wild, John Joseph
Willinger, Geoffrey L.
Wilson, Beverly
Wilson, James E.
Wolf, Allen Edwin
Wolfson, Mark A.
Yahr, Robert B.
Zebda, Awni M.

ABOUT THE AUTHOR

J. David Spiceland, PH.D., CPA, is Professor and Interim Director of the School of Accountancy at Memphis State University. Dr. Spiceland is the author of numerous accounting and tax articles in academic and professional journals. He has also served as editor of a professional journal.